Living Waters

To Dave,

Keep at the good work in saving our streams.

Yours,
Owen

Living
Waters

How to Save Your Local Stream

OWEN D. OWENS

Rutgers University Press, New Brunswick, New Jersey

Printed on partially recycled paper

Cartoons courtesy of Carl Dusinberre and Vicki Maloney; map of Valley Creek from Trout Streams of
Pennsylvania: An Angler's Guide, *copyright © 1991 by Dwight Landis, courtesy of Dwight Landis;
original map of West Valley Creek and diagrams courtesy of Todd D. Henderson; this version of the West
Valley Creek map by Ruth Strohl-Palmer; photos of Morris Run courtesy of Bryan Lambert; all other
photos courtesy of Kenneth Arnold.*

Library of Congress Cataloging-in-Publication Data

Owens, Owen D.
Living waters : how to save your local stream / Owen D. Owens.
p.   cm.
Includes index.
ISBN 0-8135-1997-7 (cloth)—ISBN 0-8135-1998-5 (pbk.)
1. Stream conservation—Pennsylvania—Valley Creek—Citizen
participation.   2. Water—Pollution—Pennsylvania—Valley Creek
3. Trout Unlimited.   Valley Forge Chapter.   4. Valley Creek (Pa.)
5. Stream conservation—Handbooks, manuals, etc.   I. Title.
QH76.5.P4093   1993   93–7641
333.91'6216—dc20   CIP

British Cataloging-in-Publication information available

DESIGN BY JOHN ROMER

Contents

Preface

W e drink water. It is critical to industry; without water our cities would die. For the most part, however, we ignore the source, taking for granted that the rains will fall, the watersheds will absorb the moisture, and the streams will continue to flow. All over the industrialized world streams have been dammed, polluted, sedimented, and dredged.

Only when drought and floods threaten, or when water becomes unsafe to drink, do we begin to pay attention to streams. Only when unthinking development has bulldozed the trees and paved the watershed, do we become aware of what we have lost. This book begins near the end of progress and development. Its purposes are unashamedly conservation, preservation, and restoration of the natural environment.

If you are already active in the conservation movement, you can learn from the experiences of the Valley Forge Chapter of Trout Unlimited. If you are interested in our country becoming more, not less, just and participatory, we believe you will find instructive our efforts to form a voluntary organization that has called government and corporations to greater responsibility. Finally, if you despair before the forces which are tearing our environment to pieces, we think you will see some hope for the future.

As I look back, I can see a number of factors why I became a stream conservationist. One of the most important was growing up in the state of Wisconsin. Conservation was in the air. One of the first sermons I remember was preached by Dean Clark Graham, a prominent Presbyterian minister and dean of Ripon College. In it he said that people were using up the coal and that someday it would be gone. We needed to be much more careful about not wasting our natural resources, he said.

My father showed me the Civilian Conservation Corps camps and told with pride how under Franklin Delano Roosevelt's administration young people had replanted trees all over the state of Wisconsin. In the mid 1940s when we would go on vacation, I looked at the green forests, and wished I could have seen the great stands of virgin trees before they were cut down. When I was in high school, I was invited to go to Camp Trees for Tomorrow, a weekend school, to learn more about conservation. My expenses were paid by a local sportsmen's group. We met some of the staff of the Wisconsin Conservation Department and learned a great deal about what people could do to preserve nature.

On the negative side I remember one cold winter in Fort Atkinson, Wisconsin, when ice on the Rock River was thick and the stream flow very low. A newspaper article reported that fish were dying in the river. The writer said that one cause was waste from the local creamery that was being dumped in the water. A few days later I walked along the river bank and observed the milky fluid going from the creamery into the water. Young people can see with great clarity. What to others may be justified as "economic necessity" to me appeared as foolishness. People had no right to ruin a stream and kill the fish! That clear vision of milk solids flowing into the water and the question about why people allowed this to happen were to haunt me for years.

Another constructive influence was Mr. Jennings, a naturalist farmer who lived near Rio, Wisconsin. When we lived in Cambria, we used to ride out to Jennings Creek to get cream. I remember comments by grownups about how strangely Mr. Jennings did things. Naturally such comments made me curious. After I graduated from seminary, I returned to Wisconsin to serve a church in Racine. It was my custom to take a few days each spring or summer and go up to fish Jennings Creek, a limestone stream fed by icy springs. One of the largest springs emerged under a spring house on Mr. Jennings's farm. I would walk up to his house and talk with him. He told me something of his philosophy of farming, namely, to do enough to make a living, but to do it in ways which, as far as possible, kept the stream intact. Mr. Jennings's lessons were reinforced by the difference between the stream as it ran through his property and the farm upstream. Upstream, cattle were allowed to graze so heavily they left the pasture like a lawn. There was little or no cover along the banks. When I fished this area, I would seldom catch or see anything. Then I would walk across the road to Mr. Jennings's land where trees shaded the stream, and shrubs and logs provided cover. Here there were always fish. The difference between farming directed by one who cared about the stream, and a farmer who didn't, was painfully obvious.

Another factor which was eventually to touch me deeply was years of traveling across North America and fishing its streams. The first trip took place in 1947, when my family spent two months touring the Midwestern and Western states. Over the next thirty years, I was to travel frequently across the entire country until I had been in almost every state. Whenever I had an opportunity, I would go trout fishing. I became very aware of what was happening to the streams in North America.

From 1965 to 1969 I lived in the Bay Area of northern California. While we were there, I remember visiting a new dam on the Feather River. I recall looking down the face of the dam to the stream below and seeing huge shapes in the water: steelhead trout and salmon who were left with no place to spawn because the dam blocked the river. I learned later that streams had been dammed throughout northern California, and that the water was sent by aqueduct to southern California to allow the continuing growth of vast corporate farms and Los Angeles.

After completing graduate work on a Ph.D. in sociology of religion, in 1969 I took a job with The American Baptist Home Mission Society near Philadelphia. To my surprise I discovered several trout streams within a fifteen-minute drive of my new home. At work I was assigned by Dr. Jitsuo Morikawa, the secretary of evangelism for the Home Mission Society, to assist in staffing a major project of strategic planning. The purpose was to give the Home Mission Society a new sense of direction, based on careful reading of critical social trends. Out of this strategic planning process the Governing Board eventually voted a goal that gave further direction to my life. This goal stated that mission programming should be done at places where concerns for ecological wholeness and social justice intersect. In essence, the goal directed us to seek structural changes of institutions toward ecological wholeness and social justice. I began increasingly to see that what was happening to the streams of North America was part of a worldwide process of pollution and destruction of whole ecosystems.

In 1972, I was enabled by the Home Mission Society to attend the Stockholm Conference on the Environment. I helped organize a group of Protestant church leaders who met during the conference. I went intending to check out the ecology-justice goal, that is to see if its reading of the issues was indeed correct. I left with the conviction that we were indeed moving toward an era in which industrial and urban expansion would be limited by ecological reality.

Thirty years of experience finally led me to action. As a practicing Christian, I knew that theory and insight are incomplete without action. I began to preach and write about the ecology-justice goal, but somehow this did not seem enough.

Then in a prayer/support group, a leader responsible for evangelism told of a sermon by Jitsuo Morikawa, in which he said that beyond one's job every religious person should become involved in some form of ministry for the good of the community. My friend found this upsetting. How could he do any more than he was already doing at work? He traveled all over the state and hardly had time for his family. But the more he thought about what Morikawa had said, the more it made him feel that he needed to do something for the greater good of people.

What he said undercut the rationalization that I was too busy at work to do anything more. It pushed me toward becoming the kind of conservationist who did something to put my beliefs into action. I agreed to serve on a township committee aimed at rewriting the local charter, but found it so boring and irrelevant that I could hardly stand it. As I looked into the future, I would never have guessed that a fishing trip to French Creek, in Chester County, would lead me to make a decision to form a stream conservation organization.

The story of our efforts from 1976 to 1992 is told in Part I—it suggests ways you can start, build, and revitalize a citizens' organization working for the good of all. Part II is my vision of new, constructive ways in which we can relate to streams and their watersheds and it should help you develop your own vision of what the streams are, how they work, and what human beings can do to preserve and restore the living waters which are our legacy and source of life. Part III comes from what we have learned in organizing a voluntary citizens' movement and from fifteen years of stream restoration—it is a handbook to which you can turn for practical suggestions and references.

In this book I have frequently used names of persons involved in conservation work. There is a good reason. Voluntary groups run on appreciation. Nobody pays volunteers, and it is important to recognize the contributions each makes. Everyone can make a contribution. Whoever one is, there is something one can do that will make a difference. Recognizing the work and accomplishments of each helps move things along.

Ecology and *economy* come from the same Greek root. If human beings are to survive, make a living, and be healthy, we will need to learn how to stop unmaking creation, and begin to start helping nature put itself together. When the worst happens, and we inherit waste land and water, and devastated forests, we can learn how to help nature become fruitful and self-sustaining again.

Finally, no matter what we plan, no matter how hard we work and how adequate our preparation, events happen which cannot be expected. Some call this factor *chance* or *luck*. Within a religious perspective it is called providence. I, myself, do believe that there is a knowing One who is moving us toward greater care for the earth and just dealing with each other.

God Speaks to Us Through Streams

The title of this book, *Living Waters*, is of course a factual one. Every stream is alive with creatures of all sizes and varieties. I must admit, though, that the title also has a religious connotation. The great prophets, informed by their sense of the immediate presence of One who is righteous and loving, pictured a future in which the rivers ran clear. In the concluding book of the Christian scriptures, *Revelation* (Chapter 22:1–5), there is a vision of such a river. Trees, many fruitbearing, are restored to its banks. Pollution is gone, and the water runs crystal clear. This is a miraculous river, indeed, because it *runs through the city*, the place human beings have created in which to live. We know, therefore, that this is not an ordinary city, but that place our best architects and planners dream of and seek freebly to form here on earth. It is the city of God, our destination. The center of that city, its visual focus, is a pristine stream.

We religious folk, however, do not always get a good understanding of our prophets' vision. The picture in *Revelation* of an unpolluted stream running through a city is so miraculous, so outside our experience we cannot believe it. On the other hand, it is in our Bible, so we have to take it seriously. Some of us, therefore, project the vision into a distant future beyond death, picturing a heaven where everything is right. That, we surmise, must be what the vision in *Revelation* is about, life after death.

A little more study of this particular book, however, discloses that it was written for trying times. The author certainly wasn't saying, "Relax, conform, do what everybody else does, and when you die everything will finally be O.K." No, instead the word was, "Keep the faith, trust God, love your neighbor and do what's right, hold on, and whether you live or die God will bring on earth at the right time an entirely new creation."

Unfortunately, the "unmaking," destroying power of evil is not restricted to streams. Our religious teachings and efforts have often been twisted. A recent Secretary of the Interior, for instance, deeply believed that someday soon Christ would come again to establish God's divine rule on earth. For some strange reason, though, this conviction seemed to allow him to give free rein to human greed. National forests were opened to unrestricted oil and gas drilling. Muddy roads were ripped through previously undisturbed watersheds. Salt, acid waste, and drilling chemicals were dumped directly into previously clear headwaters. Toxic waste dumps and incinerators were located in poor communities and where people of color lived.

When religious beliefs tell us it is alright to be unthinkingly destructive, we know something is wrong. All religions have warned us that greed gets us in trouble! We are warned so that we will change our ways. All too often we refuse to listen, however. We make up our minds what we want to do, and then justify these actions by twisting our religious beliefs. The Apostle Paul once said, "Our senseless minds are darkened." To use the second coming of Christ as an excuse for further unthinking exploitation of the natural order perverts Christianity. Jesus, who as the Prophet Isaiah foretold, was one who refused to break the bruised reed, looks with profound distaste, I believe, on current pollution. Putting the issue in biblical words, whenever we see religious faith being used to justify persecution and exploitation of others, whether it be of human beings or of nature, we can assume that these leaders are losing touch with God.

Women and men through whom God speaks see the future, present, and past in light of an immediate experience of God. Christian teaching speaks of God as Creator, Sustainer and Redeemer. In other words, God has been experienced as One who made all that is, keeps it going, and when things get all messed up, helps to put things back together again. Again and again, people who tell us that God spoke to them say that it means we are asked to be more, not less, loving and responsible. We cannot separate God's love for us from the commandments to love

God with all our heart, mind and strength and to love our neighbors as ourselves—doing justice, loving mercy, walking humbly.

According to the Bible, God speaks to human beings in many ways. I am increasingly convinced that one way God is speaking to us today is through the streams. I agree with Albert Schweitzer's emphasis on *reverence for life*. Experiencing a living stream calls forth a sense of awe. The intricate web of life, the distinctness of each living creature, the unimaginable complexity of each ecosystem, the delicate balances, leave me with a sense of wonder. All of these creatures, and the water itself, were not made solely for me to use, though I, too, eat and drink. Indeed, as I see and hear, I rejoice, and am thankful. When we human beings join together with a stream to enhance its life-giving ability, as we did that first work day on Valley Creek, the ecstasy which we experienced in a new sense of community was a sign that God that day was very close to us. After all, is it not God who draws us into community?

A sense of reverence for life is critically important. Life itself is the very breath of God. Without awe we lose respect for the "otherness" of nature. If we think of a stream only as a resource we shall find we lose the ability to see what is truly there. We will begin to lack perspective on our human activity. We will stop caring for our land and water, and we will become more arrogant. Humility, perspective, and compassion spring from reverence for life.

Acknowledgments

Many volunteers have made this book possible. Mary Kuss, long-term member of Trout Unlimited, gave the first editing comments, which set me on the right track. Joe Kohler of the Little Lehigh Chapter took the entire manuscript and put it on computer. Ken Arnold, Rutgers University Press director, not only provided editorial direction but took many of the pictures. John Dettrey provided key editorial guidance, entirely on a volunteer basis. Charles Clifton did the final editing for Rutgers Press, strengthening the manuscript greatly. Paul Nale, long-time Pennsylvania Trout Unlimited activist, provided detailed guidance on many chapters. Sal Palatucci brought a National Trout Unlimited perspective.

The Valley Forge Chapter editing committee, including Jim Clark, Ray Squires, Wayne Poppich, and Jim Leonard, read the entire manuscript and made many suggestions. Joe Armstrong,

Living Waters

PART I

The Story of a Stream Conservation Movement

Valley Forge Trout Unlimited

Facing the widespread destructions of streams and their watersheds, we are tempted to feel hopeless and frustrated, but democracy is still alive. George Washington is still looking over our shoulders, not only in Valley Forge, but also everywhere in the United States of America. Citizens who decide to do something to take care of the streams, land, and air of their own communities still can make a difference.

Since the beginning of the American republic in 1776, citizens have been organizing voluntary associations to change social and economic policy and practice. Corporations, governmental agencies, and legislatures have again and again been reformed by organized citizen efforts.

Many know that we must move from using to preserving and restoring. That means organizing. It means making an effort to find out what is wrong, discovering solutions and then seeking change from governmental agencies, corporations, local governments, and other institutions whose plans and actions will either ruin or preserve the environment.

When habitat goes, fish and wildlife go too. When a lake or river is polluted, the fish die. Muskellunge, bass, walleye, and trout require clean water. When a forest is cut down and the watershed destroyed, floods ruin the streams and rivers, and eventually estuaries are affected. Right now the entire Chesapeake Bay is sick because we are not taking care of the rivers that flow into it.

This book is being written for everyone who likes the out-of-doors. If we take for granted the health of our streams, rivers, bays, and oceans and do nothing to protect and restore them, we will be leaving a legacy of ruin for our descendants. In our own lifetime, moreover, we will see much of what we once took for granted disappear.

It is not enough to watch sports programs on television. It is not enough to go fishing or hunting. It is not enough to belong to a sporting club. It is not enough to hope that the Environmental Protection Agency or Department of Environmental Resources will save the environment. It is not even enough to join a conservation organization, though that is a step in the right direction. More is necessary. Somebody has to organize and support environmental movements in each city, township, and rural area of this country, and in other countries also.

We, in the Valley Forge Chapter of Trout Unlimited, would like to share our story. Beginning in 1976, a small group of citizens have been working effectively to save the streams of the greater Philadelphia area. We hope you can learn from our efforts. The problems we have struggled with in Pennsylvania are universal. Throughout the world, destruction of streams and their watersheds is drying up the supply of clean, cold water. Pollution makes things even worse. Our experience tells us that caring and dedicated environmentalists over the long haul make a big difference.

I Can't Stand It Anymore

W arwick Park is only a few miles from where I live; there French Creek flows through several hundred acres of meadow and forested hills. One of my favorite places in this Chester County park is a large meadow, which French Creek encircles in a horseshoe bend.

Camping is allowed here. Since there are no hookups, no on-site electricity or water, and only pit toilets, the crowds do not flock to camp at Warwick Park. One can get away from a busy life and be alone for a little while.

April is one of my favorite times at Warwick Park. On a clear night I lie on my back and look up at the stars. The landscape is dimly illuminated by starlight. To the south is the dark mass of the forested hill. Over my head I can see the delicate patterns of branches. The only signs of human beings are occasional high-flying jets heading toward Philadelphia International Airport and the soft lights of a house in the village some distance away.

In the morning I wake up with light of the sun. I look down at my sleeping bag and see that it is covered with frost. A fire quickly takes the edge off the chill. The aroma of coffee and bacon and eggs fills the air. I string up my fishing rod and get ready for the day's activities.

A Decisive Fishing Trip

One particular day in 1976 I hiked across the meadow to where the stream flows through heavy woods, leaving behind the last signs of human activity. When I fish my attention is focused on the sport itself. The "correct" fly must be chosen and tied on the leader. The rhythm of cast and retrieve, cast and retrieve, soothes the mind, and soon all my attention is focused on casting to a hoped-for fish, wading carefully to a new spot, silently applauding good presentations, and not always so silently moaning about ones that fall wide of the mark. The only interruption is an occasional snag when the fly gets caught in a bush or branch on a back cast.

Late in the day I stopped at a place where I had outlined a new rock dam. The stream in this section was very wide and shallow, and as was my custom in those days I threw more rocks together on the dam, hoping to deepen it and concentrate the flow. For a person who spends a great deal of time sitting in a "modern" building, effectively sealed off from any outside wind currents, there is something very satisfying in hard physical work. I pulled rocks out of the bed of the stream, and carried them to the dam. An hour's work and the new structure was mostly in place. Sweat ran down my face, but it felt good in the warm sun.

Soon it would be time to break camp and go home. As I waded I began to think about this stream, its beauty and the threat to it from human activity. Through my mind went what happened to the brook trout streams in southern Wisconsin. Fertile, fed by limestone streams, inhabited by colorful native "brookies," most were dredged in the 1940s and 1950s, leaving ditches devoid of habitat and fish.

I next remembered standing on the banks of the Yellowstone River the year I graduated from college, 1956, when I was struck by the tremendous fishing pressure generated by 150 million Americans. In 1990 the population was 250 million, a 100-million increase. Then I thought about the other streams I had observed on my travels, some polluted, most dammed, others with banks so covered with houses and businesses that anyone who loves to fish was excluded. Still desirable fishing places were "protected" by No Trespassing signs, while others were left so foul and littered that even though access was possible, one would have little interest in being there.

Then into my mind flashed a memory of Slabtown Cemetery, overlooking the Bark River in Hebron, Wisconsin. I had spent many hours as a young person fishing the Bark River for smallmouth bass and northern pike. Even when I was in high school, I knew that this stream was threatened by explosive expansion of the Milwaukee metropolitan area. Water would be siphoned off for drinking water and sewage treatment, and waste would be poured back. Unthinking development would fill the banks with homes and businesses, destroying the rural setting, replacing small fields and pastures with concrete and cars.

These memories flooded my mind one after another, and through them I looked at French Creek and knew that it too would probably one day be destroyed. I felt depressed and overwhelmed. Who can do anything to stop destructive development which takes place on such a massive scale?

I remember getting ready to climb out of the water. With one foot on the bank suddenly the thought hit me, "I can't stand it anymore. I've got to do something about it."

As that thought hit my mind, though, I saw immediately that "doing something" meant organizing. If I wanted to stop destruction of French Creek, that meant touching township, county, state and even national planning. One person alone could have no effect on decisions made by these bodies. My work for the American Baptist Churches involved planning, research, and helping people organize. I liked what I did, but the reason I also liked trout fishing was that it gave me a chance to be alone and get away from work. The last thing I wanted in my free time was to attend more committee meetings!

Yet I also could see that if I really wanted to do something to help trout streams survive, I would have to pull people together to do something. I reluctantly accepted that necessity, climbed out of the stream, and left French Creek with the intent to form some kind of a stream conservation organization.

Trout Unlimited

As I reflected on the decision I had made to become active in stream conservation, I began to think about the kind of organization that was needed. Since decisions affecting streams occurred on national, regional, and local levels of government, the organization should be able to influence all of these levels. Creating such an organization from scratch was obviously beyond my ability. Were such organizations in existence? Clearly some research was going to be necessary.

By talking with a few people I knew, I was able to discover three stream conservation organizations: the Isaac Walton League, Trout Unlimited, and the Federation of Fly Fishers. A little more research revealed that Trout Unlimited in Pennsylvania had a reputation for effective and aggressive conservation work. I began to feel that maybe Trout Unlimited was the organization I was looking for.

I had been discussing these matters with Chuck Marshall, a good friend and professionally an environmental consultant. During the summer of 1976 we decided to invite someone from Trout Unlimited to meet with us.

A few weeks later Chuck and I were waiting for Ken Sink, the representative of Pennsylvania Trout Unlimited, to arrive. We learned, as we had suspected, that Pennsylvania Trout Unlimited was indeed an effective conservation force. A significant number of new chapters had been started in the last few years. Members had good connections with legislators and state agencies, particularly the Pennsylvania Fish Commission. Policies developed by Trout Unlimited had resulted in changes in policies and practices of the Fish Commission.

Ken went on to tell us that the weakest area of Trout Unlimited work in Pennsylvania was in the Southeast. He had tried to start a new chapter in Phoenixville, which had met for several months but then disbanded.

A large chapter of over 300 members met in Center City Philadelphia, but Ken was very unhappy with this group. Though the chapter contributed money to stream conservation work, it was not active in local stream restoration projects. Its focus appeared to be the Poconos, where many of its members fished. We learned, indeed, that Ken had issued the chapter a challenge: "Get active, or I will ring Center City Philadelphia with several chapters, which will take away much of your membership!"

Forming a Board of Directors

We discussed how a new Trout Unlimited chapter could be organized. Ken gave us a copy of his *Cookbook*, a pamphlet which laid out very simple steps which could be taken to form a new chapter. The first step was to form a board of at least seven people. The second was to hold a kickoff meeting.

After Ken Sink left, Chuck and I talked for a while. We were both impressed with Ken. A tall, vigorous man in his late sixties, he left an impression of energy and blunt honesty. He delighted in saying what he thought, even if he felt it would make us uncomfortable. Active in his church, he clearly had a strong social conscience. He did caution us about being ineffectively radical, moving too quickly, or creating a stir in the news media in ways which would have little long-term effect.

Clearly Ken Sink was a person of substance. Chuck and I were impressed by him and felt that Pennsylvania Trout Unlimited was the group with which we wished to affiliate. A few days later I called Ken and made an appointment for him to return to Philadelphia and meet with a newly constituted board of directors.

I now faced the first of many organizational hurdles I was to encounter in the next few years. I had made a promise to Ken to bring together at least seven people, but I had no idea how we could get that many for a first meeting.

I began by asking Chuck if he would be willing to be part of this new Trout Unlimited chapter. He said that he, indeed, had been looking for an opportunity to go beyond consulting and become involved in "hands on" work. That made two people willing to attend the first board meeting, Chuck and me. I next thought about a woman who I knew loved to fish for trout when she had worked for the American Baptists. One day as I was leaving on a trip I happened to meet her in the airport at Philadelphia. I told her we were planning to start a chapter of Trout Unlimited, and asked if she would be interested in being a member. She agreed, with the stipulation that she not be asked to serve as the secretary. Knowing how people concerned about women's rights felt about always being placed in subservient roles, I agreed that she would not be asked to take that position. Now we had three people committed.

A fourth person from work became part of the initial organizing, though he agreed to stick with the effort only until we got the chapter started (because of other commitments). Somehow we found three other people to attend the first organizing meeting, which was held in the American Baptist Churches' cafeteria in Valley Forge. Ken constituted those present as the board and gave us the go-ahead to start a new chapter.

The Kickoff Meeting

The next few months were to take me into very unfamiliar territory. I read and reread Ken Sink's *Cookbook*, underlining the basic steps for starting a new chapter. Each month there was to be one board and one chapter meeting, with the board meeting held a week or two prior to the chapter meeting. Planning, organizing, and discussion should be done at the board meeting, bringing proposals for decision to the monthly chapter meetings. Ken suggested that the chapter plan meetings people would enjoy, using speakers, films, and other interesting programs. Each chapter should have active committees: environmental, legislative, fund raising, membership, etc.

To learn more Chuck and I attended a meeting of the Dame Juliana League in Phoenixville, a local organization devoted to preserving and restoring French Creek (particularly the "flyfishing only" section). We were warmly welcomed, and learned something about the work they were doing. I remember that on the way home, Chuck and I talked about what might draw people to a stream conservation organization, and how one could develop programs for it.

Finally, the date for the big kickoff meeting approached. On a cold March evening in 1977 Chuck drove to the library where the meeting was to be held. He had sent notices to the local newspapers and television stations announcing the place and time of the meeting. My job was to meet the Pennsylvania Trout Unlimited representative who was to initiate the new chapter at the exit of the Pennsylvania Turnpike at Valley Forge. He thought I could drive to the exit, turn around and meet him there. I drove to the turnpike, but found I could not turn around. I had to drive onto the Turnpike, go seven or eight miles to the next exit, turn around, come back, where I finally met him waiting beside the road. We raced to the site of the meeting. The room was packed with 55 people. The evening was exhilarating. Imagine that all these had come to start the new chapter! The Trout Unlimited leader gave a talk as did I, and then he asked for volunteers for the new board of directors. Twelve people volunteered to serve on the board. We learned later that only nine persons were to have been on the board, according to the bylaws. We asked people for their concerns about the coldwater streams in Chester County. One woman's home had a beautiful flowing spring, the source of drinking water for her family. Recent highway construction fouled the spring, and she wanted help. Other concerns were voiced by participants in the meeting. They hoped we could do something to help their streams. I was afraid, though, that for the time being their hopes would be disappointed. We would be lucky to be able to get a chapter together.

Getting to Know Each Other

When better than fifty people gathered that raw night in March to form the new Chester County chapter of Trout Unlimited, we collected a group of strangers. Even the people who volunteered to form the new board of the chapter did not know each other.

I was very aware of the lack of relationship among the new people. I was not sufficiently aware, however, as to how significant not knowing each other could be. Indeed, over the next two years we struggled to become acquainted and learn to trust each other. Relationships take time. For instance, my friend Chuck Marshall said that the reason he wished to become involved in forming a chapter was to have "hands on" experience, which he was not able to have in his work as an environmental consultant. To me, "hands on" experience means getting into a stream and throwing rocks, building structures, and planting trees. "Hands on" stands for something *physical*. Years later I found out that to Chuck "hands on" experience meant becoming active in forming an environmental coalition and setting up educational seminars. I heard the words he said, but only partly understood them. Understanding sometimes takes years.

At the first meeting of the new board, I suggested that we hold monthly meetings throughout the spring and summer, meeting each time at a different person's home. This proved to be an excellent first step. Rather than placing all of the burden on one person for refreshments, and making that home a regular meeting place, it spread the work around, and also brought us into the homes of different people who had volunteered to be members of the board. Thus we got to know a bit about the home setting in which each lived, and had some acquaintance with the families. As the years went on those who became active also got to know something about each person's work, as well as other aspects of their lives. Each board and chapter meeting contributed a bit to helping us to become acquainted. So did initial stream restoration work in which we engaged.

Creating an Organization

The next three years were to provide ample justification of the uneasy feeling I had at the kickoff meeting. Bright hopes were often dashed by disappointments and frustrations. The day after the kickoff meeting, for instance, I got a call from the library. Though we had cleaned up the meeting room, and though we left things in very good shape, somehow we omitted to check the restrooms. Someone had left the water running, and by morning the floor was flooded. We had no treasury, no money, and were in no position to make restitution. Fortunately, the library cleaned up the mess and charged us nothing, leaving us gratefully indebted.

At the first meeting the members decided to name the new chapter Valley Forge after the most well known place in Chester County. My role in creating the new chapter of Trout Unlimited was recognized as the members elected me president. I took the lead by setting up goals I hoped would be realized by the new organization, primarily to preserve and restore the coldwater streams of Chester County.

This goal was the reason I had given myself for forming the chapter. It was a direct expression of the decision I had made earlier. I expected the new organization would form around this overall objective, and would express it in many forms of action.

I was aware of the danger of being "lone ranger." The conservation movement has many stories of leaders who got a great idea and proceeded to act on it without checking with anyone else. The results of these enterprises are often painfully ineffective or even destructive. I was, therefore, committed to developing the kind of climate in which people were able to share their thoughts and feelings, giving and receiving criticism.

A second objective was to create an organization which was open to anyone, regardless of race, religion, class, or sex. Here again I had some experience and very strong convictions. It seemed to me that since a conservation organization is built out of the voluntary commitments of people, the more openness we had to different kinds of people, the more potential energy we would have. Furthermore, I believe that everyone is of worth and is needed. In forming an open and receptive climate more was involved than merely saying, "we are open to you to join." Instead, I hoped we could create an organization which would seek out new people, and make those who were interested feel wanted, comfortable and needed.

A third aim was to enable shared leadership. My first few months of experience with sports' groups and local conservation organizations indicated that they were very often organized around one person, the "leader." I knew from my experience with local churches that this form of organization had severe limitations. Suppose the leader gets tired, or needs to be replaced. That can be difficult and sometimes leads to the collapse of the entire organization.

I knew, moreover, that I did not want to create a group centered around myself. Part of the reason for this was selfish, going back to the very strong negative feelings I had about becoming active in forming a conservation movement, because of all the time demands it would make. If new leaders were identified and trained they might even replace me, which would leave me then free from all of the responsibility!

A final objective was to form an organization that desired insight and sought out information. I knew the value of research. Without it, one might grope along blindly. Listening and information gathering is threatening, however, and requires a certain amount of initiative. I felt, though, that it was essential in forming a new organization.

These objectives were not necessarily clearly stated, as I look back on the early days of the new chapter. Indeed, except for the overall goal, which was stated at the beginning, the other objectives were expressed mostly in the way I went about doing things. These objectives guided me, and in many ways did form the kind of climate which developed in the new chapter.

Forming a Solid and Orderly Chapter

At an early board meeting a statement by a member stuck in my mind. If our chapter were to attract people and do its job, two things would have to happen: first, it would have to do something about conservation, not merely talk about it, and second, it would have to be run in an orderly way, letting people know that those who were leading it knew what they were doing. Following Ken Sink's *Cookbook*, we held regular chapter meetings each month, preceding them by a board meeting. I hesitated to involve myself in all these organizational meetings, but I knew that the *Cookbook* was right. If we were going to have an organization, then we had to establish continuity: meet on a regular date at the same place and present interesting programs.

Before long we reached a decision we would meet on the third Tuesday of each month. That solved the date problem. Then through two board members we discovered a meeting place. The Episcopal Church of the Good Samaritan in Paoli opened its library to us for our regular meeting. We did not have to pay for it; we only had to promise not to smoke in the library in order to use it. I am still grateful to this congregation for opening its doors to a fledgling group, giving us a centrally located and pleasant meeting spot.

We dealt with the need of our group for money by asking people from the board to chip in. This gave us enough to buy refreshments for meetings and put a few dollars in the treasury. This was enough. Since the chapter could not do very much as yet, it had little need for money.

I remember these early board and chapter meetings as times of intense discussion. Even the simplest details seemed to require great investments of energy. At the first board meeting, for example, we talked for a long time about whether or not refreshments should be served. We decided to do so. Someone brought soft drinks, and somebody else had to find a coffeepot to heat hot water for coffee and tea.

Another baffling discussion swirled around the question of programs for chapter meetings. I had little idea of what kind of programs would draw people to the kind of conservation organization we wanted to form. Both Chuck and I felt that programs focused on learning and growing would be very appropriate for this conservation group. Others, as board member Al Frankel, were involved in organizations like Rotary Club and local sports groups. Al argued we should feature entertaining speakers, movies, and slides. Still others suggested meetings centered around fly-tying or rod building demonstrations, and other activities related to trout fishing.

Getting to Know the Territory

One of the most fascinating things about forming the new chapter was to be the opportunity to learn to know the streams of Chester County. Through the historic Great Valley of eastern Chester County, Pennsylvania, run two limestone streams. West Valley Creek flows west from its headwaters in the Church Farm School near Exton, eventually entering the Brandywine River. Valley Creek flows east, eventually entering Valley Forge National Park and then blending its waters with the Schuylkill River. Both are urban streams, flowing through housing and business developments, yet Valley Creek for many years has held the reputation of being the best trout stream in southeastern Pennsylvania. West Valley Creek, though smaller and exposed to generations of siltation from corn farming, still maintains a clean and cold flow of fertile limestone water.

Not only were these wonderful streams near where I lived, but also I discovered that there were at least thirteen significant trout streams in the county, and that, furthermore, there were quite a number of small streams with native brook trout populations.

Jerry Bullock, new board member and president of the Chester Valley Sportsmen's Association, told me about Trout Creek, which flowed very close to the King of Prussia office park where I work. In the great hurricane of the mid-1950s Jerry was living near the stream. During that storm he went out and looked at the creek and discovered that it only rose a foot or two even though the rains were heavy and long. With extensive development much of Trout Creek's watershed had been paved with roads and a large shopping center. Now when even a light thunderstorm hit the creek it flooded.

Strangely enough, I had never thought before about what happened when water fell on pavement. As soon as Jerry pointed it out I could see that water did not soak into the ground, but ran off in sheets into the nearest brooklet, which became a raging torrent. I had never thought about what happened to the water when it ran off the roads and parking lots. Now I could see (a necessary but painful vision).

Jerry also told me a great deal about the Chester Valley Sportsmen's Association, and its attempt to preserve Valley Creek. He had prepared a plan for preservation and restoration of the stream, based on

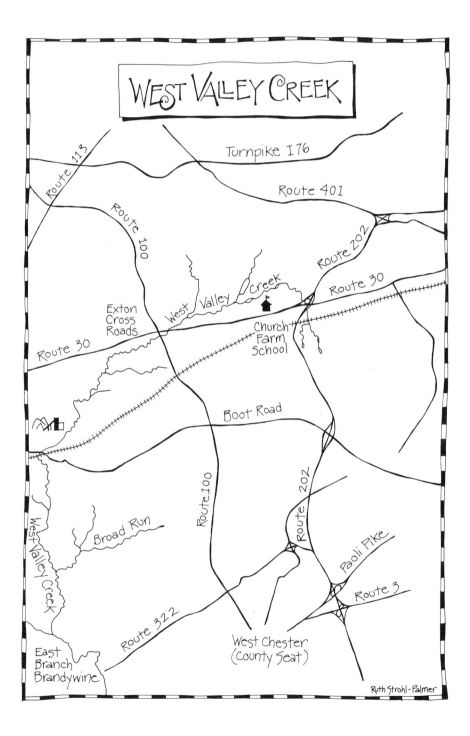

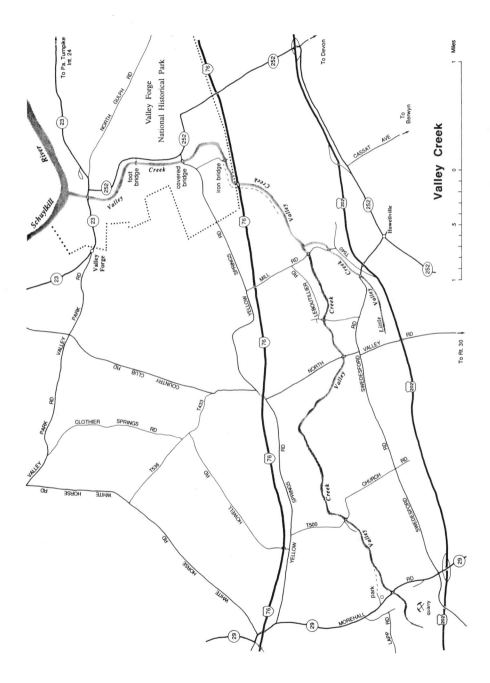

Valley Creek

his active role in conservation work throughout the late 1960s and early 1970s.

We expanded knowledge of the streams in our area by inviting leaders from other conservation groups to speak to us, and tell us what the were doing to conserve their streams. Slides of their work were informative and often inspiring. The state waterways patrolman for our area also spoke to the chapter, again increasing our knowledge of Chester County. He also told us a story showing that the efforts of a few could make a big difference.

A large mall was being built on the headwaters of West Valley Creek in Exton. During the process of building this mall, the state water-ways patrolman and the president of the West Chester Fish and Game Association became aware of the huge runoff which was going to result from paved parking lots and from the roof of the mall itself. They went to the developers of the mall and asked what plans were being made to control the runoff. Few plans had been made, and, further-more, the construction companies resisted doing more than dumping the runoff into the stream.

The two conservationists approached the woman who owned the biggest store in the development with their concern. When she stated that development would have to be stopped until the runoff question could be answered, the construction companies began to plan new designs which would channel runoff to catchment basins, so it would gradually soak into the ground. The parking lots themselves were built to reduce rapid flow of runoff into the stream. As a result of the efforts of the three leaders, the stream was kept in much better condi-tion than it would have been if mall development had been allowed to proceed with no consideration for water runoff.

Learning from Other Stream Groups

From one group we learned that it was possible to build a solid stream conservation organization by having regular work days for stream restoration. From the president of the Chester Valley Sports-men's Club, Jerry Bullock, we learned the value of developing a plan which covered an entire stream and its watershed. We also began to work with the West Chester Fish, Game and Wildlife Asso-ciation, which for many years had maintained stream restoration and trout stocking programs.

One of the most important things I discovered as I got to know people from other stream groups was that multiple memberships were common and accepted. Jerry Bullock pointed out that people who held membership in several organizations were far more likely to be active. It became clear that if we maintained a clear focus on conservation, we would not be competing with other stream groups. One could participate in the social activities of the fishing clubs and at the same time be an active member of the Valley Forge chapter.

A *Little Ecstasy*

Something happened during the summer of 1977 to restore my spirits. The new chapter had agreed to assist Chester Valley Sportsmen's Club in a stream restoration project under Jerry Bullock's direction, on Valley Creek, the stream that flows through Valley Forge National Park. One clear, hot July day we parked our cars along the road and walked to the spot where the activity was to begin. I had never seen this section of Valley Creek before. I was impressed with the cool, clear water even though the temperature already was in the upper eighties.

The project was ready to go. Someone had hauled in truckloads of large limestone rocks. Lumber and tools were at hand. The task was to construct a jack dam.

I had never heard of a jack dam before. A V-shaped structure, with the tip of the "V" pointing upstream, it is designed to raise the water level above it only a few inches. The water falls over the dam, digging a deep hole below and underneath the structure of the dam itself. One of the reasons for construction of the dam was to force more oxygen into the water as well as to provide hiding places for trout. Fifteen to twenty people must have been present. A few were eleven or twelve years old; others were in their upper seventies. Even those no longer able to get in the stream and work came out to observe and give moral support.

Jerry Bullock seemed to be everywhere. He gave instructions as to what to do, lifted planks, and pushed rocks. Soon the structure of the jack dam began to take shape.

After we had worked for a while I stood back and looked around. The temperature was now in the mid nineties. Everyone was dripping with sweat. No one was being paid. Yet all of us were working very hard, probably harder than we ever did at our jobs. A new spirit was joining us together, so that one felt close to people whom one had

never met before. Working-class and affluent people were hip deep in
the stream together. Young and old joined together in a common task,
one which would benefit others and would leave the stream better for
many to enjoy.

Lunch time came. Another surprise occurred. A local restaurant
provided, at no charge, large and tasty meatball sandwiches. Soft
drinks and beer were likewise offered. Everyone relaxed, sat down in
a cool place, and enjoyed lunch.

After lunch work on the jack dam proceeded. More people were
present than were needed. I wandered upstream with Joe Armstrong
and his daughters (a man who was to become a prominent leader of
our movement). As we walked upstream we took a good look at other
sections of stream. On the way back, we stopped and built a number
of small rock dams to concentrate the water flow. In the process, Joe
and I began to talk. He indicated a feeling of uneasiness about placing
large structures in the stream. Joe went on to say that he enjoyed
fishing in natural surroundings, and saw too much concrete, steel, and
other signs of human construction wherever he went. He believed,
therefore, that stream restoration work we did in the new chapter
should be as unobtrusive as possible, blending in with the natural
surroundings after a period of time. I strongly agreed with Joe, and a
common bond was established beteen us.

The July work day on the jack dam was a high point. Workers and
stream for a few moments were in harmony. That sense of community
between human beings and nature inspired me, motivating me to
keep going in what were to be baffling and draining times.

Few are the experiences of ecstasy in life, times in which one is
lifted out of one's self and inspired. For a day I was privileged to be
lifted out of aloneness into community. The work day showed that
people with diverse experiences and social positions could come together in common enterprise. Doing this project together generated a
sense of relatedness which never left us.

CHAPTER 3

Rats in a Maze

Trial-and-Error Learning

An experiment psychologists used to perform was to place a rat in a maze with food behind a door at the end of the maze. Rats eventually learned to find the door with the food behind it, but at first learning came slowly through trial and error. The poor animal would go down the wrong tunnel, discover it blocked, and have to turn back to where it started. It would start down another path, and usually discovered that one was blocked, too. Finally, after much trial and error the rat discovered the door with the food. The next time the rat went down the maze, however, it remembered some of the wrong turns, and so it took less time to get to the door. At last the rat mastered the maze, and could go directly from start to finish.

Put that rat in a new maze, and no matter how skilled the animal had become in running the old one, it had to start all over. No matter how good a "maze manager" the rat had become, a new situation still required trial-and-error learning.

Organizing a stream conservation group in Chester County drew on skills and insights of each, but it was a new situation. We had to get to know each other. We had to get to know the groups in the region. We had to learn the streams of Chester County, and discover the potentialities and limits of creating a conservation movement here. Looking back, I see that much of our frustration could not have been avoided. No matter what our skills and past experiences, we were running a new maze. Only as we painfully crept along by trial and error were we able to discover things which worked for us. Some of the most valuable things we were to learn came from walking down blind alleys, and then being persistent enough to go back to the beginning and start over.

Programming Problems

At the meeting when the chapter was organized fifty-five people were present. At the second meeting, twenty-five turned out. The third meeting found fifteen in attendance. For the next three years on good nights the average was ten to twelve, mostly members of the board and a few other loyal souls.

Every month a program had to be prepared. I tried to find someone who would be program chairperson for a year, but no one was able or willing to take it. We fell back on films. One of the more successful was *Way of a Trout*, a film prepared by Trout Unlimited for use in organizing new chapters. I remember the meeting when we showed *Way of a Trout*. I had borrowed a movie projector from work, carried it home, and took it to the meeting place. Chuck Marshall had a little experience in running movie projectors. We arrived early and set up the film. Something was wrong. The picture kept jiggling and jumping. Obviously either the projector was defective or we did not have the film threaded right. The time of the meeting drew closer and closer. Twelve faithful people gathered in the library of the church. We began the business part of the meeting, hoping that by the time we were ready to start the film would be ready to show. Somebody else went over to help Chuck.

As we were going through the business meeting, everybody had one eye on the movie projector, hoping it was going to work. I had a sinking feeling that despite all of our efforts to schedule a good program, we were going to have a failure. I was feeling the way I do when the monofilament on a spinning reel gets twisted and tangled just at the time a big fish splashes on the surface of the lake. There you are, ready to cast, and down between your feet is coil after coil of twisted and tangled line. Finally we managed to get the projector going correctly, after watching the first part of the film bounce and jiggle across the screen.

Those unfamiliar with voluntary associations might ask, "Why didn't you make sure that you found somebody competent enough to run the movie projector before you scheduled the film?" The answer was that there was no one competent who would volunteer! We were becoming increasingly desperate for programs for the monthly meetings, and films filled a big void. We would learn from one mistake, and discover how to correct that, only the next time to have a different problem occur. Bright hopes were often dashed by frustrations.

We kept at it. Leaders from another stream conservation group came to talk. Eight to ten people attended. In what should have been the peak time of interest in fishing, January through April, we planned meetings we felt would be specially attractive. On January 17, 1978, we showed a recreational film, *Panama Fish Bowl,* which Al Frankel had secured. That night the movie projector worked, but we still drew only a few people.

Almost a year later, in December 1978, I wrote a letter to the membership, encouraging them to come out to the next meeting for a fly-tying demonstration, and a film on the work of Trout Unlimited, *If We Don't Who Will?* We promised that refreshments would be served and that there would be plenty of time for conversation. A month before the Southeast Pennsylvania Regional Vice president of Trout Unlimited had spoken about the work of other Trout Unlimited chapters. Looking back, those programs still sound interesting. Yet only the faithful attended.

For over two years a major item of discussion at every board meeting was, "Why don't more people come?" We made changes, tried new things, but nothing seemed to work. Finally one member who seemed to have an understanding of programming agreed to accept that responsibility for the next year. He and I had lunch together one day and mapped out a list of possible programs for the next year. He agreed to see that each month a program was planned. I felt a great weight lift off my back. Now at last it looked like something was going to happen.

A week, two weeks went by, and I didn't hear from him. I began to start worrying again. I called, and discovered that there had been a serious illness in his family. He had to leave town for a time and would be unable to carry through on the programming responsibility. Perhaps I had asked him to take on too much responsibility, since he never again became active in the chapter.

Save Valley Creek?

Not only did we have trouble with monthly programs, but also our stream conservation action did not seem to move forward. In the fall of 1977 we formed a new action group, tentatively called the "Save

Valley Creek Committee." Chuck Marshall agreed to pull together a working group. I dug up names of people who seemed as though they might be interested. Then Jerry Bullock accepted a new job in Idaho: one of our strongest board members, our most knowledgeable stream conservationist, was leaving us.

The new committee struggled along with Chuck and one or two others. Month after month it seemed that we were unable to get anything moving. Meanwhile, the development of the Great Valley was rolling along. The completion of a regional sewer system allowed new construction to take place at many points along Valley Creek. Trees were being cut down, the watershed paved. Despite all our good intentions it seemed we were having no effect on anything. In May of 1978 I sent out a memo to friends and members of the Valley Forge Chapter.

> We have a loyal core of members, and we have learned a lot. But eight to ten people can't do the job of saving Chester County cold-water streams. We need people to work with the Save Valley Creek Committee, which is busily identifying sources of pollution and laying plans for action. Joe Armstrong is looking for volunteers to help with stream improvement work on West Valley Creek. Another group of us is hoping to do as much stream improvement work as we can on Valley Creek, and we need volunteers. John Hayes needs help in building our membership. Whatever your age, abilities, energy, there is a place for you at Trout Unlimited work in our area.

Joe Armstrong did take responsibility for stream restoration work on West Valley Creek. Sometimes two or three, sometimes four or five volunteers would show up. We always got something done, but the troops were limited.

A few more members moved away while others quietly stopped coming. Yet at the same time most meetings found one or two new people in attendance. We were not growing, but neither were we declining. As some left, new persons were elected to the board.

Returning to the Goal

After a year of frustration I called a friend who had been on the staff of the Wilderness Society. I shared with her all the difficulties we were having in forming this stream conservation organization in Chester

County. She sympathized, and then said something that was to prove most helpful:

> Go back to your goal of conserving streams. Use it to give people a new sense of direction. When you have done something, have the members evaluate what you did in relation to the goal: how effective was what you did in actually conserving or restoring a stream? Whatever you do, keep that goal in mind! (Conversation with Virginia Carney, 1978)

Accordingly, I lifted up the goal with new vigor. When we argued about programs and attendance, I raised the question of how these discussions related to our goal. When we did something, I called for evaluation in relation to the goal. At the end of 1978, I summarized in a letter to Ken Sink what we had done that year which had helped us move toward the goal:

> We've done some stream improvement work on West Valley Creek, and are participating in a major study of Valley Creek. We have also been focusing on building the membership, thus far with limited results. We hope that some of this work will pay off. We have been able to fill most of the positions with people who have commitment and dedication. We have discovered a young woman with a master's degree in biology, who has taken over the accountability to build the membership. Another person has shown some skill in program development and is making a contribution at that point.

Preparing a Plan

In 1978, after the first two years of experience, I sat down and prepared an action plan for our chapter. I presented this to a board meeting in the spring of 1978. The plan began by restating the overall objectives of the chapter: preserving and revitalizing the coldwater streams of Chester County.

A number of strategies were suggested:

> A. Do watershed planning
> B. Form an action group
> C. Enlist members
> D. Plan monthly meetings

    E. Generate financial support for chapter work
    F. Continue to have a good meeting place
    G. Organize

I felt this was a very good action plan. It was comprehensive, and gave a clear sense of direction as to what we might do next. To my discouragement the plan seemed to have no effect, other than giving me a clear understanding of what needed to be done. The only comment I ever got on it was from Al Frankel. A management consultant with extensive experience, he said to me that the plan made him realize that I had good skills in planning. Al's comment was supportive, but I had hoped the plan would give our chapter a stronger sense of direction.

Perhaps the plan, however, had more effect than I realized. Being able to set clear strategies marked a new phase in the development of chapter work. As the president of the chapter I was beginning to get my feet underneath me.

Learning from Others

Fortunately for us, human beings have the ability to learn from each other. Unlike rats in a maze, we can seek out people who have been faced with similar challenges, and discover how they met them. In the summer of 1978, we scheduled a joint meeting with the Delaware Chapter of Trout Unlimited. With them we hiked the lower stretches of White Clay Creek and talked about mutual concerns. I learned that this chapter had a core of only five to seven leaders. Each year they held a banquet to recruit new members and raise funds. Their chapter meetings did not have many more attending than we did. Yet this was a strong chapter which had been a conservation force in Delaware and Southern Chester County for some years. I returned from this meeting realizing that my expectations were too high. Perhaps an active, dependable group of ten to fifteen people was significant after all.

When I went to the Pennsylvania Trout Unlimited meetings, I found out as much as I could about how other chapters were organized. Ken Sink suggested I talk with leaders from the effective Blair County Chapter. I discovered that their newsletter was one of the keys to their effectiveness. From them I learned again that an active group of ten to fifteen has more influence than one might think. I asked about programs that would attract people. The Blair County Chapter was holding monthly meetings not too different than ours, featuring conservation speakers, movies, and demonstrations such as fly-tying or rod building.

Several members of the Valley Forge chapter had read about Vibert boxes, used to re-establish wild trout in streams which were unable to sustain natural reproduction. These plastic boxes look a bit like small strawberry baskets with a snap on top. They are only an inch wide and two or three inches long, but even in these small boxes several hundred trout eggs may be placed after having been removed from the trout and fertilized in a fish hatchery. Then they are put in the boxes, which are then ready to be placed in the stream.

We learned from the Pennsylvania Fish Commission that the program had produced limited results in some streams, but it seemed far wiser to attempt to re-establish natural reproduction wherever possible. When Joe Armstrong suggested that we secure some trout eggs and try planting them in the stream in Whitlock-Vibert Boxes, I was not enthusiastic.

We were learning, though, when someone has an idea and is willing to act on it, it is wise to try it, at least in a small way. So in 1978 Joe drove up to a hatchery, secured 15,000 brown trout eggs, and brought them back to plant in West Valley Creek.

The boxes were filled with trout eggs and then planted at a number of locations in West Valley Creek itself and in a major tributary, Broad Run. A few days later heavy rains hit Pennsylvania. The stream ran high and muddy. When the next weekend came, the boxes were pulled out and checked. Many were filled with silt. The eggs were still in the boxes, but were now dead. There were evidences of hatching, but on the whole the project was off to a disappointing start.

The End?

When I feel that something is moving in the right direction, I do not give up easily. Neither did the remaining members of the Valley Forge Chapter. We struggled, seeing some drop out and others come in, and we kept on going. Two years after we started, however, we hit a very low point. One summer night in 1978 a board meeting was called at my house. I got things ready and waited for people to come. Only one showed up, Al Frankel. We talked about the chapter and shared our mutual frustration. Finally as we walked down the driveway, Al asked me a pointed question, "If people don't support the chapter, are you willing to let it die?"

I thought for a moment, and through my mind ran the parable of the sower and the seed. A seed has to fall on fertile ground before it can sprout and grow. Though stubborn determination to move forward is essential in creating a new organization, there comes a time when one must be willing to let go. If one does not, in a strange way one can kill the very thing one is trying to bring into being. I looked at Al, and said to him, "Yes, I am willing to let it die."

That night was a turning point for me. I began to watch the chapter to see what people were going to do. Would they give up, or would the chapter continue? Through the fall of 1978 very little happened. The same group of 8 to 12 people came to the monthly meetings, and board attendance continued on about the same level. New officers were elected for the next year. Were people going to support conservation of the coldwater streams? I was not sure.

CHAPTER 4

Poison, Preparation, and Providence

The next few months of 1978 saw slight evidence of change. Then we risked planning a more demanding program. We invited a prominent local sportsman to come and address the chapter. We had hesitated before this to invite a well-known person fearing the embarrassment of small attendance. Notices were sent to everyone on our mailing list, and we promoted the meeting as hard as we could. We were very pleased when nineteen people turned out for the January 1979 meeting.

A Spring Thaw?

That meeting had the kind of feeling one gets after a long cold spell. Finally a day arrives when the snow begins to melt and one can smell a hint of spring in the air. Maybe our difficult times were coming to an end.

In March Dr. Ralph Heister, biology teacher at Conestoga High School, agreed to speak to us on "What is Happening to Valley Creek?" He and his students had recently completed a study of the effects of the new regional sewer system on the stream. They concluded that in a few years Valley Creek in midsummer could become a series of stagnant pools unless the remaining watersheds were preserved.

Ralph also showed slides of the continuing pollution of Valley Creek by the Knickerbocker Landfill. One particularly striking slide was taken years before when the landfill was first being constructed.

It showed an asphalt blanket laid across rough dirt fill. The blanket was to seal the bottom of the quarry so that leachate would run off into catchment basins. This photograph, however, showed huge cracks in the asphalt, clearly indicating that when the asphalt was covered, leachate would seep down through the cracks into the underground water supply. Ralph said that the massive landfill was a biological time bomb waiting to explode.

When Ralph Heister finished his address, people began to speak. It was as though a current of electricity had surged through the room. Members were angry, upset, and ready to act. Something had to be done.

Meanwhile the "Save Valley Creek Committee" had been struggling along for almost two years. Chuck Marshall continued to chair the periodic meetings of the little group. Slight interest could be seen, but Chuck did not give up. He set up a meeting of staff persons from the Pennsylvania Department of Environmental Resources, the Environmental Protection Agency, the County Soil Conservation Service, and other water-related bodies. The aim was to seek to understand and deal more adequately with pollution emerging from the Knickerbocker Landfill.

Poison

We anticipated the usual lukewarm responses to our efforts to save Valley Creek but went on with our plans. Fishing season in 1979 rolled around again. Chester County trout streams were stocked with trout, and as usual, people who loved to fish turned out in droves. Then, only two weeks after the start of the new fishing season, cyanide-laden water was pumped into Valley Creek by the 84 Lumber Company. It was later discovered that this cyanide had leaked into the underground water from the National Rolling Mills. The cyanide was so toxic that fish died all the way to where Valley Creek flows into the Schuylkill River. Of course television reporters were on the scene. After all, the Schuylkill is one of Philadelphia's major water sources. Newspapers sent their reporters. Our chapter leaders received many phone calls.

When I got the bad news, I left work and drove down to look at the stream. Dead fish were floating everywhere. Perhaps the most pathetic sight was a tiny survivor, a sucker, trying to hide underneath the dead body of a larger fish. As I walked up and down the bank that was about all the life I could see. I was briefly quoted in a newspaper. As president of the Valley Forge Chapter of Trout Unlimited I said that "we would try to do something about it." We did.

Four days after the fish kill the meeting Chuck had scheduled was held. The massive fish kill made people pay attention to Valley Creek. Twenty-two persons were in attendance. Ralph Heister, the biology teacher, showed his slides on Valley Creek, including shots of the Knickerbocker Landfill. Large drums of toxic waste were visible in one photograph taken when students had slipped in—somewhat understandably, owners of the landfill were very hesitant about allowing anyone to tour the facility. Other slides showed leachate tanks overflowing, unmonitored. We were given assurances by leaders of the Environmental Protection Agency and the Department of Environmental Resources that our concerns were heard.

Next we drafted letters to heads of agencies in the Pennsylvania state government. They were asked to act to stop further pollution. Chuck and I contacted Ralph Heister and together invited leaders of other conservation groups to meet to see what we could do to take better care of Valley Creek. The Valley Creek Watershed Coalition was formed. Our little Save Valley Creek Committee disappeared for a time, having completed its objective. Ralph Heister was elected to chair the new group.

The accomplishments of the new coalition were significant. It began by monitoring the Knickerbocker Landfill, directing press attention to the pollution coming from the landfill. During the first months of its existence, it supported the efforts of the Chester Valley Sportsmen's Association to see that Valley Creek was restocked with trout. It also monitored the efforts of the National Rolling Mills and 84 Lumber Co. to make restitution for the cyanide pollution. The steel mill, which has had a good environmental record, built new holding tanks entirely above ground so that another cyanide spill might not occur.

Pressure for change mounted. Department of Environmental Resources (DER) staff made inspections and issued a report which said that "uncontrolled and blatant discharges of leachate abound" (*Philadelphia Inquirer,* 27 September 1979). As a result, Knickerbocker was ordered to sink monitoring wells to make sure the ground water, which is used as a public drinking water supply, did not become contaminated. It was found that some ground water, indeed, was contaminated, with the chemicals polluting the underground water having some of the same constituents as the leachate.

In another report the DER noted that the landfill seemed to be generating an unusually high amount of leachate compared to calculations by consultants based on what the landfill said was actually going into it. Reports of continuing pollution continued to be heard. People living near Knickerbocker Landfill told about tank trucks regularly going into the landfill after dark and throughout the night and early morning. Foul odors blew off the landfill after these nocturnal visits.

The *Inquirer* reporter interviewed the owners of the landfill: "Theodore Rubino, who is serving a federal extortion sentence by working as a part-time volunteer in a local hospital, told *The Inquirer* that the landfill closes well before dark, and there is never any traffic at night. And Sam Rubino contended that the landfill never takes liquids: 'We don't have no tank trucks in here. Honest we don't. We run a clean landfill!' " Federal and state environmental agencies seemed to be unable to find out and report on what was going on. Rather than giving up in despair, one day Chuck Marshall drove to New Jersey. There he requested and received information on hazardous waste shipping from the Department of the Environment of New Jersey, which had a manifest system showing the destination of waste produced in New Jersey. Operators of landfills who received these wastes had to sign manifests showing they had gotten them. Chuck looked at many DEPNJ printouts. Some manifests identified hazardous wastes received by Knickerbocker Landfill!

The Philadelphia Inquirer was running a series of articles on pollution. Since Knickerbocker Landfill was allowed only to take household waste, Chuck took the information he had gathered in New Jersey to the *Inquirer* reporter who used this information in subsequent articles.

One article reported twenty-five major firms had sent hazardous waste to the Knickerbocker Landfill (during the period from January 1, 1978, to June 30, 1979). These figures are minimal because there may have been additional shipments detailed in the New Jersey records that were not discovered in the *Inquirer's* search:

Martin Aaron, Incorporated, Camden, New Jersey: 7,000 pounds of liquid and corrosive alkaline solution; 9,400 pounds of oil sludges; 6,000 pounds of pink pigment residues.

Air Products Company, Elkton, Maryland: 27,500 pounds of latex sludges.

American Can Company: 720 gallons waste oil. Franklin Pertnoy, general manager of Jonas, the hauling firm, wrote in the manifest that officials at the landfill refused to sign for receipt of the waste, so Pertnoy signed for them.

American Cyanamid, Havre de Grace, Maryland, plant: 210 gallons of liquid corrosive alkaline solutions. On the manifest, officials at the landfill did not sign for the shipment; instead Pertnoy, the hauler's general manager, signed his name where landfill officials were supposed to sign.

Certainteed Corporation, Williamstown, New Jersey, plant: 2,802,000 pounds, in what for weeks were daily shipments of 30,000 pounds apiece of wet fiberglass waste containing phenols.

Chemical Laymen Tanklines, Incorporated, Downington, Pennsylvania: 2,925 gallons of latex and oil sludges.

Dupont: 114,000 pounds of paint and pigment residues in sludge form.

Exxon: 36,100 lbs. of oil sludges. (*The Philadelphia Inquirer*, September 27, 1979)

Eighteen other companies were listed from different industries. Among them were paint and steel makers and the Salem Nuclear Generating Station at Hancock's Bridge, New Jersey.

When the landfill operators denied that they had received hazardous waste, the reporter went out and asked the gateman, Ray Howe, to sign something. Howe's signature checked with the one that appeared on a New Jersey manifest. The landfill was caught redhanded.

Hazardous waste dumping at Knickerbocker Landfill stopped. Chuck's detective work probably played a major role in defusing a biological time bomb. Since Knickerbocker Landfill was built on a limestone quarry, anything seeping down through the liner of the landfill would go directly into the clear clean water of the limestone aquifer beneath the quarry. Chuck said, "Phenols and solvents will eat right through an asphalt liner. I hope we stopped the hazardous waste dumping soon enough to protect the integrity of the liner."

As if this were not enough, the coalition then had to stop another plan which could have been even more dangerous. A proposal was brought to it to build a hazardous waste treatment site on top of the landfill. They quickly turned down that option after checking it out with the related groups.

Thanks to a few dedicated environmentalists children are again able to fish in a stream which is relatively uncontaminated. Babies will be born without the birth defects which probably would have occurred if hazardous and toxic waste dumping in the quarry had continued. The beginning efforts of the Valley Creek Watershed Coalition made a difference.

The cyanide poisoning of Valley Creek was easier to combat than slow and insidious pollution. The Paoli Railroad Yard's contamination of two different watersheds with PCBs was impossible to stop for years. The pollution of underground water by the landfill, although known by a few, caused no widespread concern. Cyanide pollution of Valley Creek had obvious effects. Once the coalition got going, however, it proved able to deal with the less visible, persistent pollution of the landfill, as well as with the immediate effects of the cyanide poisoning.

Persistence

The Vibert Box idea had captured Joe Armstrong's imagination. Wouldn't it be great if stream-bred trout could be re-established in West Valley Creek? "If water in the mainstream is too silty, what about the feeder streams?" he wondered. Along Whitford Road were two ditches. Joe and a few others took a very close look at this little tributary. They measured the water temperature and found that it was 52 degrees (F.). They walked upstream and found the source of the little tributary, a limestone spring. The tributary on the west side of Whitford Road also emerged out of a limestone spring, and maintained the same constant temperature. Each tributary was overgrown with watercress, again a sign of clean, cold water. The watercress was loaded with food, particularly cress bugs and fresh water shrimp.

Plans were made in 1979 to put boxes in these tiny feeder streams. Gravel was purchased, and over one thousand pounds hauled out to the Whitford Road area. On the day of the egg-planting people gathered at Whitford Road. Each took a bucket, filled it with gravel, and carried it out to the feeder streams. Buckets of gravel were placed in the current so that water was washing over them. Then a box was buried in each gravel "nest."

After two weeks, we returned to check out what had happened.

When boxes were pulled from the gravel this time there were few dead eggs, and when we stirred the gravel with a finger, we saw tiny trout dart out.

The hatch was excellent but would the fish survive and grow? The first big surprise was that the fish not only survived, but grew all winter. We had discovered a natural trout nursery. No matter how cold the weather became, because the little tributaries were fed by limestone springs they maintained a constant fifty-two-degree temperature. Watercress thrived throughout the cold weather, providing hiding places and an ample supply of food. The little trout gorged on the cress bugs and shrimp, and they grew and grew.

One cold Sunday afternoon in January 1980, with the temperature around 25 degrees and a strong wind blowing, Joe Armstrong and I checked what was happening to the little trout. The people looking at us from Whitford Road must have thought we were out of our minds. Joe was carrying a tiny net, the kind that is used in aquariums. There we were on that frigid day, wearing hip boots, wading up a little tributary, poking the net into hiding places no more than four or five inches deep. Again and again we caught trout. Already their colors were vivid. Red spots stood out. Each was fat and healthy. The size variation was considerable. Some were rather large, while others were not much bigger than fry, perhaps an inch to an inch and a half long (apparently fish develop at different rates, even in environments which are fertile and protected).

During the summer months, the little trout continued to grow. Many dropped downstream and took up residence in the creek itself. Stream-bred trout had been re-established in West Valley Creek.

Evaluation

People in Chester County were beginning to be aware of the Valley Forge Chapter of Trout Unlimited. They knew that we met regularly and that we did something to stop pollution of Valley Creek.

In the fall of 1979, I prepared a general letter to people inviting them to join the Valley Forge Chapter of Trout Unlimited. Initial paragraphs told the story of the work we had done on Valley Creek. The letter concluded with a summary of recent work:

> Trout Unlimited efforts have not stopped with Valley Creek. Over the past two years, we have been working with the West Chester

Fish and Game Association to improve and preserve West Valley Creek. Those who fish the stream can see stream improvements which show our common concern (deflectors, half logs, willow planting, Vibert boxes). In July, members made a fishing visit to Buck Run stream (in western Chester County), in order to become familiar with this relatively unspoiled creek. In August our regularly scheduled meeting was a visit to White Clay Creek, guided by members of the Delaware Trout Unlimited Chapter.

Our monthly meetings have featured such interesting speakers. We are looking forward to a spring event featuring Charlie Fox. We have also been collecting information about how streams work, and what people can do to preserve and restore them (which we are glad to share with interested groups). Right now we are making plans for the future. For example, we intend this winter to meet with people concerned about West Valley Creek, in order to prepare a watershed preservation plan. We hope to strengthen existing groups of people committed to preserving the cold water streams near where they live (as Dame Juliana League, the West Chester Fish and Game Association and other local groups). Where no groups committed to conservation exist, we would like to form new Trout Unlimited groups.

If trout are to survive, and provide enjoyment and sport near our homes in Chester County, they must have clean, cold water, food and cover. If our children are to have clean drinking water, the watersheds must be preserved.

As gas gets more expensive, more and more of us will want recreation close to home. But unless we act now, all we will have are spring and summer floods, alternating with stinking mud holes (where once a beautiful stream flowed). Valley Forge chapter of Trout Unlimited wants and needs your support.

A Familiar Voice Is Silenced

Al Frankel and I became good friends. When you argue and struggle with someone in a common cause, you learn to respect each other. One day I received a call at work. Al was in the hospital. He had been fishing in the ocean off Long Island, and had a recurrence of his heart trouble.

When I got there, Al was asleep. The nurse hesitated to wake him, but when I told her Al had asked to see me, she admitted me to the room. He woke up, and we talked for a little while. I remember that we joked a little about Trout Unlimited. He and I had a prayer together. I did not stay very long since it was obvious that Al was not at all well. Only a few days later I received word that he had died.

Though Al was never able to attend a work day because of his heart trouble, his guidance during the early years of the chapter contributed greatly to its development. He was one of those who helped prepare for what was to come, though he was not to see the results of his efforts. As a matter of fact, I think that if it had not been for him, the chapter would have never seen new life and energy break out. Our summer board meeting in 1978 enabled me to let go of the chapter and allow it to die if that was what people wished. Al took us through some very deep water. His guiding voice is silent, but his wisdom continues to be expressed in and through us.

Getting to Know a Tough Character
West Valley Creek

One character we came to know very well in the first three years of our work was a tributary of the Brandywine River called West Valley Creek. Indeed, in this story, it figures as a major actor. Human-caused alterations in the watershed have often made the stream appear to be a bad actor, for tons of silt and rubble wash down with every storm. Yet as we have come to know the stream, we have come to learn much more than we ever expected about the nature of a healthy stream.

In 1940 West Valley Creek was still relatively healthy. Then came development. At an old bridge was a spring from which people once drank. Road construction buried it.

Federal subsidies for farms to ditch streams and wetlands encouraged these practices on the headwaters of the stream. What had been a native brook trout fishery was turned into a barren ditch surrounded by pasture by the late 1950s. The construction of the General Crushed Stone quarry around 1970 displaced a mile section of West Valley Creek into a new dredged channel. The large spring on the quarry was covered by tons of dirt and rock.

As our struggles to start a stream-conservation organization began to show results, our attention shifted gradually to answering a pointed question: What is a healthy stream? By exploring places we might begin a restoration project we became increasingly aware of our ignorance. Many of us had fished trout streams since we were children. We had observed the riffles, pools, undercut banks, trees, and grass. We learned which areas were likely to hold trout and which ones did not. Yet when we began to think about stream restoration, we had to think about what made for a healthy stream. It was not self-evident. If we were to seek to restore streams to a healthy condition we needed far more than fishing knowledge. Clear understanding of the factors which would restore a degraded creek into a state of health was necessary.

We learned from other conservation groups how they had built their movement around in-stream work. The U.S. Army Corps of Engineers had overall responsibility for anything that happened to a waterway in the United States. It had delegated authority in Pennsylvania for restoration work to the Pennsylvania Fish Commission. The Fish Commission in turn, had established programs through which local groups could adopt part or all of a stream, develop a plan, and receive official approval for it.

Joe began to do some "poking around," as he put it. He got to know the owner of a section of West Valley Creek who was open to restoring a stretch of degraded water. He put out some feelers for a possible project on Valley Creek in Valley Forge National Park, but the superintendent at that time was not interested in such an enterprise. An obvious place for restoration was the dredged section which ran along next to the General Crushed Stone quarry, but once again the quarry was not interested in having work done on that section of stream. Vandals had taken shots at a building in which dynamite was stored, so the quarry banned hunting on its ponds and wanted nothing that would attract people to its property.

Valley Creek would have been the logical place for a restoration project, since it was a center of national and state attention because it ran through Valley Forge National Park. But this possibility was ruled off to us, so we began where we could, with the James Clark Jr., property on West Valley Creek. With approval from the land owner, we got in touch with the Pennsylvania Fish Commission and, following conversations and a site visit, were officially underway with an approved project.

Observing Stream Flow Throughout the Year

We learned much by wading right into West Valley Creek. We made small changes in the stream bed and the immediate banks of the stream, and observed what happened.

I decided to go fishing at least once a week from April to October and observed the stream under different weather and water conditions. I was amazed at the difference between the way the stream flowed during dry months and the way it ran after a heavy rain. I began to imagine the effects of seasonal changes on the living creatures in the stream.

During the high water of spring there were many places for fish to feed and hide. The whole stream bottom was accessible to them. Then came a drought, and the flow slowed to a trickle. Only a few favored spots in the quarry section held trout during that drought. The rest was barren, inhabited only by a few minnows and sunfish. Finally the drought was broken, and from a trickle the stream was transformed to a raging torrent with water four or five feet deep. All kinds of materials floated down lodging against trees and brush. The water color was a muddy chocolate. Then the rain ceased, and in a day the water would return to "normal." I became very aware that fish in West Valley Creek endured a constantly fluctuating water flow.

When chapter workdays took me out to the stream in the wintertime, I was impressed by all the conditions under which the creatures of the stream must survive. Zero-degree nights left the surface of the stream almost frozen, except in those favored sections where springs pour out water with temperatures of around fifty-two degrees F. Warmed by their flow, in most parts of West Valley Creek trout do not have to contend with frazil ice (when the stream itself partly freezes, bearing innumerable ice particles right in the current itself).

Listening to Guest Speakers

From the beginning days of the Valley Forge Chapter, we asked local conservation leaders to come to our monthly meetings and give a talk. I learned a great deal about streams and how they work by listening to these speakers.

One of the earliest presentations still stands out in my mind. Leaders of the Dame Juliana League came and spoke to us about their work on French Creek (another Chester County stream). They believed in working with nature, building small devices of various sorts. Then they observed what the stream did, modifying their efforts as they learned.

French Creek is a fairly large freestone stream. When it floods, whole trees may be torn free and float down. During one hurricane, part of the channel was diverted and an island created. The Dame

Juliana members restored the original channel and improved the habitat. They also told us of their continuing struggles to keep the stream unpolluted and open to fishing.

Pennsylvania Fish Commission fisheries biologist Mike Kauffman informed us about a major research project being done all over Pennsylvania. Each region of the state was assigned a biologist who surveyed the cold-water streams in that area. This major study has allowed classification of streams according to a carefully structured set of criteria. From Kauffman and other biologists who spoke to us I learned one could actually tell the health of a stream through study of its invertebrate life. I still am amazed that by lifting rocks and catching the mayflies and other creatures as they are dislodged and float downstream, one can tell so much about the coldness and purity of the water in a particular stream. Generally speaking, the healthier the stream, the greater the diversity and number of insects which live in its waters.

In another memorable talk, the executive director of the Mill Creek Watershed Association told us what they had learned about stream restoration in an urban setting. She had been able to establish a Vibert Box program, getting in most years an effective hatch of trout.

Each group which came and spoke to us expanded our knowledge. Gradually a picture of a healthy stream began to emerge in my own mind. I began to become aware of the factors which were critical to the life of a healthy stream.

Water quality should be high. The water should contain enough oxygen and be cool enough to sustain trout and other cold water invertebrates throughout the year. There should be a strong year-round flow of water through the stream, and it should be clean, with no pollution and little stream-born sedimentation. Acidity should be normal (usually not a problem on limestone streams).

Second, fish, insect, and other invertebrate populations are present in species and numbers characteristic of this type of stream in this geographical area (this factor is often difficult to assess, given the tremendous impact of human activity). The general stream ecosystem supports a variety of life forms, including animals, birds, reptiles, and so forth. A healthy stream produces good food for trout. Invertebrate life should be abundant, including insects, crayfish, and minnows.

A third essential is good cover. It helps if cover is directly in and over the stream. In an urbanized area, it is critically important to maintain an undeveloped, unmowed strip on and adjacent to each bank. Stepping back further, the watershed itself should also have natural cover, thus keeping run-off low and allowing rain to soak into the water table.

Fourth, regarding structure, the riffle/pool ratio should be normal. There should be adequate feeding stations for trout, and meanders should follow a normal pattern for the amount of gradient of that stream.

Fifth, a healthy stream is beautiful. Each pool and riffle is so distinct it can be named. The overall appearance of each part of the stream is pleasant to see, and enjoyable to fish and observe.

Sixth, the creatures in it are able to mate and reproduce. The stream is fertile. The riffles trout use to spawn are unsilted and are somewhat protected from predation.

Seventh, a healthy ecosystem promises to be self-sustaining over several generations (balanced). Human beings fit into this ecosystem and have access to it. Thus, the stream is open to the public, so that people in appropriate ways may be part of the total reality.

Collecting Research Reports

We also learned about healthy streams by writing letters asking for whatever reports might be available. I was struck by the limited amount of theoretical and applied research being done. With the number of streams in this country, and the obvious importance of water to all life, one might have thought that millions of dollars a year would be devoted to understanding streams and how they work. Unfortunately, this has not been the case. Little money was spent for study of fisheries. Only limited attention had been given to identifying the conditions which make for healthy streams.

We did find some reports, however, which were invaluable. Dr. Ray White, who worked in Wisconsin for many years, sent me a collection of papers which I found extremely helpful. The work of the Pennsylvania Fish Commission was frequently reported at meetings of the Pennsylvania Council of Trout Unlimited. Particularly useful was the guide to stream restoration of the Wisconsin Conservation Department (Ray J. White and Oscar M. Brynildson, *Guidelines for Management of Trout Stream Habitat in Wisconsin*, Madison, Wisconsin, Department of Natural Resources, Bulletin no. 39, 1967).

We collected research papers, studied them, and sought to apply what we learned to our own situation. Each stream in the country has unique characteristics determined by its geographical location. Learnings from a diversity of environments, however, helped us identify common characteristics of a healthy stream.

Sharpening Observation

In the quest to understand the nature of a healthy stream, I found my perceptions being sharpened. As I walked or fished the stream with chapter members, they would point out to me things they saw. One would lift up a rock and observe the different kinds of insects crawling on its under surface. Another pointed out to me trout which were invisible until I was shown where they were. Again and again, I realized how little I saw. I also became increasingly aware that some who fish develop very keen use of their eyes.

Gradually I came to see more keenly myself. In seeking to understand a healthy stream, the perceptiveness of people who fish is a tremendous source of information. Over the course of a season it is quite common for chapter members to catch and release the same fish two or three times. By the end of the summer some of our most skilled fishermen would be able to name almost every trout in the section they fish.

I began to be amazed by those who fished West Valley Creek. When there was a chemical spill, it was reported almost immediately. Someone was watching the stream, so that when something destructive happened, it was seen and reported.

Using Memories

Another source of insight into a healthy stream comes from memory. In the mid 1950s and early 1960s the quarry section was a meandering meadow stream. Large trout were not uncommon. Native brook trout could be found in the headwaters. Deep pools alternated with riffles.

When remembering, however, one should not idealize the past. I suspect that the cornfields along the banks of the stream were often as destructive to trout in times past as the current development process. To illustrate, one has only to go to where "clean farming" is practiced, as in the Pennsylvania Dutch country in Lancaster County, Pennsylvania, and see the sad state of the trout streams. An intensive farming economy which does not seek to preserve and restore streams can reduce a stream to a warm muddy ditch, just as an urbanizing development process is able to do. As long as memories are not idealized, though, they can be very useful. Reflecting back on the characteristics of streams as they once were gave us insight into what this degraded stream could become.

Learning from a Master: A Visit to Wisconsin

We learn a great deal from observation, from studying research reports, and from our own experimentation in a stream. Sometimes, though, it is necessary to spend some time with a master of an art or skill. Through his or her eyes one can see things one never would have perceived without that person's presence. English river masters, for instance, have cared for and maintained streams for hundreds of years.

I have not had the good fortune to apprentice with a river master, but in 1979 I did learn much in a short visit with Bob Hunt, research biologist for the state of Wisconsin. His pioneering research on Lawrence Creek in central Wisconsin is a classic (R. L. Hunt, *Production and Angler Harvest of Wild Brook Trout in Lawrence Creek, Wisconsin*, Conservation Dept. of Wisconsin, Technical Bulletin, 1966). Based on the best available biological information this coldwater trout stream was restructured to increase fish production. Results were astounding, with numbers and size of fish increasing dramatically during the study period.

One beautiful fall day in 1979 a friend from Racine and I drove up to central Wisconsin. We met Bob Hunt and had lunch at the local restaurant. Then he took us in his station wagon to look at streams.

The first one we visited was small. As we walked along its bank, we saw brook trout as thick as minnows. Bob told us that these fish for the most part were rather small and that people had a hard time catching them. One poor cast or the sight of a person, and a trout would become scared and shoot away. The rest would scatter, making fishing difficult. I took pictures of the little stream, noticing its golden sand bottom. Tall grasses grew on each side of the gently meandering current. Bob said that the grass next to the stream was reed canary grass. He told us how good it was for pushing the banks of the stream closer together. Its roots go down into soil and trap sediment as it goes downstream, gradually narrowing and deepening the channel, and providing many hiding places for the fish.

All three of us then splashed into the stream. Bob stuck his foot under a log on the bottom. When he showed us, we could see that it had been placed there intentionally. "It's a half log," he said. He went on to explain that one of the limiting factors in a stream with clean, cold water is cover. Increased cover means places for increased numbers of fish to rest and feed. We noticed that the log was fastened to the bottom with two blocks of wood underneath it. There was a space of perhaps six inches underneath the log for fish to hide. These logs were placed in such a way that sediment and brush would not be caught in them and were positioned so that they were immediately adjacent to the area of maximum stream flow.

I took as many pictures as I could of this little stream. Then we went on to a larger central Wisconsin stream, Roche a Cri Creek, where a major restoration project had been completed a few years before. Four to five-foot-high grass covered the banks in the swampy meadow. The area immediately adjacent to the stream was clear of trees. We could see stumps where alders had been cut and we asked about why. Bob told us that when alders are allowed to grow on stream banks, they choke the current, eventually diminishing usable habitat and making a stream almost impossible to fish.

As we walked along the bank, suddenly a hefty trout shot away upstream. It must have been fourteen or fifteen inches long, and appeared to be a brook trout. This section of restored stream looked like a normal trout stream. We could see few evidences of human efforts. When we looked closely, however, we could see rock triangles that had been placed there intentionally.

Near evening Bob took us to a project which was still in the process of being completed. Below it we could see the very wide bed of the stream, with shallow water. In the project area the triangles made of rocks were obvious, as were artificial undercut banks. We looked underneath the structures and saw how they were made: posts were sunk into holes drilled in the bottom of the stream, and planks were nailed to these posts to form an overhang. This entire structure was under water, so that the wood would not rot. Rocks were placed on top of the wooden structures, and sod was placed on top of the rocks, creating an edge of green along the stream. Then the section behind the rocks was filled in with rocks, rotten logs, brush, and whatever else was around to create a new stream bank. In a year or two this back-fill would be covered with vegetation and would become invisible, as would be most of the marks of construction. We finished the day with many thanks to Bob Hunt for his tour.

What I was able to bring back from this visit with Bob Hunt helped us greatly. First, seeing how a rock triangle may be placed in a stream gave clues to how we could make the current in West Valley Creek work for us. We learned, second, the value of undercut banks, and how they may be made. Third, we found out how to condense the flow of a broad, flat stream. Fourth, we discovered the idea of half logs. We also learned, fifth, that in restoring the natural meander of a creek, one creates much more appealing views. The stream becomes more beautiful as it becomes more varied.

One thing stood out. It is possible for people to increase the productivity of a stream by two to seven times. If we understand the characteristics of a healthy stream, we can restore degraded areas, or enhance the productivity of a stream that is already healthy. I would have never realized that it was possible to carry out such a restoration program, if I had not seen the Wisconsin results.

No Shortcuts

O ne of my initial concerns was to form a chapter with many leaders. Now I had opportunity to put this philosophy into practice. The years of struggle and discouragement sifted the chapter. Those who were firmly committed to the goal and willing to work toward its realization stayed. Disappointments, failures, and common experiences gradually melded us into a strong stream conservation organization. I was asked to become southeast regional vice president of Trout Unlimited. That meant I would have to give up the chapter's presidency.

A New Leader

Things were obviously beginning to move, but I wondered whether I needed to stay on as president a bit longer until the chapter became more solid. I decided, however, it was time to step down. There were several people in the chapter who could assume the task. Joe Armstrong's restoration work on West Valley Creek, however, had been outstanding, and he was respected and liked by everyone. The nominating committee suggested his name as the new president. When the election was held in the fall of 1979, Joe became the new chapter president. I felt a great sense of relief. Responsibilities for programs, newsletters, organizing and recruiting now fell upon someone else. I was free to become an ordinary member of the chapter—and it felt good.

Joe Armstrong did not believe in organizing for instant success. He tells a story about when as a young man he observed assistant plant managers trying to make a name for themselves in a large corporation. Each of these young leaders was assigned to head a manufacturing division. The way one became recognized as successful was, of course, to make money. The young managers rapidly discovered, however, that the manufacturing process was very stable, and little could be done to make their shop more profitable—unless they stopped spending money on maintenance. Those managers which cut the maintenance budget immediately showed an increase in profitability. Some of these "leaders" were even promoted, but woe to those who followed them. Neglected machinery began to collapse requiring expenditures far greater than adequate maintenance would have cost if it had been done all along.

Armstrong's philosophy of no shortcuts stood him in good stead. Starting with a membership of about thirty, he had to build the Valley Forge Chapter. In order to save the streams of Chester County and their watersheds, he had to see that the wellbeing of streams and their watersheds was considered in public and corporate decision-making. Beginning efforts of instream restoration had to be strengthened. There had to be education on why and how streams and watersheds could be preserved and restored.

These four objectives flowed side by side. Moving toward one could reinforce the others, provided that the chapter president saw how the objectives were interconnected. A lesser leader might have tried to get quick results in one area or another and not done the hard work necessary to build a movement that would endure over the long haul. Joe, however, set to work to accomplish all four objectives.

In 1979 Jim and Gene Clark became active in chapter work, joining the chapter when the first stream restoration project on West Valley Creek began on their property. They put in hundreds of hours building stream devices, planting streamside vegetation and pushing rocks. Nobody would have expected when we began that stream restoration work on West Valley Creek that one of the results would be finding competent new editors for a chapter paper! Within six months, Jim and his brother Gene were writing the first issue of *Banknotes*, and publicizing "An Evening with Charlie Fox," which was to be held in March, 1980.

I asked Jim Clark what led him to get active in the chapter: "It has been five generations since the Potato Famine when our family moved here. My dad loved to fish West Valley Creek, but he gave up, saying, 'Some rotten guy will come along and pollute it.' But after I went to a

Make a Difference: Report Polluters

chapter meeting, I said that as a family we had put over five generations of time into this area. Why give up?"

One night I received a call from someone who introduced himself as Jack McFadden. Calls from people inquiring about Trout Unlimited were rare. Jack was interested in stream conservation. I invited him to come to a chapter meeting. He came and as we got to know each other we became friends, particularly after we spent a few days fishing Penn's Creek on our way up to a summer Pennsylvania Trout Unlimited meeting. Jack was to become the new treasurer of the chapter, the first member to take an active interest in chapter finances and eventually the third chapter president.

Other new faces were surfacing at chapter meetings, mostly people recruited by Joe Armstrong for West Valley Creek restoration work. We got to know each other at the regular work days, sweating and struggling together. Among the new members was Jack Assetto. Jack had been attending another sports organizations, but felt that the leadership of that group was "locked in." There was little opportunity for a new person. Our attempts to establish a climate open to anyone began to pay off.

Charlie Fox Night

One of the chapter leaders, Mary Kuss heard that Orvis would give a top of the line outfit to a chapter if that chapter would be willing to fish it, and send back comments to them. Since the price was right, she pursued this, and we got a great rod, reel and line, fished it, and sent our comments to the manufacturer. We then had a major asset. What should we do with it?

After considerable debate a banquet was ruled out, but the board decided if we had a top-name speaker and we advertised well, we would be able to raffle off that rod and perhaps some other prizes and make some money.

In parallel with this, Charlie Fox, a well-known conservationist in south central Pennsylvania (and the first Trout Unlimited member in Pennsylvania) was introduced to some chapter members. We were aware of his project of planting purple loosestrife, a much maligned plant with the very positive attribute of attracting many terrestrial insects to its flowers in mid-summer. When these water-loving plants were adjacent to a stream, they would bring insects to streamside, where some would inevitably fall in, creating a lengthy and predictable "hatch" during the summer doldrums. It was decided to go visit Charlie, and pick up a few of these plants for West Valley Creek. Two chapter members went up and dug out the plants and at the same time asked if he would be willing to come speak to us. Perhaps because he was pleased that we were following one of his projects, but more likely because he was the great man he is, he accepted. We had a top raffle item and a top speaker; now we had to get into the nuts and bolts of putting together a meeting.

We were experienced in holding interesting meetings which drew only a few people. Mary Kuss argued that instead of a banquet with high overhead cost, a special night should be scheduled at a public place. Jack Assetto was given the responsibility to chair a committee, but the special event was to follow the plans given by Mary.

I remember going to a working meeting of that committee. All of the programming failures we had experienced in the past three years now became an asset. Members of the committee ticked off all the things which would go wrong in such a meeting, and made plans to make sure that they did not reoccur. The meeting place was secured, and a map prepared so that people could find it. The ten people present carefully planned the special event. Books of tickets were prepared, giving people chances on items of merchandise to be donated by local sports stores. Members of the committee fanned out across the Chester County area seeking assistance. Jack wrote letters to manufacturers, asking them to donate something to be auctioned at the event.

Posters advertising the event were placed in sporting goods stores. Announcements were made in newspapers and on the radio. The *Banknotes* featured the upcoming Charlie Fox Night.

The president, unfortunately, had to leave on a work trip. The evening of Charlie Fox Night, Joe Armstrong found himself in a smoke-filled room in Japan. His mind kept wandering away from business as he wondered what was happening back in Chester County. Had anybody showed up for the Charlie Fox Night? Was it going well? Would it be a big success or a fiasco?

Joe had arranged for a telegraph to be sent after the evening was over. He waited and waited, and finally the news arrived. Around three hundred people turned out for Charlie Fox night. Thirty new members joined and over $1,000 was raised, for the first time giving the chapter a solid bankroll for its conservation work.

This night was a seminal event in chapter history. It put us on the map. We now had some money, lots of new members, and momentum. Charlie Fox night launched Valley Forge Trout Unlimited. In many ways we have not looked back since.

From January 1 through the end of May 1980, 52 members joined the chapter, bringing the total membership to 72. The chapter received an award from national TU for the third-highest percentage increase in 1980.

The president challenged these new members to go to work, so they would not lose interest. Joe thought of all the ways he could to get people involved. One was the "Cause of the Month." Each month he identified a particularly important environmental issue. One month it might be writing to senators or congress people asking them to support constructive legislation on acid rain, or on challenging the Pennsylvania legislature to restore abandoned strip mines. Postcards were handed out at the meeting, and names and addresses of persons to whom to write were listed. Cards were collected at the close of the meeting to be mailed out.

Joe also encouraged leaders to go to their own townships to begin to monitor development projects. He gave support to chapter members who were trying to stop construction of the West Whiteland Mall, whose developers wanted to dump treated sewage into tributaries of West Valley Creek. Joe stated in chapter and board meetings how important it was for citizens to get active in understanding the development issues and making input to local governments so that the streams of Chester County would be preserved.

Stream Restoration

As if all of this work was not enough, Joe put immense energy into getting stream restoration started in Chester County. From 1977 through 1979, Joe had been trying to correct some of the worst problems. West Valley Creek was suffering from the effects of development on its headwaters. Construction of roads, houses, and businesses had increasingly removed the trees and open land so essential to a healthy watershed, replacing it with impermeable pavement. Floods had never been a problem, but in the 1970s rains brought flooding, and left masses of silt and sediment in the stream. Something had to be done.

The upper part of our project section, the Clark property, begins with a huge pool a short distance below the railroad tunnel. West Valley Creek then takes an abrupt left turn, flowing through an area where once there were a series of pools and riffles. Sedimentation had largely eliminated the pools. The lower section of the Clark property was one long pool, its bottom mostly muddy sediments. Here there was very little current.

One Sunday afternoon in January 1980, Jim Clark, Joe Armstrong, my son Andy, and I pushed rocks down a steep hill to the bank of the stream. Then we picked them up and carried them across to begin to make a bank. The weather was cold, but we got warm as we lifted those rocks. Anyone hardy enough to have been looking on might have thought we were crazy, wading around in the stream in January. We had a good time, though, no matter what anyone else thought.

Joe built a list of interested workers. Before each workday he would go to his list, calling those who had shown some interest in the stream. Each time a few more would turn out.

Then Joe became aware of a major problem. General Crushed Stone had been withdrawing stream water to assist in its gravel washing operation. After passing through several settling ponds the water was returned to the stream. Since the pond water warmed in the summer, when discharged it would raise the stream temperature substantially. During the hot mid summer months, this warm water discharge added to the heat stress on the fish.

Joe went to talk to the manager of the quarry about this problem. He listened carefully to the needs of the quarry, and then suggested a solution. A small change in operating procedure could drastically reduce warm water discharges and at the same time reduce the quarry's draw-off of relatively cool stream water. This new plan would not only benefit the stream, but also it would reduce quarry expenses.

The quarry management agreed to make the changes and began implementation in early July 1980 before the really hot weather arrived. What an accomplishment! Instead of the chapter having to consider a lawsuit with uncertain results, the quarry management was becoming supportive to environmental concerns. On the other side, the quarry was being perceived as a good neighbor. Everyone was benefiting.

Beginning Stream Restoration

We informed the Pennsylvania Fish Commission that the Valley Forge Chapter of Trout Unlimited was ready to engage in a major project of stream restoration, and wanted official approval. In the spring, a staff member of the Fish Commission, Ron Tibbott, came down and walked the stream with chapter members, reviewed plans, and recommended that an official project be approved for West Valley Creek.

When we came to the first dam in the stream, he pointed out how the stream was choked with sediment above the dam and how the dam was warming the water. He said, "Let's pull out this dam, and in a few months you will see how the creek will begin to cut a new channel; eventually it will wash away all that sediment that's above this dam." Led by Ron, right then we pulled the rocks out of that particular dam. Every month or so I would take a good look at that former dam site to see what was happening. Sure enough, the sediment above the former dam began to erode away; below the opening, a new riffle was forming.

In low-gradient streams like ours, dams are a liability, not an asset. At a later workday we pulled out existing dams on the quarry section. Sure enough, with the next high water the stream did begin to cut in a more normal pattern.

Drawing on his professional expertise as an engineer, Joe created designs for restoration structures which would, he felt, work on West Valley Creek. When he asked his new friends at General Crushed Stone to contribute stone for the project on the Clark property, in 1980 they donated, free of charge, over 85,000 pounds of crushed limestone rock of various sizes, and delivered the rock to within 25 yards of the stream.

Chapter member Jack Assetto secured permission for a second project on a free-stone stream in the western part of Chester County, Buck Run. The objective of this project was to correct eroding stream banks with appropriate structures.

The Fish Commission team offered several suggestions for adding overhead cover as well as pointing out desirable locations for bank deflectors to both narrow the stream and increase its speed, thus reducing siltation. We were also given four hundred basket willows and speckled alders to be used for bank protection and stream cover. One Sunday afternoon a few days later seventeen Trout Unlimited members planted the seedlings, and installed sixteen half logs, and checked the tributary where trout hatched the fall before in our Whitlock Vibert Box project.

This first major workday of 1980 was special because it was raining. The fact that so many showed up in the rain says a lot. Some who came had never been to West Valley Creek before got a chance to see the aquatic life in the stream firsthand. Two species of mayflies were hatching as we worked. You could not miss all the nymphs on the rocks. Stream work and getting to know the stream and its life forms went hand-in-hand.

Contributions started to come in. Philadelphia Electric gave Valley Forge Trout Unlimited some used utility poles for habitat improvement projects. They were used to form the frames for bank deflectors. Someone anonymously gave $250 for the Vibert Box program.

Twelve turned out for a Memorial Day work session, completing the frame and then partly filling in the bank deflector. Eighteen turned out for the June workday on West Valley Creek. More half logs were placed in the stream for cover, and work was started on another bank deflector. The completed deflector was already beginning to reduce bank erosion, scour silt from the bottom, and funnel food to the fish which were using the overhead cover that it provided. Until you've done it, you can't imagine how much rock it takes to fill a relatively small structure in a stream. I'm still amazed at the fact that we were able to move that 85,000 pounds of rock and put it in deflectors.

At the conclusion of that workday we sat down along the bank with refreshments which had been hauled to the stream by Joe Armstrong's wife, Ann. We looked at the work that had been done and told stories. Such times of friendship drew us close together. When people share hard, physical work together, it creates a bond of trust and caring. The sense of community included the stream, too. For us the warfare of humanity against nature was over. I was beginning to understand that friendly relationships are the center of conservation.

On a hot Sunday afternoon in July, twenty-two Trout Unlimited folks and friends assembled on West Valley Creek to complete work on two bank deflectors. One deflector was filled directly by a front end loader, and the other was completed with a bucket brigade. Over forty tons of limestone rock were put in place.

The editors of *Banknotes* recorded an unexpected happening:

> A mysterious thing happens when you leave a rock pile unattended for several weeks. Limestone piles act like a magnet for several species of garter snakes, and every-so-often one of these buggers would bullet from the pile, causing a chain reaction among the crew members who did a little bolting themselves. In keeping with our no-kill philosophy, these critters were escorted to the other side of the stream to find another haven. The deflectors and reptiles are both doing nicely, thank you. (*Banknotes*, September 1980)

It was becoming a tradition to hold a work day a month. Most had more than ten workers. Also during 1980, a smaller project was being carried out on Buck Run, a western Chester County stream. Clearly the chapter was beginning to put out a lot of energy.

In July 1980 the Pennsylvania Fish Commission fisheries crew did a stream survey on West Valley Creek. The study included sampling of invertebrates as well as of the fish population. *Banknotes* reported:

> During the last Fish Commission survey of the Boot Road section (1976) only four trout were found, or about ⅙ of the total found in 1980. This would seem to indicate that the heavier bankside vegetation, more flexible stocking schedules by West Chester Fish & Game, and cooler discharges by the quarry, are increasing the trout holding capacity of this section of stream. (September 1980)

Expanding Efforts

Despite the fact that a major shopping mall was planned for Whitford Road, 24 volunteers turned out to plant more than 25,000 trout eggs in Whitlock/Vibert boxes. Meanwhile, those who owned the property wanted to change the zoning to allow them to an on-site sewage treatment plant for the mall. When questions were raised about the effect this might have on the stream, the developers stated that they would chlorinate the water so that all germs would be killed.

People in the Valley Forge Chapter were horrified. These new little trout nurseries, which had just been discovered, would be destroyed. Imagine the effect of chlorine on the watercress, the insects, and the baby trout! The little trout, therefore, played a critical role in the fight to stop the development of this mall.

One below-zero January day in 1981, several of us gathered along the banks of the Whitford Run Tributaries. During this stretch of bitterly cold weather, large flocks of ducks had descended on the brooklet on the west side of Whitford Road and had eaten much of the watercress. Most of the cover was gone, and so were many little trout. The stream on the east side of Whitford Road, however, remained in good shape. With our tiny aquarium net we walked along the little brooklet, carefully checking the health of the tiny trout that we turned up. They were in great shape. The water steamed in the cold air.

Suddenly I stood up and looked around. The Whitford Run brooklets were both steaming, and so was West Valley Creek below the entry point of the tributaries. Above this the creek was frozen. Warm in winter, cold in summer, the limestone brooklets clearly played a crucial role in maintaining a healthy stream.

The little trout grew rapidly throughout the winter. After the heavy fishing pressure of opening day and the first weeks of the season, Jim Lowe, an active contributor to the restoration project from the beginning, and Jim Clark one day removed many little trout from Whitford Road tributaries. They were carefully carried down to the Clark and quarry sections and released. During July and August I myself caught a few of these vigorous and brilliantly colored little fish. Joe Armstrong said, "You almost forget what a real trout looks like when all you see is hatchery fish. These are the real thing."

I asked Joe how he felt about the Vibert Box program. He told me that he was pleased about the interest the program had generated and the support which had been given. "You know, it makes you feel a little like a father. Those fish are there because we put them there, and we want to see them grow up and do well."

Of course, we knew that the defeat of the Whitford mall proposal merely would give us a breathing space. The people who owned the land would not give up, but now we had additional time to develop our restoration work.

Highlights of 1981

One Sunday late in January, 1981, a hiker discovered that someone had dumped barrels of waste into West Valley Creek. They were leaking onto the ice and into the water. A call was made to the State Police, who called the West Whiteland Police, who called the Valley Forge Trout Unlimited president, Joe Armstrong. Joe promptly got on the phone and called several of us, and on the afternoon of Super Bowl Sunday, 1981, we were out on the ice of the creek, first shoveling away fluid so it didn't seep into the water, and then carefully rolling the barrels back onto the land. The substance turned out to be spent cleaning fluid. It was picked up by an EPA Superfund truck and disposed of at a site in New Jersey. Each month a workday was held on the restoration project in the stream. Chapter meetings featured interesting subjects, and were well-attended. The spring "Bash" again drew a large audience, and more than thirty new members joined the chapter that night, bringing the membership total to over one hundred fifty. The Valley Creek Watershed Coalition continued its activities, carrying out the long, and often boring, task of monitoring the landfill to make sure that past abuses did not reoccur.

One program highlight was a spring visit to another chapter of Trout Unlimited to learn about developments of the Pennsylvania Fish Commission's program, "Operation Future" which was applying a scientific approach to trout management. Through careful study of streams throughout the state, wild trout waters were identified, those supporting a robust population of naturally produced, stream-bred trout. This new approach to stream management was consistent with the objectives in Trout Unlimited and was to prove supportive to our efforts.

In addition, Joe worked with the Brandywine Conservancy in obtaining conservation easements on several properties along a local trout stream, thus limiting development adjacent to that stream. Under Chuck Marshall's leadership a county-wide groundwater recharge seminar was held in June 1981, with over forty municipal officials, developers, planners and conservationists involved. Covered were ways of reducing flooding, replenishing groundwater levels, and reducing stream sedimentation through on-site and area-wide groundwater recharge techniques.

Interest in the Vibert box project continued in 1981. Contributions from various members covered most of the expenses of the eggs and gravel (around $400). Two tons of spawning gravel was purchased. Each tiny tributary was marked out, under Joe Armstrong's direction, for a certain number of boxes. Once again eggs were secured from the hatchery. Twelve to fifteen people turned out to help plant eggs in the little brooklets. The hatch was very successful. When the boxes were pulled, very few defective eggs were discovered, and there were dozens of tiny fry around each gravel bed. Almost every weekend somebody checked the progress of the little fish.

Meanwhile the trout hatched the previous year continued to thrive. A mid summer stream survey by the Pennsylvania Fish Commission had turned up a substantial number of stream-bred trout in the Whitford Road section. Thousands of trout reared in hatcheries are stocked each spring in West Valley Creek. Not surprisingly, there were more hatchery trout than wild trout. The stream population was then surveyed again in the late winter (prior to stocking) with surprising results. Whereas in summer hatchery trout had been in the majority, by spring most of them were gone. The stream-bred trout were still present. Their mortality rate was low.

We were pleased, but not surprised by this result. Research generally has demonstrated the vigor of stream-bred trout and their ability to survive. This electro-shock finding, though, was most encouraging to us, and led to development of the project in the fourth year of our work.

Another highlight of 1981 occurred when General Crushed Stone gave official approval for a restoration project to begin on a quarry section of West Valley Creek. Two years of a mutually beneficial working relationship had finally sprung loose something for which we had long hoped. Why did it happen? Certainly the major factor was that Joe Armstrong created a climate of patient reasonableness:

> Reasonable's the word. What are the needs of the other side and how can we satisfy some of those without sacrificing our own? If a development project needs to make money, that is a reasonable goal as long as it doesn't destroy the stream, and it doesn't have to. Somebody said to me a while ago, "You are going over to the enemy." No, by being involved you can have a positive impact. Development would have gone on anyway. We know now that limestone streams can co-exist with a highly urbanized area. But the safeguards must be built in. We at this point can't stop development projects, but we can hope to modify them.

Joe's reasonable approach to the quarry paid off. So, also, did becoming active on a state and national level in Trout Unlimited. We learned through these new contacts and friendships that Koppers Corporation owned the General Crushed Stone quarry. Koppers was a major supporter of Trout Unlimited's program of stream restoration. When we let the parent corporation know of our concern, it encouraged its subsidiary to restore this stream.

The learning events, the clean-ups, and the stream restoration were lots of fun. We had picnics, a fly fishing school, and relaxed after workdays to drink and talk together.

In July 1981, the Valley Forge Chapter of Trout Unlimited received an award from Pennsylvania Trout Unlimited: *The Best Chapter in Pennsylvania*. We deeply appreciated this award, for it put a stamp of approval on our efforts.

Stream Upgrade Sought

The effective leadership of Joe Armstrong continued to move the chapter forward. Membership in the spring of 1982 was over 200, and the spring "Bash" raised over $1,500.

The Vibert Box program was continued, the stream restoration moved forward rapidly on West Valley Creek. One fall chapter meeting showed an attendance of over sixty.

In 1981, the Valley Forge Chapter submitted a proposal to the Department of Environmental Resources, Division of Water Quality, to nominate West Valley Creek for the state's special protection watershed program. This program was based on a state antidegradation policy aimed at the prevention of water pollution. While streams and rivers had established water quality standards, and the violation of these standards was pollution, degradation referred to any measurable decrease in the stream's water quality. In other words, degradation of a stream could occur before the water quality standards are violated. The antidegradation policy was aimed maintaining high quality water, which included those with outstanding state, regional or local value.

We felt that West Valley Creek had outstanding regional and local value, and in the fall of 1982, after almost two years of work with the Department of Environmental Resources, put our case in a *Banknotes* article:

> 1. The stream has potential to be a good coldwater fishery. Natural reproduction has been observed, and wild trout caught. The creek also possesses many spring-fed tributaries which provide a cold water refuge for trout during the summer months.

2. The Pennsylvania Fish Commission and West Chester Fish and Game regularly stock the stream with trout, which increases its recreational value.

3. West Valley Creek supports a diverse macro and invertebrate fauna, with twelve major fauna present. Nine of these are represented by 31 families of aquatic insects. Limestone streams are typically biologically productive, and this stream reflects this potential.

4. The stream has ecological and research value, with the Stroud Water Research Center using it to collect insects and maintaining a continuous recording thermograph.

5. West Valley Creek represents a stream that has undergone destructive impact and is making a comeback through the efforts of many people and agencies. Habitat enhancement projects have improved trout habitat and increased its fishery value. (*Banknotes*, November–December 1982)

Under the special protection program, there were two levels of protection: high-quality waters (HQ) and exceptional water values (EV). These classifications represented water protected from point sources of pollution discharge. High-quality waters were to be protected at their existing quality, but water quality could be lowered for "necessary" social and economic development if designated stream uses were protected. The social and economic justification procedures were not applicable to the exceptional values waters, which were essentially pristine, undisturbed areas. In addition, any projects on special protection waters had to use the best management practices for controlling erosion and sediment.

Challenging the DER to responsibly protect streams such as West Valley that are in a state of recovery as well as those that are undisturbed, we therefore nominated West Valley Creek for a high-quality designation. All available information from Valley Forge TU chapter, Pennsylvania Fish Commission, United States Geological Survey, local Department of Environmental Resources, and planning agencies was sent with a proposal to the Water Quality Division in Harrisburg. In response, on June 22, 1982, people from this division came out to evaluate West Valley Creek. The Water Quality Division put together a report and presented it with recommendations to the Environmental Quality Board in Harrisburg near the end of the year. The Environmental Quality Board was then to make a decision and publish it in

George Washington Appears

the Pennsylvania Bulletin, giving a 30-day period for public comment or an appeal.

The chapter had done an immense amount of work under the direction of its vice president, Pete Dodds. A conversation with Water Quality Division staff on June 22, 1992, however, showed they were not optimistic about prospects for a higher designation. This was the first Pennsylvania stream proposed for upgrading from trout stocking water to coldwater fishery. Downgrading water quality was easy. Upgrading was to be painfully slow.

Even though as volunteers we had limited energy, we were able to touch several other areas. Through the Pennsylvania Environmental Trout Unlimited Legislative committees, organized by myself as first vice president of Pennsylvania Trout Unlimited, chapters throughout the state were informed about key issues, and they were encouraged to speak up on legislation which would affect streams and their watersheds. Connections made on a state level helped us understand who our friends were and also increased the visibility of our local chapter efforts. This was of great assistance when it came time to be in touch with the Environmental Quality Board.

During 1982, we continued to be active in the Valley Creek Coalition which was monitoring Kickerbocker Landfill, keeping the pressure on to assure that what was happening there was environmentally responsible. Chuck Marshall helped to form an agreed on closure plan, so that when the landfill eventually was closed, funds would be available to monitor and take care of the leachate which would emerge from it.

Porcupines Invented

One hot day in 1982, as I was walking the stream, I discovered something new. Out in the water was our chapter president, Joe Armstrong. In one hand he held a sledgehammer and in the other a steel pipe which he was driving into the bed of the stream. I watched with amazement. Sweat rolled down his face. Before long I was out in the stream with him holding the pipes. When we were through I saw he had created a new kind of structure. Steel pipes, discarded from the company he worked for, were driven into the bed of the stream and stuck out like quills. Branches were then interwoven with the steel pipes, creating a structure which immediately narrowed the stream by two-thirds, and had all kinds of things sticking out which would trap silt and debris. Joe's daughter, Ann Baines, called it a "porcupine." We waited anxiously for the next big rain. Sure enough, silt, small branches, and debris were trapped in the porcupine. The stream, now narrower, began to cut a deeper new channel.

Other people from the chapter joined in creating porcupines at places which Joe marked out. We found that porcupines were an

Building a Porcupine

extremely good way to reduce the width of the stream and create new stream banks. One of the first structures was soon almost entirely overgrown with reed canary grass and bush willows that we had planted. The meanders in the stream which were created seemed permanent, as did the new banks.

I asked Joe Armstrong what he had gotten out of his effort. With a laugh, he said: "I haven't gotten a hernia, but I did get a couple of scars on my face. There's a satisfaction you are part of making a few good things happen. One way or another, everyone is obligated to make a contribution to the world you live in. The work we've done through the chapter is tangible. I've learned from the successes and the failures, and on the whole, we've had more successes." Joes does not talk about himself much, but I learned he keeps a fishing diary. In that diary he records the amount of time he spends each week fishing. Since he loves to fish that is a considerable amount of time! He gives

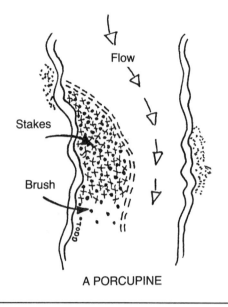

Flow

Stakes

Brush

A PORCUPINE

the same amount of time to conservation that he spends fishing. That is a big contribution.

I also asked what had held him in over these years? "It is the guy I have to look at when I shave in the morning. Society is a two-way street. You don't just take, you have to give too. I can see results from the time that I have going in, and I can see that I'm making a difference."

George Washington Joins

A renewed sense of purpose often comes by looking back and measuring what has been done against your objectives. The goal of preserving, restoring, and conserving coldwater streams and their watersheds helped us to assess what we had learned. Then with a new sense of clarity we began to move forward again. Though the key to effectiveness is what is happening to the watershed—trees, grasses, plants and animals—the dramatic focus, of course, is on the trout stream.

One of my favorite times came at the end of a long tiring work day. After everyone had left, I returned to the stream and stood and looked at what we had done. The trees swayed gently in the breeze. The sun, as it began to set, lighted up clouds in the west. The geese returned to the quarry pond, calling out as they passed overhead. The stream flowed, swirling around the structure on which we had just worked.

A good feeling welled up inside me. I could see the effect of what we had done. This time of evaluation was a time of rest, of appreciation, and of being in tune with the goodness of creation itself.

The intense efforts of establishing a chapter and the energy which began to pour out under Joe Armstrong's direction brought a time where fewer new things were happening. It was a time to take stock, look at what had happened, regroup and prepare for the future.

Electrical Evaluations

Joe Armstrong and I reflected on what we had learned thus far about restoring a stream to health. We agreed on goals for the quarry restoration project of West Valley Creek. One was to narrow and deepen the stream in ways that would make high water and siltation work for us. Another was to do our work in ways which were as unobtrusive as possible, so that after a period of time people fishing the stream would feel they were in an undisturbed area (unmarked by concrete, steel and other unnatural eyesores).

We learned a dramatic way to tell how well we are doing in stream restoration—electro-shocking. We did a stream census by measuring the number of trout in each section of stream at least once a year. We were particularly interested in the number, size, and condition of the trout (in more detailed work done by the state all forms of fish are assessed). Vital information was recorded, and then the trout were released.

Research biologists have learned that two or three passes through a stream will give a good count of the fish life. One pass in a small, clear stream may give a good estimate. Our aim was to gain such an estimate of the number of trout in the restoration project sections of West Valley Creek. Small fish tend to slip through or hide nearer to the bank much more frequently than large ones, so the count always underestimates the number of smaller fish.

One warm Sunday afternoon in September 1982, Ray Bednarchik, state waterways patrolman, brought an electro-shock kit to the stream. The kit consisted of two electrodes attached to five-foot poles, several hundred feet of insulated cord which was connected to the source of the direct current, and a small gasoline engine, which was mounted upon a board so that it can be carried.

When my son Martin and I pulled up to the stream, we saw eight or ten cars parked at the bottom of the quarry stretch. I parked next to the state waterways patrol car. We pulled on hip boots and hurried down the bank towards the water. I was surprised to find five or six people standing on the bank watching what was going on down in the stream. In the water eight or ten people were wading. Two were holding the probes. Another was carrying a large landing net. Bringing up the rear were two strong men lugging the gasoline engine. It was chugging along noisily, providing the power for the electro-shock probe. The whole company slowly moved upstream.

What was happening was that a direct current of 240 volts was going into the water. Fish were temporarily stunned by the charge. The direct current drew the fish towards the probes, where they were netted.

We joined the group wading through the water. I helped by carrying some of the coils of cord. Martin took the pail and watched for fish.

As we walked upstream again and again we turned up both hatchery and stream-bred trout. The bottom fins near the trout's head, called pectorals, are worn away by hatchery trout on the concrete of their troughs. Stream-bred trout, to the contrary, have beautifully colored, long, pale pectoral fins fanning out below them. Stream-bred trout which hatched in the fall of 1981 by September 1982 were now five to eight inches in length. They turned up in every part of the quarry section, being concentrated, as one might expect, at the most desirable holding spots (as the new stretches of pocket water). Whenever a trout was netted, it was quickly placed in a bucket, then placed on a measuring board made for this purpose. The size and any distinguishing marks were noted by Carl Dusinberre, who kept the stream census record. After measurements were taken, each fish was quickly placed back in the stream. Our chapter photographer took photographs for future presentations.

As we worked our way upstream, again and again we discovered eels. Some were as thick around as a person's arm and almost three feet long. These large fish live in shallow water and are almost never seen. As the electro-shock probes went upstream, we also turned up many suckers, some bluegills, and a few medium-size rockbass.

When we came to new deflectors with their undercut artificial banks, we wondered what would appear. Suddenly everybody shouted. A trout of thirteen inches had been netted off the very point of the deflector. Trout were holding in the new pool.

The biggest thrill, however, came when we shocked the pool below the jack dam Joe Armstrong had built. Someone netted a hefty fish. Joe Armstrong shouted with joy and raced up to see the fish. It was a fifteen-inch brown trout, fat and fully filled out, which appeared to be carrying spawn. Several other trout also turned up in the jack dam hole.

There were, of course, disappointments. No trout turned up around the huge deflector built in 1981. Over forty tons of rock were placed by hand to form this structure. Perhaps all the trout had slipped away, or perhaps we yet did not have a pool with holding characteristics.

At the very top of the quarry section, in an old swimming hole, a wild trout of thirteen inches was netted. This beautiful fish, even in the bucket, moved with power and grace. Its long pectoral fins were obvious.

After we completed the survey of the quarry stretch, we drove down to the James Clark project, where we had begun stream work several years previously. Again the electro-shock crew plunged into the water and moved slowly upstream, carefully measuring and releasing each trout caught. Finally the work was completed, and we all gathered in front of the Clark home for refreshments and conversation. The electrical evaluation had been a success. Restoration of habitat, combined with a Vibert Box program, were restoring streambred trout to West Valley Creek.

Threats

On November 23, 1982, six chapter members met with staff of McCormick-Taylor, a firm which was doing the environmental impact statement for the proposed Exton highway bypass. The meeting was held so that both groups could exchange data on sections of West Valley Creek that would be affected by construction of the bypass.

Constructing a four-lane highway has massive effect on a stream and its watershed. A huge swath of trees and grass are bulldozed away, and then during the construction process silt and sediment wash into the stream. As if the amount of sediment coming down West Valley Creek were not enough, this new construction would ruin spawning beds, fill in holes, and generally make a big mess. After the construction was over, rain which fell on the highway would pick up oil, road salts, and other pollutants on the roadway and carry them down the drains directly into tributaries and the stream itself. The increased runoff would add to floods. There was the constant danger that a truck loaded with hazardous or toxic waste would tip over and pour out its contents on the highway, with the end result that they would be flushed into the stream.

We gave the consultants information on spawning areas, habitat enhancement projects, electrofishing surveys and invertebrate counts. We also turned in a chart giving data collected by one of our members on daily temperature readings throughout the year. McCormick Taylor did electrofishing surveys of its own and discovered wild trout in two tributaries located near the quarry stretch.

Another threat to the streams the chapter dealt with was a state-

Before Acid Rain I Looked Like You

wide one: acid precipitation. Through Pennsylvania Trout Unlimited this concern had been raised with all chapters throughout the state. Acid rain, interestingly enough, is not a primary problem for limestone streams, given their high natural alkalinity. Yet when anglers from Philadelphia went to other parts of Pennsylvania to fish and enjoy the waters, they were finding many streams being devastated by rainfall which was extremely acidic. According to the Pennsylvania Fish Commission, the state-wide average pH was then 4.0 (1,000 times the acidity of neutral water). The chapter placed articles in the *Banknotes* about acid precipitation. Carl Dusinberre, one of the newer members, drew a cartoon featuring E.T. and President Reagan to dramatize the threat of acid rain.

A third threat to the streams was posed by expanding development. New roads were appearing throughout the townships through which West Valley and Valley creeks flowed. New buildings were sprouting up here and there, and each month one could see fewer trees and open space. Chapter members began to meet with developers, reviewing their plans, and they began to go to township meetings. Yet the threats continued.

Soil erosion, a fourth threat, goes with poor construction practices. For instance, as one chapter member drove along West Valley Creek after a big rain, he saw a muddy torrent pouring off a construction site and flowing directly into the stream. Returning home, he called up the township officer responsible for monitoring development. Fortunately, sedimentation control laws enforcing responsible development were in place. Within a few days, the officer had worked with the construction firm, and this abuse was corrected.

A fifth threat to streams was the erosion of the Pennsylvania Clean Streams Act. Pressures from corporations and government to encourage development, no matter the environmental cost, increasingly were moving the Pennsylvania Department of Environmental Resources to approve plans which would have serious negative environmental impacts. For example, enforcement of the Clean Streams Act was modified in a significant way. Instead of monitoring pollution where it came out of a factory or municipality into the stream, an "administrative decision" was made to monitor the water quality at the point of the next intake. This made it possible "administratively" to allow the stream to accept a great deal more pollution. Though this threat was serious, efforts of state environmental groups to change the ruling had no effect.

A sixth threat surfaced close to home. In March 1983 the Department of Environmental Resources for the first time told anglers planning to fish Valley Creek that meat from brown trout stocked the previous year was found to contain low levels of PCBs. Native trout collected from the south branch of Valley Creek, Little Valley, were found to contain even higher levels of PCBs in the whole fish analyses. PCBs collect in fatty tissue, and are responsible for causing birth defects, spontaneous abortions, and cancer. This new threat was reported in the March issue of *Banknotes* and discussed in chapter meetings. Some new action by the chapter appeared to be called for. We would have to see what was called for as events developed.

When we stood back and looked at the threats, we saw a great deal that was discouraging. Though our efforts to preserve streams and their watersheds were moving in the right direction, we were still having about as much effect as a proverbial drop in the bucket. If the streams were to be preserved, we needed to do a great deal more. Sometimes we were tempted to despair. However, when we met threats with hope, there were things which could be done. A clear threat can be a challenge, encouraging a person or group to work harder, think more clearly, be more effective.

Education and Communication

Since the chapter newsletter was started, six issues per year of *Banknotes* had been written and mailed. With a chapter membership of around two hundred, this meant that a substantial number were being

Washington Supervises a Work Crew

informed on the work of the chapter to preserve local streams. Among those included on the mailing list were an increasing number of township and state officials whose work brought them in touch with streams. We were getting our message out. Cartoons by Carl Dusinberre were beginning to appear in *Banknotes*. A cartoon is often worth a thousand words, dramatizing in a humorous way what is happening.

Slide presentations were prepared on the restoration work of the chapter. One particularly memorable presentation was made to the Eastern Chester County Planning Commission by the incoming chapter president, Jack McFadden, and me. Being able to see before and after pictures of in-stream restoration work is something that folks got excited about (including Planning Commission members).

Board member Jerry Bullock in 1977 had said that an effective organization needed to have a sense of purpose, and be effective in its management and action. In 1983 there were many signs that we were moving in this direction. The spring fund raiser held in March netted over $1,700. Thirty-seven new members were signed up, making a total of 192 (a slight drop in reenlistment left us with a few less total members than the year before). Under the direction of the new president, Jack McFadden, plans were made to expand chapter efforts to include other streams in Chester County. The restoration project on Buck Run was reactivated, and plans were laid for beginning a new project on Pickering Creek. These were not planned as major projects, but to get three or four people working to improve each of these streams.

Measuring Stream Restoration

A highlight of chapter effort in the years since we started was stream restoration. By 1983, an estimated 2,500 hours had already been invested in the project, typically in fishing season when members might have been out fishing themselves. Regular work days, averaging at least one per month, had now been held for five years. The chapter had directly spent about $5,000 on such things as rental of heavy equipment, sawmill work for logs, purchasing trees and so forth. Over 350 tons of stone had been moved and placed into deflectors or placed as random boulders in riffles to increase holding cover and velocity and scour the bottom of silt. About 2,000 trees and shrubs were planted adjacent to the stream, increasing cover, shading the stream, and providing leaves for aquatic and terrestrial insect food. Nearly

150,000 trout eggs were planted in tributaries of the stream over the past five years, with a result that in a day's fishing an angler would be likely to encounter at least one stream-hatched trout.

To get a clear picture of what had been happening in the restoration project areas, we took slides of each stream section before we started. Then we took pictures as we went along. Each year we measured the depth and width of the project section. After five years the stream was becoming narrower and deeper as we had hoped. Readings taken in 1980 showed an average width of 31.5 feet while the average depth was 10.6 inches. By July 17, 1983, the average width was 23.5 feet with average depth of 13.4 inches. As this narrowing occurred, the speed of the water flow increased, helping to keep the water cool. The bank cover, some of which we planted, along with rapidly growing trees, were indeed reducing summer water temperature. Baseline data surveys of insect life were made (since one of the primary indicators of a healthy stream is the diversity and type of insect populations). We also looked at water flow, both in quantity and quality.

Stream restoration had been a dramatic focus of chapter efforts in the early years of its life. To strengthen our efforts, we applied to national Trout Unlimited for a Project Restore grant of $1,000.00. In May 1983 the chapter was very pleased to learn that this grant was made to improve the trout-carrying capacity of West Valley Creek.

Goals Flow Together

Beginning under my leadership, and continuing in a much more intense form under Joe Armstrong's direction, we moved forward on four goals. Chapter development gave a stronger base for institutional action. More active members and more chapter money gave more energy to preserve and restore the stream and its watersheds. Stream restoration took us into the stream, placed us in direct relationship to its living waters, gave us intimate knowledge of what was happening, and began to provide us with credentials of a group which seriously cared about the stream. By educating and communicating, we were able to reach out to our members and beyond through our chapter newsletter. Slide presentations sharpened our understanding of what we were about, touched some people who became new members, and began to create a climate in the county more conducive to stream conservation.

Saving a Vital Tributary

In 1983 Mitsie Toland of the Open Land Conservancy and Valley Forge chapter board member John Renshaw began a long and uphill climb. A tiny tributary of Little Valley Creek, called Little Crabby Creek, was threatened by plans for massive new developments.

Mitsie returned from a trip to California to discover that the township had unanimously passed a plan for an office park which would eliminate a big section of Crabby Creek, over 1,200 feet of free-flowing stream. These plans threatened a tributary vital to the entire Valley Creek watershed:

> Little Crabby Creek's excellent water quality, gravel riffle areas, spring-influenced temperatures and stable food organism community and provided conditions conducive to brown trout. The stream serves as a spawning area for wild populations, a nursery for young trout, and a low temperature summer refugee for stocked trout. Little Crabby Creek, according to the Pennsylvania Fish Commission and Weston study results, harbors the most trout. (Raymond Wilguardis, Curt Philipp, Gerard Dinkins, "Trout and Community Development: The Story of Little Crabby Creek," *Weston Way*, Summer 1987)

Office development had used up the most desirable land and now it was spilling over into areas which were far more environmentally sensitive. Mitsie called John Renshaw of Trout Unlimited, and together they went to the Tredyffrin township supervisors. As usual this civic work was done with no pay. John and Mitsie sat for hours through tedious township discussions until finally their concern appeared on the agenda. They pointed out that the developer had misrepresented the environmental impact of his proposed Westlakes project.

At a public meeting on November 19, 1984, they raised the following points of concern with the Board of Supervisors:

1. Replacement of the free-flowing stream by a warm water pond and dam.
2. Relocation of two segments of the creek totaling 350 feet to allow for the access road and parking.
3. Encroachment within the 50-feet buffer zone (a violation of the township zoning ordinance).
4. The sanitary sewer crossing a major spring that provides a significant flow of cold water to Crabby Creek.

5. The storm water retention basin designed to discharge into the spring feeder.
6. Undefined landscaping of the natural vegetation within the buffer zone.
7. One-hundred-year flood plain not shown in the drawings. (*Banknotes*, winter, 1984–1985)

Fortunately the supervisors listened. They decided to hold up on other aspects of the project to put pressure on the developer to change his plans. Open Land Conservancy and Green Valleys Watershed Association then joined Trout Unlimited in a complex process of negotiations. If Little Crabby Creek were dammed, it would flood the spawning grounds, block upstream fish migration, and increase downstream temperatures. Straightening the channel would eliminate precious feet of stream habitat, and these changes would also have eliminated trout populations in the creek.

Fortunately the developer responded to citizen pressure. Negotiations worked through plans agreeable to conservationists. Finally an agreement was reached that was acceptable to conservationists and the developer.

Then one day early in 1984, Mitsie heard a rumor that the Westlakes project had been sold to Trammell-Crow, a large national land development firm. Would all of the effort be lost now that a new company was coming in? She immediately called the project lawyer, who was astounded that she had already heard the news. Representatives of the Trammell-Crow Corporation were coming to visit, and he invited her to meet with them that afternoon. In that session the Trammell-Crow partners agreed to do the development in an environmentally responsible way.

George Washington Joins

For the 1982 Trout Show, our "Spring Bash," Carl Dusinberre had prepared a cartoon of George Washington fishing with delight in Valley Creek. In 1983, Washington again appeared, this time at one of our chapter workdays on West Valley Creek. In 1984, however, George Washington really got involved in stream conservation. Carl pictures him looking over our shoulders, asking us to save Valley Creek and the other cold water streams in Chester County.

Listening to Washington's call, many came to the "Spring Bash" to

And Help Us Save Valley Creek

hear Penn State professor Bob Bachman tell about what he had learned from years of careful study of trout behavior. Following the event, chapter membership increased to 227, making Valley Forge Trout Unlimited the second largest chapter in Pennsylvania.

The Fly Fishing School in 1984 drew thirty-four students. The day was beautiful and all enjoyed great food, made new friends, and a few caught their first trout on a fly.

Workdays on the restoration project proceeded in high gear. In midsummer, front-end loaders and backhoes were rented to move mountains of stone provided by General Crush Stone. Over 100 tons were used to fill in the two new deflectors, and some large boulders were placed in the stream for cover. The stone was also added to older structures where settling had occurred.

Though the slow process of seeking upgrading for West Valley Creek was still dragging along, the chapter took the first step in seeking to upgrade the water quality classification of Valley Creek (to ensure that water temperatures would remain within the tolerable levels for trout).

Banquet tickets were passed out to members to get advance sales. Prizes were secured, some through National, some through local efforts. On November 7, 1984, the chapter hosted its first banquet. A total of 110 people showed up for the event and a profit of $2,200 was realized which was split equally between the local chapter and National Trout Unlimited. All who came enjoyed themselves and had an excellent dinner.

Heartened by reports of many catches of stream-bred brown and rainbow trout throughout the year in West Valley Creek, the chapter continued its planting of trout eggs in the tributaries. Once again, 40,000 eggs were placed in the stream, soon to hatch and bring new life.

CHAPTER 8

Bigger Chapter—Bigger Challenges

In the winter of 1984, Joe Armstrong designed and built a small experimental structure on the upper section of the West Valley Creek restoration project. Christmas trees were fixed in place on top of a deflector in order to catch silt. The trees acted like snow fences in a blizzard, and silt was indeed trapped in them. The stream narrowed and deepened as Joe had hoped. Planning to build on this accomplishment the "Banknuts" restoration crew visited ten Christmas tree merchants to relieve them of any unsold trees after Christmas. Merchants had a disposal problem; we needed trees. We hoped we might end up with about two hundred trees.

We succeeded beyond wildest expectations. One luckless firm ended up with hundreds. At our work session in January we faced a mound of over seven hundred trees. Undaunted, thirteen hearty chapter members installed and wired in place trees from this used Christmas tree mountain. It took several other workdays, however, before all trees were in place.

After a few weeks there was a heavy winter rain. One of our VFTU board members went out to check how the Christmas trees were doing. He noted oil on the water and traced it to a drain pipe which came from the sewage pumping station operated by West Whiteland township.

A phone call to township officials resulted in a test being run which positively identified a buried fuel tank on the property as the source of the problem. The township immediately dug up the leaking tank, junked it, removed some contaminated soil for proper disposal, and installed a new tank inside the pumping station (where leakage would be immediately noticed).

West Valley Creek's Water Quality Upgraded

In 1985, three years after the chapter had made application to the Department of Environmental Resources (DER) the water quality designation for West Valley Creek was finally upgraded from "Trout Stocking Fishery," (which allowed trout killing summer discharges of water which could raise the temperature to eighty-seven degrees Fahrenheit) to "Coldwater Fishery." The new classification recognized that trout do indeed hold over through winter in West Valley Creek, and that young of the year are found in some sections. Letters, pictures and articles about the upgraded classification appeared in the local newspaper, and a very impressive column was written in the *Philadelphia Inquirer.*

We received a very special surprise, also. Broad Run, the major tributary to West Valley Creek, was studied as part of the DER investigation and found to have a population of wild brown trout and other evidences of high water quality. It received, therefore, a more stringent water quality designation than West Valley Creek itself, further protecting it and in turn West Valley Creek. The three-year effort of Pete Dodds, chapter vice president who handled this project, thus came to a successful conclusion. A quote from Ralph W. Abele, then executive director of the Pennsylvania Fish Commission, summed up our feelings: "Politically attractive hatcheries are no substitute for improved water quality—in fact, they are a dangerous diversion of effort" (*Banknotes*, spring 1985).

Joe Humphreys, noted angler from Pennsylvania, was the featured speaker at the 1985 spring trout show. Almost 400 persons attended, a new record. The event raised over $1,500, and best of all, 61 new members and 4 transfers were recruited. Membership rose from 230 to 300. The chapter, furthermore, won a National TU funding grant for stream restoration and educational presentations of $2,000.

As if this were not enough, the 1985 fly fishing school held on May 19 drew forty-two enrolees. The weather was fine, the instruction rated superior, and the food was outstanding. The only disappointing note was that twenty additional persons who were interested in enrolling had to be turned down.

Noted Stream Biologist Consults with VFTU

We had spent eight years learning stream restoration, and felt it was about time we brought in a consultant. Increased funds from national grants and local fundraising efforts made it possible to pay the expenses for a visit by Ray White, specialist in stream research and restoration and co-author of our restoration "bible." On March 25 1985, Ray came to Chester County. Several of us took time off from work to spend the afternoon with him. We started on West Valley Creek, walking the Clark and quarry stretches. White made many helpful suggestions as to further improvements of specific devices.

Then we drove to Valley Forge National Park, where we met with park rangers and walked the lower part of Valley Creek. White strongly suggested that dams be removed and restoration plans be developed for a demonstration project. At dark we retired to a barn in the park and saw slides showing how streams messed up by human activity have been restored to health.

White's visit restored our spirits. We began to imagine a fish for fun stream, from headwaters to the mouth of Valley Creek. Despite pollution of the stream by PCBs, all was not lost. We began to dream of pools filled with schools of stream-bred trout! A demonstration project which restored a section of Valley Creek might generate national attention, perhaps enough to save the stream.

Tackling the Railroad

We were having a wonderful spring. Everything was going well. The chapter was the second largest in Pennsylvania. Money was coming in. Membership was the highest it had ever been. Then, not long before fishing season, the Pennsylvania Fish Commission announced that it would no longer stock Valley Creek because it was too contaminated with PCBs.

A major recreational resource was lost to area residents who loved to fish. The PCB pollution was traced to the Paoli car shops of Amtrak/SEPTA. Amtrak owned the property; SEPTA, the South Eastern Pennsylvania Regional Transportation Authority, operated it. Investigations revealed that as far back as the mid 1930s, when the site was owned by the Pennsylvania Railroad, PCBs were carelessly handled there. Evidence obtained by both the DER and EPA showed that the careless handling of PCBs had continued and had been cause for legal action by both agencies. Neither were getting far. Fines levied by the EPA were not paid! Cleanup orders issued by the Department of Environmental Resources were appealed and ended up in what appeared to be limbo.

Yet every time it rained, PCBs were washing off the site. Adhering to soil particles, they eventually washed into Little Valley Creek and then into Valley Creek. Once in the stream, the sediments settled into the stream bottom where they were injested by insects, thus entering the food chain.

PCBs are extremely durable and break down very slowly. Studies of trout in Valley Creek showed astoundingly high levels of PCBs in their fat. White suckers, bottom feeders, had even higher levels of PCB than brown trout. Not surprisingly, the fish in little Valley Creek below the Paoli railroad yard showed the highest levels of PCB.

What could be done? Since the Fish Commission had prohibited removal of any fish from Valley Creek throughout its entire watershed, we could emphasize the positive aspects of a catch-and-release fishery. Though trout flesh contained unacceptable concentrations of PCB for human consumption, there was a flourishing wild brown trout population. Patient fishermen were rewarded with fine fish, some quite large in size.

Some might have felt that what we should do is sit back, relax, and enjoy the fishing, but the purpose of Valley Forge Trout Unlimited was stream conservation, preservation, and restoration. Could we sit by, as others had done, and allow the pollution of Valley Creek to continue? If not, what could we do? We learned that to thoroughly remove PCBs from the whole stream system would require stopping the continuing pollution from the Paoli railroad yards, dredging up the silt in the bottom of the streams, and removing all fish and other life from the stream (as fish and insects die, the PCBs in their flesh were being recycled). It was likely that human lifetimes might be involved before the PCB problem at Valley Creek dissipated.

A complete cleanup was beyond the capacity of the chapter. It would, moreover, destroy the life in the stream. At the June summer board meeting, we discussed the whole matter, and felt we had to make a start by cutting off the source of pollution. That meant tackling the railroad.

Meanwhile on West Valley Creek, chapter members had been attending many Planning Commission and supervisors' meetings in the township, patiently indicating Trout Unlimited's points of view on matters affecting the stream. Finally, these years of effort paid off.

BOARD APPROVES MAX EFFORT VS. RR's PCB's; BANQUET SET

BANKNOTES

VOL 5 NO. 7   SUMMER 1985

PCB's AND VALLEY CREEK

As many of you are aware, Valley Creek, which flows through Valley Forge Park has been deemed polluted to the point where the Pennsylvania Fish Commission did not stock trout in it this year for the first time in about 50 years. The stream has been taken off the stocking list, and a major recreational resource has been lost to many area fishermen.

Continued on Page 3

NOT THIS TIME, DRAGON-MASTER. *Not* UNTIL YOU CLEAN UP YOUR ACT AND YOUR YARD !!!

COME ON JESSE JAMES - LET'S CLEAR THE TRACKS !!

Suing the Railroad

A summer meeting of the West Whiteland Township was a Trout Unlimited dream. A development project was under discussion, embracing a considerable stretch of West Valley Creek. It could have had a disastrous effect on the stream. After considerable discussion, the supervisors reached agreement with the developer to have an easement on either side of the stream to insure fishermen access, unhindered by future land owners. Furthermore, vegetation in this corridor was to be undisturbed, so no "golf course" setting would be allowed.

The fall meeting of the Pennsylvania Council of Trout Unlimited brought us an award as the best chapter. The VFTU were cited "for outstanding effort in the preservation and enhancement of the cold water resources of the Commonwealth." Joe Armstrong himself received an award as outstanding Trout Unlimited Member Conservationist of 1985.

Crabby Creek Project

Back on the tributaries of Valley Creek, working through an agreement with a developer was only the first step in a new construction project. Plans had to be made and reviewed in order to relocate the stream, build a road and bridge, and construct a roadway to give access to the site. Trammell-Crow hired Roy F. Weston, an environmental consulting firm, to develop a conceptual plan which would satisfy the requirement of various permits and the concerns of the conservation groups. The Pennsylvania Fish Commission, the U.S. Fish and Wildlife Service, and the U.S. Army Corps of Engineers were also involved in the discussions.

The Weston plan limited the disturbance to Little Crabby Creek to only one area where it would be crossed by the access road: "A new stream channel would be created to cut off an existing meander, and the 270 ft. meander would be filled and covered by the roadway embankment. A 180 ft. relocated channel would be covered by earthen and berm to bridge the stream for the road. Overflow basins and twin box culverts were designed to reduce storm flow surges during site development" ("Trout and Community Development," *Weston Way*, Summer, 1987).

Weston designed a new stream channel, developed a sediment and erosion control plan and conducted pre- and post-construction ecological surveys. Everything was going along very well. Then one day we heard the news that there had been a massive fish kill on Little Crabby Creek:

> Ken Salamon of Weston's Life Systems Group first visited the site in September, 1985 with Charlie Durkin of Curtis, Cox, Kennerly, to begin initial discussions for the stream relocation. While approaching the stream they were suddenly surrounded by representatives of

the U.S. Fish and Wildlife Service, the State of Pennsylvania Department of Environmental Resources, Trout Unlimited, and local interest and media groups. Since their visit had been unannounced, Ken and Charlie were truly startled by the sudden attention. When they reached the stream, nearly 100 brown trout were seen lying belly-up throughout the very stretch of stream designated for relocation. An upstream release of a chlorinated swimming pool was suspected of causing the kill, although the exact cause never was established. ("Trout and Community Development")

Later it was discovered that a drinking water line had broken. Chlorine in the water killed the trout! As we have found on other occasions, however, a destructive event can focus attention on a stream and result in constructive changes. The number of dead fish showed there was a large trout population in this tiny tributary. Plans for stream relocation took on new importance.

Summer Work Sessions

As we struggled to think through whether or not we should sue the railroad, four times during the summer work sessions were held on West Valley Creek. Three new structures were built to further narrow and deepen the channelized section of the stream. More boulders were placed in the stream to increase cover and previous structures were covered with stone to increase their permanence. The efforts of the chapter members were increased as an Eagle Scout candidate took on a project and brought Boy Scouts along to help.

We tried hard to get a clean up of the Paoli Yard PCBs without a lawsuit. Joe Armstrong wrote SEPTA Management. No one replied. He decided to set up a meeting with SEPTA to discuss the matter. SEPTA declined to meet with us. We also wrote to the Department of Environmental Resources, asking it to pursue its cleanup order of June 28, 1979. The chapter became increasingly aware that if these actions failed we might have to pursue the matter in the courts. We had never sued anyone, and were very hesitant about so doing. We wrote letters in mid summer, 1985, to the EPA and Pennsylvania Department of Environmental Resources, and sought meetings with SEPTA and other parties. Nothing happened. Finally on February 4, 1986, we issued the following news release:

The Valley Forge Chapter of Trout Unlimited (VFTU) today announced the filing of a law suit last Thursday in Federal Court in Philadelphia, seeking a clean up of PCB contamination at the Paoli Car Shop, a train maintenance and service facility located in Tredyffrin and Willistown Townships, Chester County, Pennsylvania. The defendants' names in the case are the South Eastern Pennsylvania Transportation Authority ("SEPTA"), Consolidated Rail Corporation ("Conrail"), and the National Railroad Passenger Corporation ("Amtrak"), each of whom, according to the suit, have either owned or operated the site. The suit alleges that storm water runoff from the site contaminated Valley Creek and Little Valley Creek, two nearby trout streams. According to the complaint filed in the case, Valley Forge Trout Unlimited members have been active in fishing the streams and maintaining their environmental quality.

According to the suit, PCBs are suspected carcinogens which cause chloracne, liver ailments, infertility, birth defects and other serious health problems. The toxic chemical has been deposited on the sites since the 1930s by employees of the three defendants and their predecessor companies, according to the complaint.

Conclusion

In 1985 the Valley Forge Chapter was bigger and stronger. Our work to save the coldwater streams of Chester County was showing good results. Now we are faced with a big challenge—could we get the Philadelphia mass transit system to stop pollution of Valley Creek with PCBs?

CHAPTER 9

Watersheds Produce Trout

Ten years after Valley Forge Trout Unlimited had its first beginnings, Joe Armstrong wrote an article entitled, "Watersheds, Not Streams, Produce Trout" (*Banknotes*, Winter 1986). All the stream improvement in the world, the best stocking and catch-and-release regulations could not produce good fishing if the watershed was being abused. Drawing on an address by Benjamin Dysart, president of the National Wildlife Federation, Armstrong went on to say that the key to producing trout is the integrity of the lands that surround the waters, and what is allowed to go on upon those lands, and how those activities are conducted. Chapter activity in 1986 reflected the degree to which Armstrong's advice was taken to heart. One group was working with an attorney preparing a lawsuit against the railroads to end the PCB contamination of Little Valley and Valley Creeks. Another chapter leader continued to keep watch on sources of siltation from new construction projects in the Valley Creek watershed. Others were working closely with the developer to prepare a good plan for work to be done adjacent to Crabby Creek. Under the Pennsylvania Fish Commission's "Adopt a Stream" program, the chapter adopted Valley Creek as its watershed.

Working with lawyers, developers, and township officials was often tedious and seemingly remote from the streams. As Joe pointed out, it is certainly less satisfying than rolling rocks to create instant habitat, or planting trout eggs and watching them grow. Without effort focused on the health of the watershed, however, all the other efforts would be of little value.

What was needed to protect the streams and watersheds? More

volunteers: "We need more help, as so much remains to be done, and a few people should not have to do the whole job by themselves, nor can they. No matter what skills you have, it can be useful in our increasingly diverse activities. And it is fun when we win some!"

Trout Show 1986

Many had seen the big signs in red print along Valley Creek put up by the Pennsylvania Fish Commission, warning that no trout could be kept and eaten. The posters warned that eating trout would be detrimental to health. The stream thus became "a catch and release" project. On the publicity inviting people to come to the 1986 Trout Show, George Washington is reading a poster which prohibits taking fish from Valley Creek because they are contaminated by PCBs.

The Trout Show, featuring Lefty Kreh, a Baltimore newspaper columnist, was another success. Three hundred fifty people attended; over one thousand dollars was raised, and twenty new members joined the chapter. Those attending were informed about the PCB contamination of Valley Creek by the railroads, the railroads' lack of responsibility in cleaning up the mess they had made, and our suit to try to get a clean-up.

Not long after the suit was announced and made public at our trout show, others also sued SEPTA. Citizens who lived downhill from the railroad years discovered that their homes were contaminated. They began to put two and two together, and realized that miscarriages, birth defects and other health problems might have something to do with poisonous PCBs on their property. Businesses who saw property values declining also filed suit.

Residents staged demonstrations calling for public action. Senator Heinz and Congressman Schultz came to learn what was going on and listen to local concern. Suddenly the EPA and DER began to pursue their suits against the railroads more vigorously. The Valley Forge Trout Unlimited suit of SEPTA dropped into the background, but it ground on in the courts.

For the third time we organized a Trout Unlimited committee focused on preserving Valley Creek. Each time before a small group had gotten started, done some good work, but then disbanded. We had been unable to find a leader who would mount an enduring effort.

We made another try. Members of the committee inspected several areas where erosion and sedimentation were major problems. One

The sign on the right reads:

ATTEN
ALL
FISHER

The Pennsylvania Fis
anglers that fish tak
VALLEY CK may p
therefore,

NO FISH MAY BE
IN POSSESSION

Results of pollutio
vania Departmer
indicate that trou
these waters may
chemicals which
consumption.

PENALTY

1986
TROUT
SHOW

1986 Trout Show

involved a large clothing store with a defective erosion basin. Another
was a Pennsylvania Department of Transportation storm drainage system at an important intersection. The large Chesterbrook development had several areas of soil erosion. There were major problems
along the sanitary sewer line near Valley Creek.

Surveillance by Trout Unlimited members led to enforcement of
control measures by the township. A letter was written to Pennsylvania Department of Transportation about a planned intersection on the

upper section of Little Valley Creek. As a result of this letter, officials promised informally to eliminate the most objectionable aspects of the project.

Conversations were begun with leaders of Valley Forge Park on the possibilities of establishing a demonstration project within the park to restore about one-third mile of trout water which was largely a biological desert. We also sought to remove a large dam which was warming waters above it.

Perpetual Land Preservation

All of this work to preserve the stream and its watershed was focused in a special general meeting held in May, 1986, featuring Open Land Conservancy. Led by Mitsie Toland, the Open Land Conservancy for years had been quietly laboring to preserve a corridor of open space along Valley Creek and its tributaries. Years ago Mitsie observed how this beautiful creek flows right through a federal park. If open lands could be protected along Valley Creek, she thought it could be a model for other communities.

Founded in 1939, Open Land Conservancy is a nonprofit, tax-exempt land trust supported by a membership of over four hundred. It has received five conservation easements on eighty-three acres of environmentally sensitive land and has received as gifts from private owners and developers twelve separate parcels which have been combined into five major preserves totaling two hundred thirty-five acres. All of these preserves are open to the public during daylight hours.

Mitsie Toland cut her teeth on the struggle to preserve the Chesterbrook lands by adding them to what was to become the Valley Forge National Park. This effort failed. Undiscouraged, she then gave herself to new efforts which have been effective in preserving open space. Over a twenty-year time span, she has gone to hundreds of township and county meetings.

> I feel it is important for people to establish connections with the natural world, and not lose them all. In nature we see messiness, struggles between vines and trees. We escape from human sounds and sights and experience the natural setting. This not only refreshes our souls, but also gives birth to care and respect for the earth. Experiencing nature is my driving force. (Conversation with Mitsie Toland)

When Mitsie was brought up she was taught to serve the community. Members of her family were active on many civic boards. She also liked action and thrived on challenges. Since she had four brothers, she learned to hold her own and not be cowed by men. From the time she was a child she loved to spend a day alone out under the sky. Mitsie studied insects and learned to understand how critical they are to all of life and to the food chain. She learned about the amazing strategies insects have for nest building, surviving and eating, and she then found out more and more about natural selection and the interdependencies of nature. Her husband shared many of her interests and also took an active role in the community. More and more she felt that she wanted to take care of our planetary home by preserving open space.

Trout Unlimited has contributed to land purchases by Open Land Conservancy since it began. We recognized that preservation of open space is essential if the watershed is to be maintained in some degree of health, but we have been in no position to manage open lands. We have, therefore, encouraged conservation easements and actual gifts of land to the Conservancy and to other entities who would protect the land and natural systems on it.

Keeping lands open is not an easy task. Nor is it easy to protect lands once set aside from destructive human use. Some sneak in with chain saws and cut down particularly valuable trees. Others dump trash and waste, or run motor bikes through these sensitive areas. A few property owners seek to extend their lawns onto conservancy property, or break down fencing. Beer parties and drugs are a minor problem, but are still an irritant.

As Mitsie told about these problems, I began to wonder how it would be possible to preserve open lands in perpetuity, at least over the next 100 to 200 years.

> That will take vigilance. The worst threat is taxation, for a little group like ours could never afford to pay taxes on these lands. Another threat is condemnation. Right now there are 18 acres of land which Chesterbrook has deeded to the municipality to construct a municipal building. In the development agreement, however, this land was to be preserved as open space in perpetuity. To use it for a municipal building is violating the trust of the citizens in the township that open space be preserved. Then there is apathy, so that lands begin to get abused and nobody cares to enforce the terms of the old deed and agreement. (Conversation with Mitsie Toland)

Education becomes an extremely important part of the Open Land Conservancy's work. Many enjoy spending time in an undisturbed natural setting. The Conservancy seeks to teach those who enter Conservancy lands respect for nature and sponsors programs that enhance appreciation and understanding. An informed public willing to take action in its long-term interest is the strongest force for preserving land.

The number-one tool in open-land preservation today is the conservation easement. Suppose an owner wants to protect 30 out of 100 acres from all future development. If a conservation easement is placed on that land, it restricts its use in perpetuity. The agreement is signed with a conservation organization which is obliged to watch over the land forever. The land owner continues to hold title on the land and as the property changes hands the easement goes along with the deed.

Sometimes future owners go to court to try and break an easement, which is expensive for a conservation organization. Without support from *pro bono* lawyers like its counsel, the Conservancy would be unable to take care of lands entrusted to it.

Conserving open lands is a challenging task. Not only is it difficult to preserve sensitive environmental areas from destructive development, but it is also essential to keep these lands natural in perpetuity. That requires an organization which endures for generations.

While the Valley Creek Committee was keeping a watchdog eye on the stream, Mitsie and her colleagues were attending township meetings and negotiating with developers to save little spaces of land so that our children could see and experience a beautiful shifting world other than the one which human beings have built to make money. Together they and others were laboring to take care of our planetary home.

Valley Creek Watershed Revisited

In 1986, 37 members of the advanced biology course at Conestoga High School in Berwyn participated in a stream study of Valley Creek, under the direction of long-term conservationist Ralph Heister, their teacher. Their report evaluated the status of water quality in the creek, using data for comparative purposes from similar studies conducted in 1972, 1978 and 1983. It showed that the stream is an excellent indicator of the status of the watershed. Since much of the precipitation that falls in the watershed runs over the land and into the stream, the characteristics of the land can be seen in the water quality of the stream. The report identified several major problems within the watershed that impact the water quality of the stream. One was the dewatering operation at the Warner Limestone Quarry. In 1986, 3–5 million gallons of water per day were being mined and pumped into Valley Creek. This large volume of water changed the water temperature and, therefore, affected fish and animal life. The quarry proposal to increase its operation and deepen its pit (possibly pumping 11 million gallons per day) could, in a drought year, cause a severe water shortage (*Valley Creek Watershed Revisited*, 3.).

Second, the Knickerbocker Landfill had contaminated the stream with heavy metals from its leachate. Though this was improved with the closing of the landfill and reopening of it under careful supervision, it was still a source of some siltation and perhaps PCB contamination.

A third problem came from the Paoli Railroad yard's PCB contamination. A fourth was the toxic chemicals which had been dumped on the EPA Superfund site by Chem-Kleen over the years. These poisons contributed to the high background level of many toxic chemicals throughout the watershed. Furthermore, the decrease in ground water would concentrate the background chemicals contributed in part by the landfill and Chem-Kleen, making their hazardous effects more potent. The study concluded that water shortage could be the watershed's biggest problem. In a severe drought year, the Warner Quarry would mine approximately half the water available within the watershed.

An additional impact was excessive enrichment and sedimentation while some areas showed much higher ratios of fecal coliform to fecal streptococcus ratios than in earlier studies. This data indicated the large amount of human waste still being loaded into the creek, perhaps coming from leaky sewage connectors, and/or pumping stations, and/or septic tanks. On the positive side, Valley Creek showed a decrease in levels of heavy metals and the diversity indices of fish and benthic macroinvertebrates had improved or remained the same.

A few weeks after Ralph Heister presented his original finding to the chapter at a meeting in 1979, cyanide poisoning had killed fish throughout the length of the stream. Seven years later, we were involved in many issues affecting the well-being of the stream and its watershed. Chapter members joined with persons from other conservation groups in seeking to end pollution of the stream, and protect the remaining parts of the watershed. Yet we could see in Heister's new 1986 study that although there was some progress, as in the Knickerbocker landfill operation, at many other points the stream was getting worse. Would our efforts to seek responsible development have enough effect to save the watershed, and thus Valley Creek?

Porcupines and Triangles

In 1985, I learned through Joe Armstrong of a trout stream habitat improvement workshop, to be held in August 1986 at Lockhaven University in Pennsylvania. I wrote to the Pennsylvania Fish Commission and found out what they were looking for in the line of papers and prepared an article on results of our stream restoration project on West Valley Creek to present to this assembly of researchers and biologists. In August 1986, I presented a paper titled "Porcupines and Triangles," based on what we had learned, including techniques for stream restoration as well as their effects. The conclusions were (1) stream-bred trout population increased as a result of stream modification, coupled with a trout egg restocking program using Vibert boxes; (2) the project led to immediate betterment of trout habitat through in-stream efforts; (3) the artificial devices employed were beginning to assume a natural, aesthetically attractive appearance (though they still had some distance to go); (4) working on the restoration project had strengthened the local conservation movement, bringing out to the stream a dedicated crew of "banknuts" workers whose activity led to increased involvement in other chapter work; and (5) the project had significant impact on public policy toward preserving and restoring this stream and, interestingly enough, others in Chester County. The presence of wild trout in the stream had a positive effect on many environmental impact statements (as in locating new four-lane highways).

Township planning for housing and industrial development was increasingly influenced by awareness of the presence of an extremely valuable stream flowing through its boundaries. As environmental leaders we ourselves received a great deal of education and encouragement from carrying out the project and using it to teach others how healthy streams work and can be restored. "Before" and "after" slides taken of the project were used in presentations to give many a better understanding of ways officials could be better stewards of the land and water their decisions were affecting.

Destroying a stream takes no knowledge. Restoring a stream to health takes understanding, teamwork, hard physical work, and lots of patience. Joining the Creator in restoration, however, brings new life to human beings, as well as to the stream. It leaves one with a deep feeling of parental delight. ("Porcupines and Triangles: *Restoration of a Dredged Limestone Stream*," presented to the 5th Trout Stream Habitat Improvement Workshop, Lock Haven, Pa., August 1986, by Owen D. Owens)

As I drove home after presenting this paper, I reflected that I had learned new ways we could begin to make more effective the work we had begun. I was also left with a peculiar feeling that this restoration project was in some way the soul of the entire environmental movement we had started. On the surface it seems that getting in a stream and throwing rocks would make little difference to what was happening to the watershed. And yet, in some strange way, the fact that we cared enough to initiate this long-term restoration project seemed to be very significant. I wondered what was going to happen next.

During the fall we did our annual electrofishing. The results were very satisfying for those who had rolled rocks, planted willows and tied in Christmas trees to collect silt. About double the number of trout previously noted turned up in the restoration section. We had twice the wild fish, twice the keeper-size fish, twice the wild fish of keeper-size. A total of 68 trout were reported, of which 34 were stream-bred wild. A few weeks later, Mike Kauffman, regional biologist for the Pennsylvania Fish Commission, walked the restoration stretch of West Valley Creek. After offering helpful suggestions for further improvements, he said that it was the best stream restoration project he had ever seen.

Other chapter activities were also encouraging. The fall banquet raised over $2,700, once again supporting local and national efforts. Over 30,000 eggs were planted in the tributaries of West Valley, hopefully to ensure a good stream-bred trout population in years to come.

Development

All over the Exton area, the headwaters of West Valley Creek, developments were mushrooming. Through the inspired leadership of one of its members, the West Whiteland Planning Commission had developed an ordinance designed to protect the limestone aquifer which underlay much of West Whiteland township. In 1987 I prepared a plan for West Valley Creek based on preserving the stream and its watershed. This plan was presented to the West Whiteland Planning Commission and from there went to the township supervisors. We hoped that maintaining groundwater recharge would be kept front and center as plans for development proceeded, and that a green belt on both sides of the stream would be preserved.

Then big news hit the papers. Church Farm School contracted to sell 1,500 acres to the Willard Rouse Corporation. This was the largest open space left in eastern Chester County. Its estimated worth was approximately $45–$50 million. Much would depend on how this development was done. If groundwater recharge were maintained and rainfall allowed to soak into the land, it could be that the development might leave the stream in better condition than the bare corn fields eroding throughout much of the year. On the other hand, a thoughtless development of massive size could ruin the stream.

At the same time as these plans for development were being aired, the Downington Regional Sewer Authority was debating how they might get rid of the wastewater being produced by the rapidly increasing population. Since all the tributaries flowed into the Brandywine River, the question was how much sewer water would the Brandywine accept? The other question being debated was the source of the water needed for projected new industries and homes. Little attention was given to the long-term consequences of unregulated development. As Joe Armstrong observed, it seemed like people were thinking that there would always be water when one turned the tap and that once the toilet was flushed, everything would disappear!

We received unofficial word that studies were well underway to site a sewer plant on West Valley Creek. If such a facility were sited well upstream on the Church Farm School property where much of the sewerage would come from, and were built to be very reliable, it might be a benefit to the stream during drought periods. It appeared, however, that the likely site would be at the head of the restoration project. Sited here, such a facility would wipe out the stream, making it little more than a flowing sewer.

To this very depressing news was added a tragic loss. Gene Clark, first editor of the chapter newsletter, who thought of the name *Banknotes*, was killed in a motorcycle accident on March 29, 1987. Few work days passed without Gene giving his enthusiastic efforts. Issue after issue of *Banknotes* came out because of his commitment. We would miss Gene a great deal.

Meanwhile, the Route 29 bypass project connecting with Route 202 was producing heavy siltation in Valley Creek below where the work was being done. When questioned about the poor quality construction evidenced, the project engineer reputedly said, "Why are they worried about the trout? When we are done, they won't be there anymore!"

Trout streams and Trout Unlimited members, however, do not give up easily. At the spring trout show on March 26, 1987, 337 attendees saw the Trammell Crow Company and Roy F. Weston Company presented with an award recognizing their significant contributions to the preservation of an environmentally sensitive area on Little Crabby Creek. Little Crabby Creek was still alive because the developer had secured the services of a competent, environment consultant firm, developed careful plans, monitored the construction and completed the work effectively. The results of the first of several follow-up surveys was reported in the summer 1987 issues of the *Weston Way*. They were very encouraging. Thirty-seven brown trout were collected and beneficial insect colonization of the new stream section substrate was evident. Four years of hard, untiring work by Mitsie Toland and John Renshaw had paid off handsomely.

Work was advancing on Valley Creek, too. Stream improvements began in Valley Forge National Park for the first time as we planted native willow shoots on the eroding banks of some sections of the creek. Another major new development planned to go in near Crabby Creek submitted plans which were reviewed by chapter members. The developers made corrections which would more adequately protect the tributary and insure adequate ground water recharge.

There was a good side to the story, however: an unexpected explosion of naturally reproducing brown trout in Valley Creek. Protected from heavy fishing pressure, natural reproduction was very successful. Though anglers could not eat the fish, they were taking delight in pursuing wild brown trout in the stream from which Washington's troops drew their drinking water.

Conclusion

For years the *Pennsylvania Angler* had featured a column by Ralph W. Abele, director of the Pennsylvania Fish Commission. Abele's honesty and sometimes abrasive commitment to conservation had made enemies, but to all who cared about the streams of Pennsylvania, he was a legendary figure. His last article was reprinted in the *Banknotes*. In it, Abele said that it was natural to want to leave behind something noteworthy and worth remembering. Throughout his life he had

Responsible Development Saves Crabby Creek

preached the need for a conservation ethic. This was not an easy message to get across, for everywhere there was evidence of a throwaway society.

He went on to say that a unique power was bestowed upon each human being to work for results that would benefit all humanity and even change the course of history. This power was often quite underestimated.

One person with enough stubborness can dig in his heels and say, "This much and no more." Beware of the cause that you choose for this kind of stubbornness, because you will surely prevail! There are great causes to be followed, and victory always starts with one person hanging on by his teeth and saying, "I will never give in." All the greed and shortsigntedness of the exploiters and developers—and that includes people in state and federal governments—will not prevail if that one individual rises up and says, "Why should we put up with this?" I insist that if one is stubborn enough—unmovable, unchangeable—that person can and will prevail. (*Pennsylvania Angler*, May 1987)

Making a Difference

What can one person do alone? One day Wayne Poppich was fishing Crabby Creek. He saw oil in the water, and wondered from where it was coming. Upstream a little farther he saw a pile of paint cans, some open, spilling into the creek.

When he got home from his fishing trip he called up the Department of Environmental Resources and reported the pollution. The small painting contractor responsible resisted doing anything, but the DER increased the pressure. Finally the painter went down and hauled out all of the cans. Wayne's next fishing trip found the stream running clean and clear again.

Church of the Yawning Precipice

In January 1988 newly elected president Jim Ferrier found himself in a rapidly moving current. For five years we had been part of the Great Valley Coalition, which addressed concerns about a proposed expansion of the Warner Quarry. Through the persistence of Coalition members, letters to state representatives and their direct interceding in the process had held up the permit for the longest period in history.

There were serious flaws in the permit issued in March 1988, however. Even though unprecedented restrictions were placed as conditions for the 113-acre expansion, at least eighteen wells could be lost from increased groundwater pumping resulting from the deepening of the quarry pit. Warner would be allowed to mine sixty feet below sea level and pump up to 14 million gallons a day. The lowering of the water table due to increased pumping rates could lead to dewatering of up to a mile of Valley Creek. There were no provisions for monitoring groundwater quality, despite the United States Geological Survey's "urbanization" studies' findings that toxic chemicals were being drawn into the area's groundwater by the quarry's pumping. Quarry discharges into Valley Creek would result in a significant degradation of its water quality, both allowing too much sediment to go into the stream and the water temperature levels to rise.

The coalition prepared for more years of effort and expense. Based on the past performance of the Department of Environmental Resources in inspecting and enforcing its own permits and regulations, enforcement mechanisms in the permit seemed vague and inadequate.

Perhaps the most striking effect of the development, however, was on the historic St. Peter's Episcopal Church. The proposed expansion would totally surround the church property and leave it perched on a yawning precipice. It would hurt the congregation's ability to continue to function as a parish church, and desecrate the 300-year-old historic site.

A Good Deed by the Scouts

In the fall of 1987, Mike Cattell had undertaken an Eagle Scout project on West Valley Creek. He had to put in several hundred hours of work and organize a group to assist him. Having completed the approved plan and picked the site, the scouts began work late in the fall of 1987. Weeks and several workdays passed.

One January day, 1988, eight young people splashed back and forth the pool in oversized hip boots. Buckets of small-sized stones were passed by human chain and dumped on top of a slowly rising deflector. Larger rocks were carried one by one. Shovelers continued to dig into the bottom to produce a good-sized hole in front of the deflector. Christmas trees and small branches were piled behind the stones and staked securely into place. Several large rocks were placed on the opposite bank to further concentrate the current. By March, Mike and his troops had completed the deflector, a deed which would tell of their good efforts for years to come.

Cleaning Up Paoli

The end of the Philadelphia Main Line, Paoli, is an unlikely spot for a Superfund site. Yet, as a result of the PCB contamination of the Paoli car yards, the EPA designated the Paoli Car Yards as such a site. When a problem is acknowledged publicly, it becomes possible to study it. The EPA carefully examined the Paoli railroad yards. Its studies showed that PCBs had not only contaminated tracks and downhill properties, as well as the stream and its trout, but were also poisoning those who used the busy Paoli commuter station. PCBs were discovered everywhere: on floors and smeared on telephones. They certainly had been tracked into hundreds of houses throughout the area. They had washed with soils off the site and poisoned surrounding residential areas. No wonder the Paoli yards were designated as a Superfund site.

In the summer of 1987, a limited amount of work was done to stop PCBs from running off the site. In 1988, the clean-up went into high gear. Houses downhill from the site were covered with plastic up to the second story. Contaminated soils were removed from throughout the affected area. Barriers were placed around the yard to end contamination. The goal of the law suit we had begun three years before had been realized. PCBs were no longer polluting Valley Creek.

We then received an unexpected dividend. The poster for the 1988 Trout Show pictures George Washington holding up a check for $43,750. Around him are chapter members with big smiles on their faces. The funds, emerging from a lawsuit against Conrail in upstate New York, had to be used to further coldwater resource work within 50 miles of Valley Forge Park and could not be used to pursue action against the railroads. The chapter immediately invested the funds, planning to use only the dividends for its work.

Our suit was for a clean-up, not for damages. We never expected that money would come back to us from the lawsuit, but it did. These new funds gave us financial backing to deal with the larger and larger problems facing the streams and watersheds of Chester County.

Baffling Crabby Creek

Little Crabby Creek has four major highways going over it. Box culverts allowing the tributary to go underneath the highways had been

ANNUAL   VALLEY FORGE
Trout Show
APRIL 1988

Valley Forge Chapter Receives a Conrail Check

constructed with concrete bottoms, effectively blocking fish migration and providing no habitat. Joe Armstrong came up with the idea of putting wooden baffles in each of these culverts, in effect producing a series of tiny meanders which would provide cover and concentrate the flow.

Conversations had to be held with the Pennsylvania Fish Commission and the Pennsylvania Department of Highways (PenDot), as well as with a home builder with a project which called for widening two more roads which crossed Crabby Creek. A deal was struck with the builders to install such baffles as part of their project. They also agreed to deed 17 acres of steeply-sloped wetlands and springheads to Tredyffrin Township rather than build in the area.

The Crabby Creek story was not over. We received permission to restore habitat in the tunnels. On Independence Day, 1988, I found myself down on my knees in a culvert underneath the four-lane highway. I was tapping a star drill with a hammer, gradually eroding a small hole in the concrete bottom of the culvert. I was not alone. Several other obsessed Trout Unlimited members were there with me preparing to install wooden baffles. One by one we fastened 4 × 6 wooden beams to the bottom of the culvert. As each went into place, a new meander was created. The water rushed around the end to bump against a new baffle which we put behind it. Foot by foot, we moved through the concrete culvert to its end. Deep enough water was created to hold small trout and to allow easy passage for spawning adult trout when they headed upstream.

Every time I drive across these culverts, I think of what is underneath them: little trout, insects, a healthier ecosystem. Sometimes our efforts are not as "baffling" as they seem. Furthermore, now that these matters had been brought to the attention of developers and Pennsylvania Department of Transportation, perhaps future construction of culverts would leave a natural stream bottom underneath them.

Chlorine

Valley Forge Trout Unlimited board member Jim Leonard was out on Valley Creek looking for some early blue-winged olive mayflies. Instead, he found a pool service pumping some very dubious-looking liquid from a swimming pool into a Valley Creek feeder. When Jim asked them what they were doing, he was told to "jump in the creek." He got on the telephone and in short order had representatives of the DER and the local police on the scene. The pool cleaners were indeed pumping out potentially harmful materials which could have killed trout.

Fish kills occur again and again on suburban streams when swimming pools are drained into them. Chlorine is poisonous to trout and beneficial stream insects, as are the noxious cleaners used in pools. Fortunately, a fisherman's willingness to leave the stream and make a few phone calls kept the worst from happening. It also educated local police, who might in the future be more likely to keep an eye out for similar incidents.

Throughout the spring, fishing was great on Valley Creek. Chapter members caught many fish when caddis flies were coming off the water in late March and April. The sulfur hatch brought fish and fishermen out in droves. The population of wild brown trout from Valley Creek was exploding.

On July 11 and 12, 400 meters of Valley Creek and about 100 meters of Crabby Creek were electro-fished by the Pennsylvania Fish Commission and volunteers. Valley Creek yielded 122 trout, mostly small and medium-sized fish, but a few "rod-benders" were also captured. All these fish were released into the water. Catch-and-release fishermen of the future would have more opportunity for good sport.

Valley Forge TU had requested that the Mill Road and Route 202 culverts on Crabby Creek be electro-fished. Forty-two fingerling brown trout turned up in this census. The baffles in the culverts had converted zero trout habitat to a very desirable one.

Members of VFTU met with project managers of Pennsylvania Department of Transportation and their consultants to discuss again the upcoming four-lane highway bypass project which would cross West Valley Creek as well as a number of tributaries. For five years we had been writing letters, attending meetings, but had received little feedback from PenDot as to designing this new roadway to minimize the potential devastating impact on the stream.

Armed with access to advice on current state-of-the-art roadway construction from a member who was engaged in constructing a major Philadelphia four-lane highway system, we approached the meeting at PenDot local headquarters with considerable apprehension. We were delighted to note that previous contacts with us had been carefully noted, and the features we had been suggesting were indeed included in the design work. We reviewed proposed construction in detail. A number of points were found where some of our concerns had not been adequately met, but these were more of an oversight than willful deletion.

As this highway would involve considerable heavy industrial traffic, it was predictable that a truckload of hazardous material would at some time overturn right above the stream or one of its tributaries. Facilities to contain the spills were a key part of the design of the new roadway. Further nonpoint pollutants such as lead, oils, asbestos, carbon black, acids, glycols, and other materials related to transport vehicles could also be expected to wash off the roadway and cause large problems in total (although each event might be minute). These problems, too, had been addressed in the design work for the new road.

Years of frustrating and persistent work appeared to be paying off. While there would doubtless be problems during construction, Pen-Dot had made a major effort to include design features to protect the stream. When built, these features would represent the highest level of stream protection of any roadway in the state.

Stream Classification Upgrades

When we began our efforts years previously to gain an upgrade of West Valley Creek, we learned that it was the first time in the state that a local group had originated such a request. Most requests were for downgrading water quality classifications. Accordingly, it took some time before West Valley Creek was upgraded. Our request for the upgrading of Valley Creek dragged on even longer, though it was obviously a high-quality fishery with a substantial wild trout population.

Under the previous regulations of "trout stocking" designation, it would have been legal for effluent to enter the stream which would have warmed the whole stream past tolerable limits for trout during the late summer. The logic of this designation was that stocked trout do not survive the summer. While that may be reasonable for some streams, Valley Creek now supported a fine population of wild brown trout that could have been legally destroyed under the "trout stocking" designation. The designation which was finally given after three and one half years of work, was "coldwater fishery." Would-be polluters would have to jump over another strand of barbed wire. It was a major step forward.

Changes in Department of Environmental Resoures procedures emerging from the persistent efforts of ourselves and others to upgrade cold water streams resulted in an unexpected bit of good news. The Department of Environmental Resources, while responding to a complaint about a package sewage plant on Broad Run, a tributary to the West Branch of the Brandywine Creek, did some invertebrate sampling that turned up surprising results. They decided to recommend that the stream be classified as "exceptional value, coldwater fishery," based on their samples. Our long and often discouraging efforts, therefore, had made a difference.

Making a Difference

What makes a difference? First and foremost, one person makes a difference. One person seems so small, so insignificant, and yet the stories of the changes that have occurred in Chester County again and again tell about individuals who got involved and stuck at it.

Mike Cattell built a deflector, an Eagle Scout project that restored one part of West Valley Creek. Buck Plank picked up trash for years, never expecting that would affect a decision by the the West Whiteland supervisors. Chuck Marshall went to New Jersey to check out manifest ladings and gave the information to a newspaper reporter, never expecting that this might defuse a biological time bomb, the Knickerbocker Landfill. Mitsie Toland went to hundreds of meetings, hoping that her efforts to conserve open lands would make a difference, and often they did. When people get active in the community to look out for the creation, sooner or later the Creator honors their efforts and miracles happen.

Second, research makes a difference. Knowledge gives power. Ralph Heister and the students of Conestoga High School over the years gathered information on Valley Creek which proved to be invaluable. Without that information, changes in the watershed would have never been noticed or documented.

Third, a network makes a difference. When people work together for the good of all, they are much stronger than when they go it alone. The Valley Creek Watershed Coalition played a critical role at many points. So did the coalitions which came into existence to deal with the expansion of the Warner Limestone Quarry.

Fourth, legal advice makes a difference. The environmental lawyers who worked with our citizen's group gave us much help. Without their aid the PCB cleanup in Paoli would not have happened.

Fifth, some money helps make a difference. Chuck Marshall chuckles to himself about the size of the war chest that the Valley Forge chapter now has and how it happened. Having money to back up one's ongoing work makes a group formidable. Over the years the chapter raised the money it needed by fund raisers and contributions. Having an endowment fund to back up its work made it even stronger.

Sixth, being honest persons of integrity makes a difference. Even their adversaries respected Chuck Marshall, Mitsie Tolland, Joe Armstrong, and worked with them. Chuck observed:

It is really neat seeing Trout Unlimited being a respected voice in the community. I felt that with Churchill, when people outside referred to you. For example, the first time we met with the Rouse Corporation one of the staff called Trammel-Crow and asked about Trout Unlimited. The response was: "They are formidable but a good group to work with." Being respected makes it easier to open doors and get somewhere in the social-political process. I feel now that there is no issue that we could not rally support to deal with.

We had faced large institutions which were deciding to unmake creation. Their leaders had money and political power. A few years before, it seemed impossible that a few persons could make any difference. Yet, when we worked together for the good of all, good things happened. Often we do make a difference.

CHAPTER 11

World-Class Sewage

During the 1980s Chester County was rapidly urbanizing. Land-owners and developers made a great deal of money. The tax base of townships was expanding so that they and other governmental bodies were gaining new revenues, although the new services demanded often outran the larger tax base. Constructing office "parks," housing projects, roads, sewers and utilities provided many jobs—even if they were short-term. In the rush to develop, one thing determined whether or not a given project was done—whether or not it would make money! Building a sustainable community in balance with its natural environment, therefore, was a secondary priority, when it was even taken into account at all. Even less important to the developers was the polluted and deteriorating city which they left behind in Philadelphia.

Thus far, development in eastern Chester County had devastated and paved much of the watersheds of West Valley and Valley Creek, provided little or no housing for poor and working people, and greatly increased traffic and population density. What made Chester County valuable and desirable was rapidly being eliminated. Conservationists who wanted to preserve cold water streams and their watersheds could begin to feel despair. One was tempted to complain and say, "Isn't it terrible! Does anything I do make any difference?"

A new Department of Environment Resources computer model was completed on the Brandywine River. For the third time in a little over a decade, the computer study showed that the Brandywine could accept far more sewage than previous models had estimated. In a somewhat cynical mood, one of our chapter wits said that instead of dumping the sewer water in the Brandywine a few miles away from the intake valve of the city of West Chester, what should be done is to connect the outflow sewer pipe to the West Chester water system and simplify matters! In either case residents of the West Chester area would be drinking recycled sewer water.

Carl Dusinberre, our chapter cartoonist, said:

> I am amazed that trout are still in West Valley and Valley Creeks. I was willing to work, cheerlead, donate, but was not that optimistic. Even now, I am not sure there will be trout in these streams in ten years. The future looks bleak, with acid rain, global warming of the atmosphere, and rain forest destruction in the news. It appears that only a small percentage of the population knows what is going on. Many of those do not believe what they read. There are a disturbing number of persons in key positions who don't do anything. John Johnson, West Chester Fish, Game and Wildlife Association leader, said that wetlands in the past were destroyed from ignorance, but now when they are being destroyed, it can only be from greed.

A Pistol at Our Heads

Valley Forge Trout Unlimited members and John Johnson, leader of West Chester Fish and Game Association, were invited to meet with officials of the Rouse Corporation to share concerns to work through plans which would be mutually agreeable. Several meetings were held. One day in December 1988 the community and public relations director of the Rouse Corporation laid out the colorful plans for the huge development, now to be called Churchill. As he extolled the virtues of the new plan, more and more time passed. Suddenly, Carl Dusinberre, reflecting on his years of work as a real estate developer, in pointed language said, "Give it to us straight." After the PR man swallowed a bit of anger, he said that they had decided their best option to get rid of the sewage was to dump it into West Valley Creek at the head of the restoration project. Since there already was a pumping station there, it would be easy to expand it and put the effluent into the stream at that point. There were, of course, other options, but this seemed to be the most feasible one.

Joe Armstrong said, "You're putting a pistol to my head and asking me how I like it! Dumping your sewer water would destroy a fine trout stream, and it's right above the project we've sweated on for over a decade."

At our next board meeting we assessed the realities, looking at the different options that might be available for dealing with the sewerage. We knew we had to come up with an alternative proposal. There was no question about whether or not the chapter would act. The Rouse plan would destroy West Valley Creek as a trout fishery. Joe Armstrong wrote:

> We appear headed for a major problem with a proposed Rouse Development of the church farm property near Exton. The property involved will be a virtual mini city when finished with a shopping center the size of the biggest one in the world (presently located at King of Prussia, Pennsylvania), housing on a scale of Chesterbrook (a densely constructed area near Valley Forge National Park), and office space about like Great Valley Corporate Center (the huge Rouse development in East Whiteland). This will involve a lot of water, both clean and dirty.
>
> We are still concerned about using wells to provide water for the development which might deplete ground water and hence springs feeding the stream. Of even greater concern is the handling of the sewage generated. At present, plans are pretty well along to build a sewage treatment plant at the Clover Mill Road pumping station, and discharge directly to nearby West Valley Creek. The flows envisioned will be between three and ten times stream low flow. That is a stream channel full of sewer water, with a little stream water mixed in. Given the record of frequent misoperation of sewer treatment plants, this will kill the stream. It is ironic that the discharge point is immediately at the top of our ongoing stream restoration project, which is now about a dozen years old and has involved about $10,000 worth of material and close to that number of volunteer hours. We have to fight this proposal with everything at our disposal. In effect we have been painted into a corner, and we have no option but to fight or roll over and play dead.

Joe went on to outline alternatives:

> First, water conservation features could be built into new construction, thereby reducing water usage by up to one third. Second, "force main" sewer lines, built to be nonleaking, could be used in

the new construction, reducing infiltration of clean ground water into the sewer system. Third, the Rouse plan should use water collected in storm water basins and spray it on a proposed golf course; sewer water could be used for this purpose, further reducing the effluent loads. Were a sewer plant to be built, it could be located on the Church Farm property itself, rather than three miles downstream; thus when a sewer plant malfunction occurred, there would be several miles below that discharge point for natural processes to partially mitigate the spill. Each of these four options would substantially reduce costs of sewering. (*Banknotes*, February 1989)

I wondered whether Willard Rouse had made a big error. Eighty-five percent of the land for "Churchill" was in West Whiteland Township, 15 percent in East Whiteland. Major zoning variances would be required from each township to do the development.

In more than ten years of effort the chapter had experienced significant successes; in its suit of SEPTA, negotiations with Crabby Creek developers, work with PenDot and DER, and many other efforts. Each expenditure of time and energy had prepared us for a larger struggle. We could not back off. If the Willard Rouse plans stood as proposed, West Valley Creek would be destroyed. The "Churchill" development plan which Willard Rouse's subordinates had presented was a slap in the face to all conservationists in Chester County. Our restoration project was an effort to improve the stream and make the environment in Chester County more fertile and desirable. Here was a massive "world class" developer, heavy-handedly planning to destroy part of what made Chester County desirable. We were being presented with a wonderful organizing issue, provided that the development did not move so rapidly that the stream was ruined before we could get started.

We learned that the Rouse Corporation was pressing West Whiteland township to amend its 537 plan sewering ordinance. Carl Dusinberre agreed to stay on top of township meetings and coordinate chapter efforts. Chapter counsel Howard McGarvey, Chuck Marshall, Joe Armstrong, I and other chapter members agreed to do our best to stir up support to testify at the township hearing for the 537 sewer plan. Jim Clark began to prepare a special issue of *Banknotes* which would set forth constructive approaches to sewage treatment and groundwater recharge in the West Whiteland area. Joe Armstrong checked with leaders of other groups to alert them as to what was going on and seek their support. John Johnson alerted the Civic Association and the West Chester Fish, Game, and Wildlife to developments and joined us in preparing for the 537 hearing.

Though this was a difficult time for me in my family life, I set aside these troubles. I called the Pennsylvania Fish Commission, "You once said that the West Valley Creek restoration project was one of the best in the state. It would be really helpful if we could get an award which would call attention to the project's value." The Fish Commission was very supportive and indeed soon publicly announced we were being given an award for a fine restoration project. In a letter to chapter president Park Messikomer, David Houser, chief of the Adopt A Stream Section wrote:

> In a decade of cooperation between the Valley Forge chapter of Trout Unlimited and the Pennsylvania Fish Commission, a great deal of accomplishments have been achieved, too many to realistically depict in a letter. One project does seem to stand out: the West Valley Creek Habitat Restoration Project. It is one of the few total restoration projects in the state that has made a real difference. The once barren habitat and fishless stretches of stream are hard to recognize today. This comes from cooperation, imagination and a great deal of hard work. I hope that nothing would ever jeopardize West Valley Creek's quality, because it is quite clear that the Valley Forge chapter of Trout Unlimited is truly an "Adopt A Stream parent" that loves its children.

I called the newspapers and gave them a story on the West Valley Creek restoration project. A reporter came out and took pictures on a January 1989 work day when we attached Christmas trees to the tops of deflectors. A few days later a major article appeared with pictures telling about the work of the Chapter. Jim Clark wrote:

> Hah! You thought that just because somebody wants to murder the creek, you might be able to get out of going to work sessions. Wrong, Banknut. In January, Owen Owens, Joe Armstrong, Wayne Poppich, Ray Squires, Park Messikomer, Jim Leonard, Ed Penry, Todd Henderson, and I secured the vast majority of about 300 donated Christmas trees to the tops of our silt catching devices known as porcupines. The rest will be put in as time permits. (*Banknotes*, February 1989)

I asked Mike Cattell, the Eagle Scout who had built a restoration project, and Harry Cattell, his father, if the Boy Scouts might come to the 537 plan public hearing. Harry and Mike responded that they would be glad to come and felt that other Scouts also would want to be present. After all, these young people were due to inherit what was left after development, and they wanted to make sure the trout stream would survive.

Over the Christmas vacation I took the township manager to see the restoration project. It was a cold day, but he got a good view of the work that had been done. I also arranged to take the man in charge of engineering for the sewer project for the Rouse Corporation out to see the restoration project. He was impressed but seemed to feel that little could be done to avoid dumping the treated sewer water into the stream.

On Monday, February 6, 1989, the 537 sewer plan was to be presented before the West Whiteland Township supervisors for approval. That very day Tom Tatum wrote in the *Daily Local News:*

> The preliminary plans for a new sewage plant in West Whiteland Township have been drawn up and, from an environmental perspective they do not present a pretty picture. In fact, they're stone cold, drop dead ugly. The environmental ecological havoc the present plan would impose, not only in West Whiteland, but throughout much of the county would be monumental. Two of the most vocal opponents of this project are Trout Unlimited and the West Chester Game, Fish and Wildlife Association. Their concerns are centered on the sewage/waste chemical effluent which would be discharged into West Valley Creek and the Brandywine. At a potential two to three million gallons of effluent per day, we're not talking minor problems here, we're talking ecocide.

Carl Dusinberre had kept in contact with the township to determine when the hearing would be held on the 537 plan. The night before the hearing, a premeeting was held with Carl, Chuck Marshall, Howard McGarvey and myself. Howard was to prepare to speak on legal realities. Chuck was to critique the proposed draft of the 537 plan based on his extensive experience as an environmental consultant. Carl was to address issues of real estate development, drawing on his own extensive experience, and I was to deal with reasons why the township should preserve the stream and not dump sewage into it.

Speaking Out

The big night came. When I got to the township building the hall was filled. Over 30 Scouts and their leaders were present, and they came in uniform! Leaders from other groups were ready. The township had cleared time on its agenda for Trout Unlimited to respond to the Rouse presentation. When the time came we spoke out. In my presentation I commended the township supervisors and their staff for the efforts they had already given to protecting West Valley Creek. I

Exton Mall: Headwaters of West Valley Creek

Checking on Streambred Fingerlings

Valley Creek

Washington's Headquarters: Valley Creek

Crabby Creek

OPPOSITE
Morris Run, a tributary of Valley Creek,
before and after "development."

Baffles in Highway Culvert: Crabby Creek

Christmas Tree Deflector

Wing Deflector with Christmas Tree Spine

Point Bar Below Deflector

mentioned the dump truck they had sent when we had picked up trash along its banks and the diligent efforts made to enforce regulations on construction to keep silt and sediment from washing into the stream. I concluded by asking the supervisors to continue to provide support to protect the stream and its watershed. Chuck gave a fine critique of the proposed 537 plan, shredding the roughly put together proposal and indicating desirable alternatives which had not been considered. Carl identified other real estate realities which had not yet been considered in this planning.

We kept our presentations brief, and at the end the chair of the three-person board of supervisors stated that the 537 plan would be sent back for further consideration. He publicly asserted that he and the supervisors wished to do nothing to make the stream worse and hoped that their work would indeed make it better.

We realized our goal, to slow down the "railroad." The 537 hearing was decisive. If the 537 plan as proposed had been adopted, the Rouse project would have moved forward so rapidly there would have been little time for anyone to organize. Now there would be time for other groups to pay attention to what was going on, and deal with the larger issues.

Looking for a Miracle

When we feel absolutely alone and overwhelmed, we can take heart that George Washington is looking over our shoulders. Washington, Jefferson, Adams and the other founders of democracy in the United States of America had their faults, just as we do. But they sacrificed much for the good of their country. If Washington's "bottom line" had been making money, he never would have refused the presidency when it was offered to him for life. Nor would he have made decisions for the good of the whole people at his own expense.

In the sketches and cartoons Carl Dusinberre has done for chapter events, we frequently see George Washington participating or looking on. Carl thinks our first president would be pleased to see the democratic system he and others helped to found still working. I asked Carl what some of the main things he had learned from his years of work in the chapter: "I am not so sure it is what I have learned, as what I have relearned. The system sometimes works. As an American it helps to realize that our government system works, and the voice of the people is heard. One person can become vitally important, though at the end you need a larger group, a coalition. One or two carry the load and do the actual work."

If citizens organize and do the hard work that nobody will pay them for, miracles do happen. There are no advance guarantees, however. In his article in the February special issue of *Banknotes*, Joe Armstrong discussed options for saving the stream, some of which would actually cost less to implement and maintain than expanding a high-tech package plant. Joe concluded by saying: "It is not reasonable to come into an area, and have as the first act of what will presumably be an ongoing participation in local affairs, a public execution of a much-loved and labored-over stream. It is also not necessary. We hope to have our views prevail." On the next page of this same issue of *Banknotes* was a special cartoon, commemorating the Willard Rouse Company's plan to turn Valley Creek into a treated sewer water stream. It features the "good neighbor" himself, adding his contribution to the water of the stream.

Tens of thousands of hours and a great deal of money had been spent to keep the stream beautiful and clean. In a world increasingly filled with concrete jungles and asphalt parking lots, this living stream was providing thousands with a place where they could get in touch with nature. Would a developer be allowed to undo all this effort and kill West Valley Creek?

Grinding On

The struggle to save West Valley Creek dragged on. The chapter took a position that we would fight to maintain the stream and its watershed but not oppose development itself. Indeed, given the extensive corn farming carried out by Church Farm School with its attendant soil erosion, a careful and responsible development could actually leave the stream and its watershed in better shape.

When you are facing a developer who commands hundreds of millions of dollars, it makes a little stream conservation organization feel very small, indeed. The Rouse Corporation continued to insist on dumping its treated sewer water into West Valley Creek. It pursued amending the township 537 sewering plan to allow it to do so. After several months, however, its "loss leader" (a drug company), so called because the first tenant corporation to build would pick up much of the costs of the next parts of the development, decided to locate elsewhere. Since drug companies work with hazardous materials,

The Good Neighbor

chemical as well as biological, this loss meant that someone in the future would have to do less monitoring than would be the case if the drug company actually had stayed and built. It also removed some of the financial steam from the Rouse Company pressures.

George Washington continued to look over our shoulders, reminding us that being a citizen could be costly and required constant public activity. The dedicated few kept on. The Brandywine Conservancy took the lead in forming a coalition. Supported by West Chester Fish, Game and Wildlife Association, Harmony Hill Civic Association, and VFTU, alternate plans were prepared for the development of the Church Farm School site that stayed within existing zoning and had far fewer environmental impacts than Churchill.

VFTU's major concern with the Rouse Company's plan for Churchill were three-fold:

1. Discharging treated sewage at the Clover Mill site on West Valley Creek at the rate of 2.2 million gallons per day (mgd) would ruin

the stream as a fishery. West Whiteland township wanted to piggyback its sewage to make it a 3.0 million gallon per day plant.

2. Withdrawing 1.0 million gallons per day of water from the aquifer that supplies base flow to West Valley Creek would mine ground water.

3. Increasing storm water runoff would reduce aquifer recharge and increase peak storm flows.

What Are Nature's Realities?

This "world class" developer's plan to kill Valley Creek by dumping an immense amount of treated water into it forced us to look more deeply at the realities of nature. Both water supply and effluent had to be considered. In a worst-case scenario, dewatering the stream and dumping effluent into it could combine to cause its annihilation. Should waste water be pumped out of the basin to the Valley Forge or Downingtown regional sewage plants, there would be a decrease in ground water available to recharge the streams which feed West Valley Creek. An increasingly impervious surface due to construction of rooftops and pavements in the developed area would further retard ground water recharge during rainy periods while diverting this water directly to the streams. This change in runoff patterns would raise flows in floods while diminishing base flow in droughts.

Water for drinking, sanitary, and process uses is essential for any domestic, commercial, or industrial development, and that water has to come from somewhere. On the other hand, that water has to go someplace after it's used. Were there not plans which could clean up the water and allow recharge of the ground water at the same time? Through research done by the Brandywine Conservancy, many alternatives to dumping treated sewer water into the stream were discovered, with the best waste water handling systems those which most closely mimicked nature. "This means the ideal system would use Mother Nature to help in breaking down objectionable components, would not create a point source of considerable flow, and would be relatively immune to plant upsets. While no system is perfect, land application of treated sewage comes close to addressing the various concerns raised" (*Banknotes*, June 1989).

The underlying principle of land application is that sewage is treated by conventional means, then undergoes a relatively long stay in a storage/treatment system where objectionable components can be broken down, as in a pond. With this long-term treatment, short-term upsets which would be devastating with a "state of the art" sewage package plant can be controlled and damage minimized.

Nutrients in the water used for irrigation are for the most part absorbed into the plants and trees; thus little fertility infiltrates the ground water. With ground water irrigation, of course, the underground water table is recharged so springs keep flowing and the base flow of the stream will be maintained. Responding to worries of residents as to what "that stuff" might do to them, a leader in the field of designing such systems stated that normal fecal coliform bacteria standard for public swimming pools was forty times higher than that coming out of his systems.

For a developer who wants to squeeze as many buildings as possible onto the land in order to maximize short-term profit, a land application system is viewed with distaste. In order to have land to irrigate, there must be open space. Even here, however, use of water-saving devices in new construction which could save up to 30 percent of the requirement, according to the Delaware River Basin Commission.

Another substantial savings could be derived from construction of sewer lines tightly sealed against leakage. A typical gravity flow system allows infiltration into the sewer line of clean, cold ground water, often up to 15 percent of the total.

Furthermore, the history of operation of package plants in Pennsylvania was dismal:

> The problem with mechanical sewer plants is, in essence, that they don't work. A study done by the Chesapeake Bay Foundation on sewer plants in the Susquehanna Basin indicated that, according to a monthly report submitted by each sewer plant, 59 of the 69 plants studied had at least one reported problem of exceeding water quality standards during the year. This data is very sobering since these records are based on reports submitted by the sewer plant operators themselves. In at least one case, good results were later documented as fradulent. These figures given are on a monthly basis, and may not pick up a short term malfunction which, however, could be devastating to the aquatic life of the stream. (*Banknotes*, June 1989)

Drawing on a recent study prepared for the Brandywine Conservancy on the east branch of the Brandywine River below the existing DARA sewer plant at Downingtown, effluent entering the stream at a rate of about one part effluent to five part stream flow (at low-flow condi-tions), the Brandywine exhibited classic evidence of stress, with oxy-gen depletion being the most noticeable result. Without sufficient oxygen in the water, fish are stressed, or die. The proposed plant for Clover Mill Road would propose to put four times low flow into West Valley, or essentially twenty times the loading which already had caused problems in the Brandywine.

Try Not Breathing

As Joe put it, try not breathing for a day, or even an hour, and see how you feel! One failure in a package plant, even if it lasted for a day, could destroy the life in West Valley Creek. Fish, like people, have to breathe all the time.

There are times when popular treatments of information do not do the job. Careful examination of the effects of proposed actions need to be made, and new plans developed which are environmentally and socially responsible. A series of public meetings were held by the Brandywine coalition to inform people. Hundreds turned out to one I attended at a local school. Experts described types of development which would maintain the environmental quality of Chester county. Suggestions were given for alternative plans which would even cost less to developers and public bodies. Newspaper articles picked up the information sent out in publications of the Brandywine Conser-vancy and in *Banknotes*. Civic associations gave support, not only because they were concerned about the environmental impact of this 1500-acre development, but also due to worries about increased traffic and taxes.

The Rouse Corporation took its plans to the West Whiteland and East Whiteland planning commissions and sought zoning changes, but now the process moved slowly. A Trout Unlimited member kept environmental considerations up front in deliberations of the East Whiteland planning commission, and continuing input was made to West Whiteland.

Meanwhile, behind the scenes negotiations with the Rouse Corpora-tion moved forward. We were very clear that we were not trying to stop its development. Indeed, we felt that it was probably better to deal with one large developer than with a hundred small-sized ones. For each little development the same issues of mining ground water and producing sewage would have to be faced. Chapter members spoke in favor of environmentally responsible waste handling methods at public meetings.

Rouse sent several staff to Chicago to observe spray-irrigation systems there. Finally, the corporation developed its own plan to create such a system for Churchill. We were very pleased. By September, it was beginning to appear that it might be possible to reach an agreement which would be acceptable to all sides. "Stopping the railroad" during the spring of 1989 had allowed time to make reasonable decisions to the benefit of all.

Restoration Continues

On a lovely late spring day, I was down on my knees again in Crabby Creek in a culvert underneath a big highway. Once again we were drilling holes in concrete, this time with gasoline-powered star drills. The drills, contributed by a local contractor, speeded up our process immensely. However, the foul smell of exhaust fumes and the noise somewhat reduced my pleasure in the whole process. We drilled and put into place baffle after baffle. Then we went down to look at the work we had done in 1988—instant success! Even conservationists can use some of that! In the midst of the drawn-out struggle to save West Valley Creek from becoming an open sewer, it felt good to see a small project like this making a difference.

We also continued West Valley Creek's restoration project. Howard McGarvey, chapter counsel, and I designed and built a sill to deepen the channel at a particularly good point. Rock was secured from the General Crushed Stone quarry to strengthen and heighten deflectors already in place. I noticed, however, that all the work was being done now by persons with old familiar faces. I felt a little tired out myself.

One development we never anticipated when we went to speak at the West Whiteland township hearing on a new sewering plan was that less than a year later more than 80 percent of Chester County voters passed a non-binding referendum to spend $50 million through bond issues to maintain open space in the county. The vote mandated county commissioners to assist municipalities to purchase land for parks of their own, buy new county parks, assist conservancies to protect open space privately and to purchase agricultural easements to help make farming a viable economic activity in the area. The margin was passed by a large majority, which left us hoping that it would be implemented justly, effectively, and rapidly.

The stream-restoration group of the Pennsylvania Fish Commission sent one of its staff to West Valley Creek to learn more about the techniques we evolved for restoring the low-gradient streams. They were particularly interested in how we have used "porcupine" structures to catch silt and narrow the stream. Christopher Hunter, in *Better Trout Habitat* (Washington, D.C.: Island Pr., 1991), highlighted the West Valley Creek and Crabby Creek restoration projects as among the fifteen best in the United States.

Knickerbocker Landfill Closes

After years of bad relations with the community, Knickerbocker Landfill was finally going to close. Leachate had continued to leak into Valley Creek, producing a desert as far as trout were concerned for some distance below the site. As a result of eleven years of work by the Valley Creek Watershed Coalition, it now appeared that the closure would be done in an environmentally safe way. The Coalition had successfully sued the landfill to get it to post a higher bond in order to insure ongoing maintenance with leachate collection and treatment. Enough funds had been set aside to monitor the operation for years into the future.

Remembering all the times Chuck Marshall had inspected the site, I asked, "What kept you going over all these years?"

> I like to do things I don't have to struggle with. It's been fairly easy to deal with these issues and get something done. When I called the Knickerbocker Landfill lawyer, he respected me enough so that when we made a request, he would see that it was done. That happened even though we were in an adversarial relationship. The quarry owners respected me. Thinking about what to do came easy so I kept going with it. It is hardest when you have to struggle with questions like whether or not you did the right thing, and when others are yelling at you. The difficult job is organizing a lot of people into action, but fortunately that was only required for three or four years. There Mitsie Toland's support was helpful, having someone to stick with me as we worked on it.

Chuck went on to say that in recent years it was hard to get the current operator to cooperate with Trout Unlimited and the state. A final closure plan was not delivered, and it took a long time to settle whether closure of the landfill would be regulated unless rules existing when consent to develop the property was assigned, or whether it would be done under current regulations. A soil engineer studied the project to determine what steps need to be taken to care for the site so that in the future it did not become a source of danger to the community.

Even when closed, a landfill is dangerous for a long time. It will take a generation or two, and perhaps longer, before it ceases to be hazardous. Remembering back to the time when Dr. Ralph Heister, Conestoga biology teacher and environmentalist, had spoken to the chapter I said to Chuck, "It does not look like Ralph's prophecy is going to be fulfilled, namely that the biological time bomb of Knickerbacker Landfill may explode." Chuck responded that he felt that although there were many dangers, probably the bomb had been defused. He did feel that if there were major problems like breaches in the liners, there would be more massive ground water contamination that is apparent at present. He feared, moreover, that the liner would not last as long as the trash is potent.

All the work which had been done by the Valley Creek coalition, however, made a big difference. Certainly Chuck's activities in stopping hazardous and toxic waste dumping played a major role. The landfill was safely capped with soil, a bond was in place to monitor leachate collection, and inspection procedures were being carried out.

Then came the best news of all. Willard Rouse announced publicly that he was willing to put in a sewage handling system which would not involve stream discharge at all! Instead, the Churchill Development would employ a land application system. The "world class" developer finally was planning a system which would recharge ground water and protect the stream. We breathed a sigh of relief.

From prospects of a "world class" mess, we had moved to a plan providing a state of the art land application system. The biggest issue we had tackled to date had come to a successful conclusion.

CHAPTER 12

Sustaining a Movement

The year we started the Valley Forge chapter one of the chapter members, Jerry Bullock, told me a painful story. A tiny stream flowed down a beautiful wooded valley. A few citizens in an adjacent housing development heard that the sewer authority planned to cut down the trees in this valley and run a sewer line underneath the bed of the stream. They organized to get the sewer authority to adopt a more responsible plan. After months and months of work they were finally able to get an agreement. The line would be constructed in such a way that the stream would be protected.

The association turned its attention elsewhere. Some of those who had been involved moved away. Years passed, and then the day came when it was time to build the sewer. The construction firm ignored the plans that had been agreed upon and drove the sewer line straight down the bed of the stream, cutting down every tree that stood in the way.

Such a cynical, destructive thing to do! Yet Jerry's point was that it isn't enough to organize and win short-term victories, even though that is critically important. You have to sustain a movement for the long haul. Plans must be monitored, and those who implement them must be held accountable to carry out agreements reached.

Tiring Out

It was the spring of 1990, fourteen years after the chapter was formed. We had built a chapter with over 350 members, held meetings consistently for almost a decade and a half, and had effectively tackled large agencies and corporations in seeking to preserve the streams in Chester County. All of this work was done on a voluntary basis, and now as the struggle with the Rouse Corporation was coming to an end, we seemed to be tiring out. Board meetings were down to a faithful ten or twelve persons. The same ones were in attendance at every meeting. No new faces were in evidence. Chapter meetings seldom drew more than fifteen to twenty. Wayne Poppich moved away to the Poconos, leaving a big hole among our leaders. Others became less active for different reasons. Losses were not being replaced by new members.

In an organization made up of a long-term members who have become friends it may be increasingly hard for a newcomer to break into the inner circle. At a meeting it is natural to go and talk with your friends, but it takes a special effort to speak to those you don't know. The place where we held our monthly board and chapter meetings had limited space, with the result that when we scheduled a large meeting there was not enough room for those who came. It was almost impossible to find a parking place, and the West Chester location had never been easy for a newcomer to discover.

The restoration project on West Valley Creek won an award from the Pennsylvania Fish Commission, and it was beginning to receive national attention. Yet those who had taken the lead in organizing workdays were beginning to wear out. Whereas once we had scheduled a work day every month, winter or summer, rain or shine, we now would go for months without any workdays.

Joe Armstrong was working on a book on the limestone streams of Pennsylvania. In his free time, he was traveling to different parts of the state to fish the streams and prepare field notes for his book. My own life was affected by family problems which required increased attention, so I had less energy to give, even for organizing work days. Jim Clark stepped in to keep work days going, but he was already carrying heavy responsibilities as editor of the *Banknotes*. No one volunteered to organize regular work days.

For several years we had held a fall banquet. Now no one was willing to take on the responsibility of organizing it. We decided to let it drop. Here was another sign that we were wearing thin.

Meanwhile, Valley Creek was becoming known as a vital fishery. More and more were coming to fish the stream and enjoy catching wild trout. The attention given to West Valley Creek in the media by the Rouse Corporation's plan to dump treated sewer water into the stream also increased the visibility of the Valley Forge chapter of Trout Unlimited. There was great potential for expanding our work.

Sal Gives Us a Hand

We needed help. In the spring of 1990, Sal Palatucci, national staff member of Trout Unlimited, drove down to have dinner with Jim Ferrier, Carl Dusinberre, Ray Squires, and me.

The wear and tear of conservation work can tire out the most effective group. As Sal listened to us talk about the fall banquet, he sensed that we were running out of energy, and he gave us the following helpful tips to rebuild the chapter:

1. Think back over the last few years and list your best ten chapter meetings. Which meetings were best attended? Who were the speakers? What were the topics of the presentations? Go back and reschedule meetings which worked very well.

2. Create an attractive meeting format. Re-invite the best speakers. Everything starts with an exciting, fun chapter meeting. Unless people get in the door, no one will volunteer for anything.

3. Plan a year's schedule of meetings. Start your plans with September. The prime months are January–June. Most chapters have very good April and May meetings. Have an October meeting, whether or not you have a banquet. Plug in top speakers for each month. Revamp your meetings, keeping in mind the purpose which is that those attending will have a good time.

4. Consider this example of an evening format:
   - Earlybird session: fly-tying or rod building every month (6:45–7:30 p.m.)
   - Business meeting: (7:30–7:45 p.m.)
   - Reports of the treasurer and secretary.
   - New business
   - Letter writing (or formal conservation report on a special issue) 7:45–8:00 p.m.
   - Coffee break (8:00–8:15 p.m.)
   - Speaker (8:15–9:00 p.m.)

5. Chop business to the bone. Start the meeting on time and keep to the schedule. The president will have coordinated with those who are to give reports, with reports being limited to three or four minutes apiece. Each report should be succinct and excit-

ing: "You will be enthused about what we are doing." "We are going to have a work project, and if you want to, sign up." Make sure there are reports only when there is something to talk about.

6. Hold a big meeting in the spring, as late as you can, in April, or perhaps even May. That opens up your schedule to take advantage of your best meeting times of the year. Don't hold any meetings in July or August. Give yourselves a break.

7. Maintain a regular schedule for several years. Follow your new schedule, keep up-beat attitudes, enjoy your own meetings. In two years you will see the chapter move forward in new ways. Ask yourselves, "Are we doing everything we can to get every member to be a part of what we are doing?" "Are we doing what we can to get people excited and come out of their house to a meeting?

8. Recruit leaders. One chapter lists the jobs to be done on a big posterboard, including every project and committee. Next to each responsibility is a line for the chairperson. If there is no active chairperson, there is no name listed. Every meeting the president says, "This is what we could be doing." There will be names on the posterboard that anyone can relate to, so someone who wants to try something can go up to somebody and ask, "What can I do?"

   Don't forget the "buddy system" works. Help each new person feel "I can take a little, tiny bit."

9. Keep up the enthusiasm. Keep excited and enthusiastic members on the board. Only have people on the board who want to be an active part, and see the chapter be great. People who are not producing and are negative are murdering you. Identify such persons and if you have one, suggest that person may want to take a vacation for a year or two, so they have a chance to recover from being burned out.

10. Hold a banquet. Look at the flow of chapter life. An exciting banquet emerges out of what leads up to it. It will take a couple of years of renewed attention to chapter programs for that to flow into the banquet.

11. Do demographics. Find out where your members are, where they cluster. You might think of the chapter as a business. Look at the market. Poll the members. What do they like? Learn what is causing them not to get active. Then apply these questions to your programming.

12. Build the chapter newsletter. Aim to have frequent newsletters, as many as possible, even if you have to mail an issue with only one article. Remember to get something into peoples' hands before the meeting so they don't forget. Remind them two weeks before. Keep your newsletter strong. It will pay off for you.

I took notes on what Sal had to say and had them typed up. He had given us excellent suggestions to revitalize our chapter, suggestions which fitted what we already knew, namely that there is no path that instantly leads to success. Two or three years would be needed for the chapter to be renewed. Someone, also, would have to take hold and begin to apply his insights.

New Location—New Program

Sal Palatucci's suggestions were mailed by the president to each board member and were discussed at a summer 1990 board meeting. Those present agreed that Sal had some good ideas. We needed more entertaining and dramatic meetings, and we needed a better place to meet. As was so often the case, however, we knew also that unless somebody took responsibility for program and location, a year from now would find us right where we were, but with a little less energy and fewer people.

Carl Dusinberre said he would be willing to see if he could find a new location, and would work on programs for the next year. He also wanted authorization to spend enough to secure well-known speakers. He presented his ideas as an experiment which he was willing to carry forward. The board gave him the approval to go ahead.

The first thing Carl did was to find a new location for the chapter meetings at a fire station with access from all parts of Chester County and the Greater Philadelphia area. This would cost us $50 per meeting, but the room was pleasant and could hold over one hundred people.

Paul Nale, former executive of Pennsylvania Trout and high school biology teacher, spoke in September on catching trout with spinning gear. Twenty-five persons came out to hear his witty and provocative presentation. Those attending enjoyed a most interesting evening, we raised a little money, and were very pleased at the good turn-out.

In October, Greg Menzer, long-term Trout Unlimited activist from the Delaware Chapter and now a guide in Montana, came to speak about river float trips. Carl publicized the event widely, spending notices to local papers, sticking up posters, and putting an article in the *Banknotes*. Carl also had a Trout Unlimited sign made giving the meeting night and time which he stuck out by Highway 100 the week before the meeting. Once again about twenty-five turned out for the meeting. The talk was enjoyable, the slides were excellent, and evaluations of the meeting were positive.

Despite the fact that we were moving into late fall, when people's attention is supposed to turn away from fishing to other interests, at the November meeting a guide both in Alaska and on the Salmon River in upstate New York drew forty five people.

At each meeting Carl inquired where people lived. He found some attending from nearby cities and suburbs who had read about the meeting in the paper. One man told Carl he saw the sign, and changed his plans to go to the meeting. He ate a quick supper and came back for the night. Carl concluded that the advertising as well as the content of the meetings was beginning to pay off.

In December some felt it would be better not to have a meeting, since the third Thursday might conflict with Christmas preparations. Carl, however, invited leaders from the Phoenixville Dame Juliana League to come and put on a program. Before the meeting, Carl called those who were coming and "talked show business talk." He pointed out that it was important to get their act together and rehearse what they were going to say. Once again the presentation was excellent. Even though it was December, forty people showed up.

Late winter and spring are the seasons of the year when people begin to think about trout fishing. In January Carl scheduled a former Pennsylvania TU Southeastern regional vice president who had recruited me to become a regional vice president. We had known each other for a long time, and I was pleased to hear that he was coming. His subject was fishing the trout streams of Siberia. About sixty showed up for the meeting, a high for the year and for Valley Forge Trout Unlimited. Then in February Ed Koch came down from his territory on the Letort River in central Pennsylvania, to speak about midge fishing. Author and conservationist Koch drew better than eighty people. We were amazed and very pleased.

What Makes Someone Volunteer?

In some chapters many turn out for entertaining monthly meetings. In our chapter having eighty people turn out for a monthly meeting was previously unheard of. Carl's programming for us, therefore, was a big step forward. I decided to talk with Carl and find out what had led him to volunteer and schedule these programs.

He said that board meetings were interesting and gave everyone a chance to talk. Board members did the conservation work, and did not care if they were entertained or not. Carl, however, was getting tired of doing more work than he needed to do. The people in the group were doing all the work, yet the chapter now had 360 members. He began to feel himself getting tired, and noticed that his ability to drag along others declined as he wore out. The same thing was happening with the rest of us. Then Carl went to a meeting of the Cumberland Valley Chapter of Trout Unlimited at a centrally located restaurant, and it drew a big crowd. Carl felt that the location was luxurious compared to the basement where we had been meeting.

He wanted to get more people involved. The chapter was getting dry rot. Somebody had to do something to get a new injection of new bodies, Carl felt. It seemed, comparatively speaking, that we of the Valley Forge chapter were the best conservationists and fishermen and the worst party givers Carl had ever seen! The organization was mainly vested in twelve people, and he could see us getting more tired and less interested each month. Carl then said:

> Because of my situation I feel an extra obligation. Twice God has saved me when I went through bypass heart surgery so serious it left me on total disability. I've been looking for what to do, and maybe there is a little bit of religious fervor there. I do believe one person can make a difference. I've seen it in politics and in the chapter. "Who's going to do this," I wondered. The answer was clear, "Nobody, unless I do." While I'm not a rocket scientist, I do have a faint sense of humor, a little common sense, and a sense of what would be interesting to others.

If he were working on a career path, he wouldn't have had the time, strength or interest, he said. Some forced to live on disability give up, but Carl saw necessity as mother of invention.

New Life Flows into the Chapter

One of our goals when we formed the chapter was to establish a climate which was open to everyone who wanted to move in the direction of stream conservation. I tried to start a chapter in which anyone would be welcome, regardless of color, economic status, or gender. We benefit from individual differences. Every person's experience is different as are everyone's gifts and talents. Carl, for instance, has a tremendous sense of humor, which was a great asset when he began to plan the programs: "I like to shock people a little bit. I like to kid people and keep them off balance. I try to be a little bit different. That's why I led off the programs with a spin fisherman, and tried to stay out of the groove. I didn't want four consecutive fly fishers, but wanted a mix. And I didn't want to pay for every speaker to come from outside."

Just as Sal had predicted, new energies were released into our chapter work. At a February 1991 work day at West Valley Creek, four new volunteers showed up. All had attended recent meetings. They volunteered when I asked those interested in helping with a workday to sign up. Three "old timers" joined the newcomers rolling rocks and building two new spines on old deflectors. These volunteers would not have appeared if it had not been for new life coming into the chapter through the meetings. The Valley Forge Chapter of Trout Unlimited was moving forward again.

PART II

Living Waters
A Shining Vision

H uman activity flows from a vision. We see, hear, sense, and our
minds go to work. We begin to see what is happening to streams
and their watersheds. We ask why these things are going on. Like a
powerful searchlight the mind begins to focus attention on what we
wish to know, understanding emerges. "Without a vision, the people
perish," says the ancient proverb. Part II of this book deals with some
of my learnings about watersheds and streams and how we may relate
to both in ways in which are constructive, leaving the environment
better than we found it.

Keepers of the Stream

Our struggle to save West Valley Creek was succeeding. The Rouse Corporation had finally planned a spray irrigation system instead of dumping treated sewer water into West Valley Creek. We knew we would have to begin intensive monitoring once construction began, but that was in the future. In October of 1990 we continued restoration efforts by adding a rock spine to a bank deflector. In November we planted 30,000 brown trout eggs in tributaries of West Valley Creek.

As 1990 was quietly coming to an end, West Valley Creek was very much alive, and we celebrated Christmas on December 29 by putting up signs in the restoration project area announcing that in 1991 this would be a *special regulation area!* For the first months of the season it would be open to catch and release fishing. After July a low catch limit of three per day hopefully would enable many fish to survive to spawn, as well as providing much sport for all concerned throughout the year.

Awards and Commendations

At the 1990 annual state meeting of Pennsylvania Trout Unlimited, Valley Forge Chapter of Trout Unlimited received two awards. For the third time the best chapter newsletter in Pennsylvania award went to *Banknotes,* edited by Jim Clark. The second award was for best chapter project, given for the "Porcupine" stream deflector structures that were invented by Joe Armstrong. A few months later the winter issue of *Pennsylvania Trout* featured "Valley Forge: A Winter Home to Our First President and One of PATU's Top Chapters," by John Mc-Gonigle. The article provided evaluative highlights of the work of the chapter.

First, the chapter was now second largest in Pennsylvania. Second, the spring trout show had been consistently effective, featuring noted speakers. Third, stream improvement work had been done on Valley Creek, Crabby Creek, and West Valley Creek, with the latter restoration project receiving awards from the Pennsylvania Fish Commission and PA Council of Trout Unlimited. McGonigle felt that Crabby Creek was a textbook example of cooperation between big business and a conservation group, resulting in retaining the creek's natural fish producing capability. Fourth, on the legal front the suits against the Conrail Train Yard in Paoli and Knickerbocker Landfill resulted in wins for the environment. The former removed hazardous PCBs from the environment due to cleanup of the superfund site, and the latter controlled the threat due to hazardous leachate from the landfill. Fifth, along with other chapters, VFTU put on a yearly banquet fundraiser, along with a full slate of monthly meetings. Sixth, the chapter's fly fishing school had been popular for years with area anglers, both members and non-members. Seventh, in 1990 the chapter, working with West Chester Fish, Game and Wildlife Association, successfully petitioned the Fish Commission to make a section of West Valley Creek an "artificials only/delayed harvest project."

Awards and McGonigle's commendations had a strengthening effect on our movement. Someone else noticed that we were moving in the right direction, and having limited successes as we went along. Such awards are like little inconspicuous signs that hikers in wilderness territory sometimes leave to mark the trail. They say, "We got this far, and you can too." We had made progress toward our goal of preserving, restoring, and conserving the cold water streams in our area of responsibility, Chester County, and taken steps to live out the philosophy of Trout Unlimited which is printed in every issue of *Banknotes:*

> We believe that trout and salmon fishing isn't just fishing for trout and salmon. It's fishing for sport rather than for food, where the true enjoyment of the sport lies in the challenge, the lore and the battle of wits, not necessarily the full creel. It's the feeling of satisfaction that comes from limiting your kill instead of killing your limit. It's

communing with nature where the chief reward is a refreshed body and a content soul, where a license is a permit to use—not abuse, to enjoy—not destroy our cold water fishery. It's subscribing to the proposition that what's good for trout and salmon is good for fisherman and that managing trout and salmon for themselves rather than for the fishermen is fundamental to the solution of our trout and salmon problems. It's appreciating our fishery resource, respecting fellow anglers and giving serious thought to tomorrow.

A glance backward over the trail we followed showed how far we had gone. Then we turned around and looked to the path into the future. No one has yet called a truce in the warfare against nature. Huge construction projects were underway on every watershed in Chester County. Increased development, traffic, and public disregard was resulting in even more junk being dumped along the banks of the stream. More roads meant more polluted runoff. The watersheds themselves were still losing their integrity, as more land was paved and trees cut down. Members active for years were aging and could no longer do what they once had done. Others, tired by the struggle, had dropped out. We had a long way to go. But we were still in the fight.

Valley Creek Committee, III

Under the direction of Chuck Marshall the first Valley Creek Committee was formed in 1978. Out of it came the Valley Creek Watershed Coalition, which supervised clean up of the cyanide spill on the stream, and after years of effort had successfully closed Knickerbocker Landfill, with a plan and funds in place to provide for monitoring of leachate and underground water contamination for years into the future.

Valley Creek Committee II was formed in the 1980's. For two or three years it was active in monitoring erosion throughout the watershed, and focusing chapter efforts to preserve the stream. It was not able to achieve one of its primary goals, though, which was to begin a visible restoration project on Valley Creek, preferably in Valley Forge National Park in certain degraded areas of the stream. In 1989 Valley Creek Committee III was formed. In the spring of 1990 a public meeting was held to seek more involvement, with a good turnout. Out of that meeting came active cooperation between Trout Unlimited and Valley Forge National Park. Ray Squires, chapter president who had "cut his teeth" as a conservationist in efforts of the Valley Creek Committee, wrote an article on movement which was beginning to occur through this committee:

1. Surveillance of the watershed by VFTU members. The committee had been particularly effective in keeping a constant vigil on the waters of Valley Creek and its tributaries, resulting in the enforcement of sedimentation and erosion control laws by township and Pennsylvania Department of Environmental Resources.
2. Performance of water quality studies and biological surveys. A project entitled "Turbidity Monitoring" was done jointly by several VFTU volunteers and officials of Valley Forge National Park. The Pennsylvania Fish Commission performed electro fishing of three sections of Valley Creek, assisted by VFTU volunteers. The results yielded an abundance of wild trout which certainly classified this creek as a Class A trout stream.
3. Participation in the Great Valley Coalition. Through two different coalitions the chapter helped correct the ongoing bad effects of Knickerbocker Landfill on the watershed, encouraged the Department of Environmental Resources to examine the Warner Quarry proposed expansion extremely closely and issue the most stringent permit in the history of the Commonwealth to regulate this mining operation. Members served on the steering committee, and the chapter often contributed money from its own treasury to support these efforts.
4. Negotiation with landowners. Project plans for developers of a tract on the south branch of Valley Creek, Little Valley, yielded some modifications of the project plan. The hope was to preserve coldwater springs and prevent excess runoff into the stream.
5. Planting willow shoots along Valley Creek.
6. Organizing an active ongoing Valley Creek Committee.
7. Contributions by VFTU to purchase and preserve undeveloped land along Valley Creek. Through the Open Land Conservancy we helped keep these multi-acre sites undeveloped and accessible to visitors and those who loved to fish.

As I read this article by Ray Squires, I was impressed at how far the Valley Creek committees had gone. Yet, one thing was missing. We lacked a chapter organizer who would take hold of the Valley Creek Committee, and enable it to move forward with vigor, the way Joe Armstrong had done years before with the West Valley Creek restoration project, or the way Chuck Marshall had done with the Knickerbocker Landfill. For years Joe Armstrong and I and others had wished for more volunteer organizers. The reader who has followed our story to this point will recognize the names of such persons. They crop up again and again. They not only do work themselves, but they enable a movement to come into being. For a voluntary association seeking change in public policy and action to be effective, someone must organize. Someone must step forward, take responsibility, contact others, and as assignments are accepted and given, follow up and see that the work is done. As all of this is going on, one must also be the kind of person to provide the food which powers any voluntary association for social change, namely recognition and approval. A leader affirms, affirms and affirms, and encourages, encourages, encourages, always seeing some hope at the end of the tunnel.

Where do such leaders come from? We would watch and encourage, but few appeared. Sometimes we would go a year or two, and then, like a miracle, some new person would take hold of an area where work needed to be done, and new energies would be released.

The key to the accountability of Valley Forge Trout Unlimited was Valley Creek. It runs through Valley Forge National Park, which in 1990 was recording 4 million outside visitors per year. Valley Creek has national and even international visibility. As a trout looking up and seeing a tasty mayfly floating down toward him, we looked up with hungry anticipation at the prospects of a restoration project on Valley Creek in collaboration with Valley Forge National Park. Imagine the education and communication which might occur! Young people would get a new vision of healthy streams and how to restore degraded ones. Senior citizens might get some hope from seeing that our nation was beginning to take care of its water heritage. All could enjoy a clean, beautiful stream flowing through the wooded hills and broad fields of the park. Yes, we could see that mayfly of a strong Valley Creek Committee floating over our heads, but without an organizer to take hold, each mayfly floated on untasted.

I had taken as my primary responsibility organizing each Valley Creek Committee only to see one after another fade away. In starting Valley Creek Committee II, I got to know Ray Squires, the young man who in 1990 became president of VFTU. I remember nights where Ray, Wayne Poppich, who contributed so much to our restoration efforts, and I alone discussed the problems of Valley Creek and what could be done to correct them. In these discussions and our limited efforts, I learned something important. New persons coming into the chapter had to apprentice for two or three years before they felt they knew enough and had enough confidence to take accountability for organizing themselves. Given the pressures on myself, however, I knew I was not going to take on responsibility for organizing Valley Creek Committee III. To do this job right would be even more demanding than becoming president of what was now a large conservation movement in Chester County. So I stayed behind the scenes, encouraged, and from time to time put my energies into holding a public meeting, as the one in 1990. In January, 1991, Valley Creek Committee III met again at the Visitor's Center in Valley Forge National Park to discuss activities affecting the watershed. About thirty-five people came out on a windy, chilly night. We passed around a signup sheet and recorded names, addresses, and phone numbers. Volunteers were requested for several projects, and we were heartened to see a number signing up.

The meeting, however, did not realize my main objective. I was casting my fly over the water of this meeting for an organizer who would take hold and move the Valley Creek Committee III forward. The potential was there, but the leader was not.

Churchill Turned Down

Membership meetings in the spring of 1991 averaged fifty at each event with some even larger. The annual trout show featuring Charlie Meck was attended by over three hundred people, with thirty-one of them becoming new members. Our "rock'n rollin'" work sessions on West Valley Creek continued to be held once a month. We put out about 100 Christmas trees on various deflectors. I continued to coordinate work sessions. In the fall of 1990 I seriously injured my back. No doubt the years of rolling large rocks had contributed to a slipped disc. We needed younger and stronger people who would do the work. Until that occurred, I continued to stick with the project.

For three years chapter members had been attending, as Joe Armstrong put it, "excruciatingly boring township meetings where the Churchhill development was discussed." We had strongly opposed the wastewater handling proposed by the developer, which would have inundated the stream with up to six times low flow of treated sewage. The proposal would have wiped out the stream as a fishery and our award-winning restoration project with it.

After lengthy discussions and community pressure, the Rouse Corporation embraced land application of treated effluent so that there would be minimal stream impact. The corporation finally even agreed to eliminate limited discharges in winter. We thought we were finished with the whole matter.

Then, Churchill plans were rejected by the two townships principally involved, East and West Whiteland. The primary reasons for rejecting the plans were traffic, open space, historic preservation and fiscal impacts, none of which were central VFTU concerns. Joe Armstrong wrote:

> Where does this leave us? At this point no one really knows. The worst of all worlds would be wall to wall houses on the site. The best would be if the interested parties could get together and come up with plans which remove the objectionable parts of the Rouse plan, but still allow for an economically viable project on the land. This should be possible if all parties to the matter are willing to enter into discussions with large doses of good will and small amounts of rhetoric.

As we talked about the matter, we agreed that now we would have to deal with many developers on this site rather than just one. Monitoring construction would be far more difficult with a host of developers than with one. Yet at the same time we could celebrate that the work of the chapter had made a difference. West Valley Creek was alive in 1991. If it had not been for our efforts, the murder of the stream would be well under way.

The Grim Reaper Reappears

For three years the Downington Area Regional Authority (DARA) had been considering sewage treatment in the area. During these years it met monthly, with most meetings attended by VFTU members. When DARA presented its study in three large volumes for public comment, six VFTU members made input to the hearing. We helped pay for part of the cost of a critique of the DARA report by an internationally prominent designer of land application systems for waste water. He was present at the hearing and gave excellent testimony on the strengths and weaknesses of the proposed sewage handling plan.

Many groups testified. Pennsylvania Federation of Sportsmen's Clubs, The Sierra Club, Cleanwater Action, West Chester Fish, Game and Wildlife Association, The Brandywine Valley Association, French and Pickering Creeks Conservation Trust, Green Valley Association, the Town of Downington, the State of Delaware, the Brandywine Conservancy and individual citizens were present. The testimony was overwhelmingly in favor of land application, and offers of assitance were made in locating suitable land.

An expanding industrial economy threatens the environment. "You can't stop progress," say the developers. Watersheds are paved, trees cut down, streams polluted. People must stand up for their land and water. We had seen considerable success in so doing in Chester County, but true progress came hard.

In 1991 the economy was in trouble. The vast national debt and the attempt to maintain infinite industrial expansion and growth in a finite world was beginning to come up against its limits. People were talking about acid rain, breakdown of the ozone layer, global warming. We heard that the EPA was shifting its attention to these broad global concerns, which probably meant there would be less money to clean up less politically visible problems such as the Paoli Superfund Site.

In the April 1991 edition of *Banknotes*, an article was reprinted which was written by Leonard Hess, past president of the Pennsylvania Federation of Sportsmen's Clubs. It highlighted a new and dangerous anti-environmental organization which had arisen in our state, the Pennsylvania Landowners Association (PLA). Masquerading as a group of small farmers and land owners concerned about the loss of property rights to governmental regulations, particularly concerning protection of wetlands, it and its allies were attacking on a wide variety of environmental areas. Hess said, "Their basic philosophy seems to be that it is the right of every property owner to do as they please with their property, regardless of the impact this may have on the greater good of society as a whole."

The association's first tactic was to post members' property against hunting, in order to force the Pennsylvania Federation of Sportsmen's Clubs into abandoning its own strong stance on wetlands protection. Suddenly the association received support from the Pennsylvania Coal Association and Pennsylvania Independent Petroleum Producers. Its "posting for support" program was picked up and promoted nationwide by the American Farm Bureau.

One of the founders of PLA was arrested in 1986 for filling 130 acres of wetlands on the headwaters of Elk Creek. the U.S. Fish and Wildlife Service called it "the most serious wetlands violation we have seen in Pennsylvania in recent years." The article went on to document that the PLA organization was not a group of family farmers, but instead an organization of corporations and industries that historically profited from the exploitation of the land and its products.

In the *Banknotes* reprint, Leonard Hess concludes by saying,

> Where does it end? Is it the right of the property owner to strip for coal without reclaiming his land? Is it his right to bury hazardous waste on his property and then sell that land for housing developments, as was done at Love Canal? Can he discharge mine acid, drilling brine, or raw sewage into streams and ground water without concern for others? Can he rape and pillage the land simply because he is the present owner? The American Indians believed that no one can really own the land, that it belonged to the Great Spirit, that they were only the custodians of it. This concept is also found in the Old Testament. The promised land of Israel was given to the ancient Hebrews by covenant with God, but there were restrictions that made it quite clear they were care takers, not owners.

The appearance of this front for corporate exploitation would certainly affect Pennsylvania Trout Unlimited. If effective this new organization would destroy cold water streams throughout the state. Once again the question posed by Senator Gaylord Nelson, founder of Earth Day, would be voiced, "Must we destroy tomorrow in order to live today?" New efforts would be required to answer that question with a resounding, "No!"

Summer 1991 was a pleasant time. Fishing was good in southeastern Pennsylvania, despite a drought throughout the entire Commonwealth. Buffered by our limestone streams, cool clear water continued to flow through West Valley and Valley creeks. Then one day in mid August I received a call from Carl Dusinberre. A special meeting was to be held by East Whiteland Township. The Rouse Corporation was proposing to build another package plant, which would dump hundreds of thousands of gallons of treated sewer water, this time into Valley Creek. The Grim Reaper had reappeared.

For some years intensive housing development had been planned for a parcel of land in East Whiteland Township. Chapter leaders were aware of this proposed development, but it did not appear that it would have significantly negative effects on Valley Creek. Then a week before the meeting in which this plan was to receive final approval, we learned that the Rouse Corporation was proposing to build a package sewer treatment plant which would dump all of the water from this development and future ones into Valley Creek. Just as had been proposed before with West Valley Creek, the stream would become a conduit for treated sewer water.

We had one week to get ready. This time we would probably have little chance to get township supervisors to take a close look at the package sewer plant proposal. The developer owed hundreds of thousands of dollars in back taxes to the township, despite having made millions of dollars out of developments in that area. It seemed that Rouse Corporation had argued that it would be able to pay its debt only if it were allowed to dump its treated sewer water in the stream. It appeared that a deal had been made.

The Rouse Corporation had gone back on painfully achieved agreements to move forward with a land-application project. Perhaps it did not want to take land out of development for a spray irrigation system. Perhaps it did not care about the fact that package sewer plants have an appalling record of effectiveness, again and again breaking down and dumping raw sewage into the streams. But whatever its rationale, we had one week to get ready for a critically important meeting. One of our new members worked out a campaign to alert all 350 chapter members to what was going on, and others contacted related groups. Whatever happened, we needed to show political leaders that there were many concerned citizens who are not in favor of destroying tomorrow to live today.

The night of the township meeting arrived. When I drove up the parking lot was already full, and people were parking anywhere they could find a space. When I walked into the meeting room, I found over two hundred citizens gathered that August night in 1991. Despite the fact that many residents were away on vacation, the council chambers were packed. Some could not get in the room and stood outside the open doors to hear what was going on. The three township supervisors entered and began promptly by moving approval of the Rouse proposal. One courageous supervisor, Glen Cockerham, refused to keep silent. He forcefully documented the effects that building a package plant would have on the jewel of our nation's heritage, Valley Creek. The other two supervisors ignored him, and then refused to allow anyone in the room to speak. They insisted on voting, and by two to one approved the plan for the development.

I could feel the anger burning in the room. Imagine a public meeting, here in America, in the suburbs, right next to the center of America's independence park, where citizens were not allowed to speak to an issue which was going to affect their well-being. Indeed, the chairperson of the supervisors refused to allow anyone to speak out after the vote was taken! Then a civic leader stood up and argued that at least they should listen to the concerns of people in the meeting. The chair grudgingly consented to hear, though making it very clear that what was said would make no difference. Joe Armstrong spoke, so did John Johnson of West Chester Fish, Game and Wildlife, and so did I. Others did too.

We could see, however, that we were going to be in another long struggle. The threat to Valley Creek was even worse than it had been to West Valley. Ignorance can be met with enlightenment, provided parties are well intentioned and listen to each other. Joe Armstrong's prophecy was that if common sense prevailed all around, perhaps a well-planned, economically solid, and visibly attractive community might be built on Rouse Corporation land, and incorporate state-of-the-art storm and wastewater management. It appeared, however, that instead of mutual good will, we were being faced with greed in both civic and corporate leadership.

Political as well as corporate leadership was involved in this "railroading" of a package sewer plant. There had to be strong interests involved for the developer and township to take the risk of being sued in violation of the state's sunshine law.

With other concerned citizens we sued East Whiteland Township for violation of the sunshine and other laws, seeking redress in court. At every chapter meeting the progress of our lawsuit was reviewed. We hoped to win in Chester County courts, but the first results of the lawsuit were a judge's decision that we had no standing to sue the township in this matter. The coalition spent over $20,000 in the first months of legal action. Our contribution to this effort was over $5,000, a serious strain on our now-shrinking treasury.

In January 1992, I stepped back and took a look at where we were. This threat to Valley Creek was probably the most serious challenge we had faced to date. Opponents were entrenched, with significant economic and political power. We could very well lose Valley Creek this time. We had to again "slow down the railroad," stopping immediate construction long enough to allow opponents of the project to organize. Then we had to mount long-term and very large-scale education and communication highlighting the value of Valley Creek and the patriotic reasons for keeping this part of our nation's heritage intact and alive. And of course, chapter members would need to attend the endless and boring meetings which would go on for years. Our president estimated that in 1992 we would need to raise over $10,000 to break even for the year.

Once again, though, the Rouse Corporation had presented us an organizing issue on a silver platter. West Valley Creek was a relatively insignificant stream in the eyes of most people, but as one person put it, Valley Creek was the jewel in our nation's heritage, flowing through the shrine of independence, Valley Forge National Park. Once again George Washington was looking over our shoulders and asking what we were going to do. Over two hundred angry citizens knew what was happening. One chapter member said:

> I always thought our public leaders watched out for our interests. I had not gone to township meetings. I guess I was naive. I now see that they aren't looking after our civic well-being at all. It makes me angry.

If we could somehow mobilize the energy in those who left the August 1991 township meeting hot with anger, perhaps we could save Valley Creek from the largest assault to date.

Cleve Corner, newly elected chapter financial advisor, proposed a fundraising plan. A letter would be sent to every member asking them to make a contribution of $100 or at least $50 to pay for the lawsuit. At a January 1992 board meeting Cleve asked each of us to take part of the list of chapter members and follow-up the letter with personal phone calls. Every board member agreed to make phone contact with at least thirty members.

Our goal was to raise at least $2,000. As a board member I made my phone calls. Only one person was cold and unresponsive. Most were supportive, some had already contributed, and others promised to send in their donations. By March 1992 over $3,400 had been contributed, one-third more than we had hoped for. At the board meeting in March, Cleve Corner came in late. When he did, everyone applauded him for a job well done.

A Letter from the Editor

In August 1991 I learned about how an environmental group in Montana had communicated its message to a wide audience by placing a full page advertisement in the local newspaper. I took the advertisement with me to the next board meeting, and suggested that we needed to do something like this to get our message out. We agreed that we probably could not afford a full-size advertisement in a local paper. I offered, therefore, to pull together a communications group to state our message, and to think through ways that we might get out what we wanted to say. Three others joined me.

One agreed to prepare a series of eight brief messages with cartoons, highlighting stream conservation issues and suggesting steps people could take to make things better. Another said that he would explore having major articles put in a national magazine, featuring the fishing in Valley Forge National Park. A third suggested that he might prepare a letter to the editor of the *Philadelphia Inquirer,* focusing on what was going to happen to Valley Forge National Park if this package sewer plant was allowed to be developed as planned.

Within a few weeks a rough draft of a letter was brought to a meeting of the Valley Creek Committee. Five or six Valley Forge Chapter members read the letter carefully, and suggested changes. One was to remove any expressions of anger. Another was to answer questions which one might anticipate being raised in response to the letter by those in favor of the package sewer plant.

I took all the input, and carefully rewrote the draft. My goal was to maintain the integrity of the substance and style and yet strengthen the content of the letter. The writer very graciously accepted the suggestions and incorporated them into a revised draft of the letter. Connections he had with persons on the *Inquirer* staff helped to gain a positive hearing for the letter. On March 7, 1992, it was published along with a cartoon.

"Valley Forge is threatened again," reads the headline. The editorial placed the new threat in relation to the efforts of those who for many years had been working to preserve Valley Creek and Valley Forge National Park. More than "a miraculous home of wild trout," Valley Forge Park is used by thousands for close to home recreation. It is visited by millions of tourists yearly because our nation was born here, and therefore, it should be protected at all costs:

> Take the family out to Valley Forge this weekend. Walk along the creek down by Washington's headquarters. Imagine the creek transformed into a sewer. Then express your outrage to the National Park Service. Write to your legislative representatives in Harrisburg and Washington. Tell them that you won't stand for the trashing of Valley

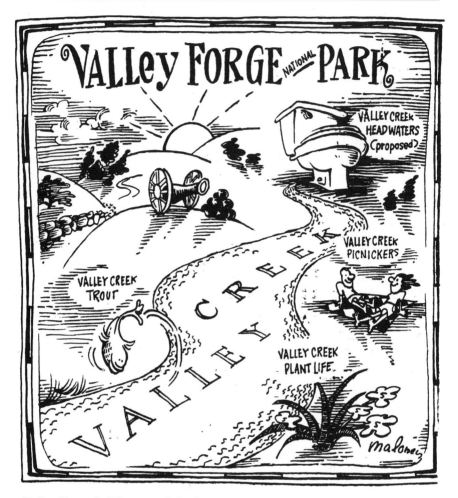

Valley Forge Is Threatened Again

Forge. Fight for it the way you would fight to protect your own
backyard. (*The Philadelphia Inquirer*, March 7, 1992)

For the next week Ray Squires, chapter president, began to receive
a call or two a day from concerned citizens asking what they might do
to help. Letters went to congressional representatives and senators
about this threat to Valley Forge National Park. One wrote directly to
the head of the National Park Service. Administrators at Valley Forge
National Park were alerted even more to the effect this plant might
have on the park itself. A Pennsylvania Congressman wrote directly to

the Department of Environmental Resources asking it to deny a sewage treatment permit to the Rouse Package plant!

When we formed the Valley Forge Chapter as a stream conservation movement in Chester County, one of my goals was to see that the watersheds and streams were preserved and restored. I did not know how this might be done. How do constructive changes in public policy occur? How do citizens have a say in matters which affect their own and their children's well being? This letter to the *Inquirer* helped answer these questions. It raised issues and concerns. The letters and phone calls which were written in response affected people in agencies and corporations. Increased interest in the stream allowed staff people and managers within those agencies already concerned about the environment to take more aggressive steps to see that it was cared for.

Because one person cared enough to use his writing skills and connections with people in the news media, changes occurred which helped us move forward. Once again, one person, working as part of a supportive community, made a difference.

Keepers of the Stream

For ten years we had been looking for a leader who would take hold of a Valley Creek committee and form a powerful movement centered on Valley Creek and Valley Forge National Park. The foundation had been laid for such a movement, but no organizer had ever emerged. One day a member stepped forward who had joined the Valley Forge chapter of Trout Unlimited in 1989 and actively participated in stream restoration work on West Valley, as well as attending meetings of the Valley Creek Committee when I asked him to participate in some of the work and planning of that little group. He began regularly to fish Valley Creek, and in an article in *Banknotes* said:

> The greater my experience on Valley Creek, the more apparent its significance, uniqueness and importance to Trout Unlimited members became. A limestone stream with a vibrant population of reproducing wild trout, flowing through a National historical park, it is enjoyed by thousands of people (fisherman, visitors from around the country and the world, joggers, bicyclists, and other recreational enthusiasts). Also here is a flow of life and natural beauty enhancing the properties of homeowners and businesses along its meandering course. And yet because of its proximity to a highly populated,

commercialized and industrialized area, the stream is currently polluted with PCBs and is constantly endangered in many other ways. (*Banknotes*, September, 1991)

He then noted that he had gotten to know many who were interested and willing to work to save Valley Creek. He also acknowledged that he had seen some volunteer and then not be fully incorporated into the effort, so that it was easy for them to feel left out.

He was correct. We were touching many who were interested in doing something to save Valley Creek, but we had not been able to incorporate them into an integrated effort. Wes saw a need to involve more members in the activities of the chapter and to concern ourselves in a deeper way with Valley Creek. With these two concerns in mind he volunteered to attempt to coordinate some of the efforts of the chapter regarding Valley Creek.

This new leader began to think about a book he had read concerning trout and fly fishing called *Keeper of the Steam* (by Frank Sawyer, New York: Pueblo Publishing 1985), authored by an English river keeper who was responsible for a six mile stretch of the Avon River. Wes decided to formalize our Valley Creek efforts by using that book title for the name of our program, so those who participated were going to be called "Keepers of the Stream." Who would become excited about belonging to a group called Valley Creek Committee IV? That name does not "sing." Keepers of the Stream—that summarizes who we are. It catches up the goal which has guided us for years.

More than that, the *Banknotes* article set forth a program. Each was asked to become involved to make a commitment in the form of "the eight-hour pledge."

> I want you to make a pledge of eight hours total time over the course of 1992 to some effort that contributes toward the preservation of Valley Creek. You can fulfill the pledge in whatever segments of time you wish and in any constructive way you choose. If you simply wanted to spend one half hour collecting stream side trash following a fishing visit, that is great. I would appreciate it if you would keep me informed relative to your activities so that the efforts can indeed be documented and coordinated with the other members and with other groups and individuals involved with Valley Creek.

The mark of an organizer is to allow people to focus their wishes and desires in a common effort. The name Keepers of the Stream helped us understand who we were. The eight-hour pledge was small enough so that any person could contribute to making the stream a little better. As we have seen, essential to the formation and maintenance of a voluntary institution is holding oneself to account for what you are volunteering to do. The new organizer, therefore, saw that unless the volunteers reported back to the coordinator, little would happen.

A person could volunteer to be a project director in a general area of activity, or volunteer to help on a specific project. He promised to complete an annual updated account of what was done. A "Keeper of the Stream" would be recognized by a patch which could be sewn to a fishing vest. Carl Dusinberre, chapter cartoonist, agreed to provide an original piece of art in color of a brown trout which would be framed for presentation to the person who makes the greatest total contribution to Valley Creek over the course of 1992. At the end of the year a print of the original would go to that year's winner; the original would be awarded to the next year's winner.

The activities of the new program might include:

1. Develop an informational booth at chapter meetings, trout shows, and other events to tell our ongoing story.
2. Develop a stream-watch pamphlet to homeowners, businesses, township, visitors, and others who share boundaries with the stream and spend time adjacent to it. This pamphlet would highlight the importance and value of the stream, make known dangers to the health of the stream, and provide phone numbers and names of agencies or person to whom these could be reported.
3. Organize an Earth Day stream-wide trash pick-up or similar event.
4. Provide informational research, for instance dealing with chemical pollutants, sewage, and erosion control; someone would need to collect and summarize these facts.
5. Take pictures, visually documenting the conditions and changes occurring at various sites over the course of the year. Possible photos could include construction site negligence or poor practices in run-off basin construction, or document some of the scenes of beauty along the stream for use as publicity or in public education.
6. Publicize and educate with a speaker's bureau that could provide programs to schools, men's and women's clubs, and other groups.
7. Coordinate work on the fishery with the Fish Commission.

8. Set up a spills, silt/sedimentation/pollution monitoring and correction unit.
9. Organize a political unit for zoning, development, highway, ordinance, storm water management and other actions within the various governmental units as might impact the stream.
10. Ensure a protective green zone surrounding the stream by forming a ripariam zone group.
11. Form a long-term database on aquatic insects to better understand the supportive food chain which reflects the health of the stream.
12. Set up a fundraising unit.
13. Form a communications group to telephone people and remind them of work sessions, meetings, and perhaps spread information to residents and businesses along the stream.

Reminding readers that the Keeper of the Stream effort would need to be extended over many years, the article concluded:

Remember, you can do as much or as little as you desire. You can start out leading a particular unit and if time does not permit you sustaining the activity, you can back off. Or you can just lay your one brick in the wall and go home. You will still have contributed to the effort, and after a few years we will have a wall with your brick helping to support it.

In this article Wes had disclaimed being a leader. He said he was a worker and helper, but his detailed program with title, pledge, and list of activities allowed persons to volunteer. This was a program for which we had been looking. He had taken a comprehensive plan for the stream, and turned it into a program!

Leaders Begin as Apprentices

In 1981 I wrote a letter to the then president of Valley Forge Trout Unlimited with reflections on a long-term goal of forming a large differentiated organization with several action and social centers. I saw then how important it was to develop a chapter that would provide spaces for all new persons who were interested. Unless we could create a structure in which each active leader assumed responsibility for defined areas of work, however, we would end up with a group of about fifteen to twenty who were active, friends with each other, and who were mostly unable to allow new persons to become part of this central core. We would be unable to expand the number of active conservationist leaders beyond this small involved group.

In the 1981 letter I said that the task of the leader was to designate clearly the committees and groups we wished to form, and define the responsibility of the leader of each committee. I also identified three objectives for a chapter president:

1. Cultivate and develop new leaders.
2. Find out what each person does and does not want to do, and encourage each to act on his or her desires and concerns.
3. Use one's own responsibility as a leader to involve others.

Though these three objectives were very clear to me in 1981, how they were to be realized was not clear at all. I did see that it was important to draw new persons together in some common form of activity, such as a work day on the restoration project:

> People become informed, you have a chance to talk about what you want to do and don't want to do, and it becomes possible then as a leader to encourage a person to act on one's desires and concerns. By finding out what a person does not want to do you can give that person the freedom not to worry about becoming involved at work at those points, thus removing a major form of resistance.

Over the years we learned that volunteers need a time of apprenticing before they feel ready to tackle organizing efforts. Leaders emerge from followers. Good leaders allow followers to take accountability and don't push them back because they feel threatened by those who might take away their jobs. You use your responsibility as a leader to involve others. Indeed, the task of any leader of a good voluntary organization is to allow your work to be taken over by others, drop into the background, and continue to work on things that you yourself feel are critical to give yourself to.

I had no idea that he would develop a plan which would become the "Keepers of the Stream" program. By inviting him to join, it opened a door, he saw the need, and he volunteered to do the one

Keeper of the Stream

thing that was necessary to move us forward at this critical point of time in 1991: organize the Keeper of the Stream program for Valley Creek.

"Keepers of the Stream"—I could see a program enlisting hundreds working to save Valley Creek. Also, I could see the development of such a program on every cold water stream in Chester County. Our original goal for the Valley Forge Chapter was to form a large differentiated organization with many centers of movement, with a coordinating and financial center. The Keepers of the Stream program would allow such an effort to be mounted. Each stream could have its own group, call forth new volunteers, and tackle responsibility for the streams in its areas. Big issues requiring coordination across the county could then be dealt with through the chapter itself.

Exceptional Value

E very stream and river in Pennsylvania has a water-quality designation. The lowest are Warm Water Fishery and Trout Stocking Fishery. A designation of Cold Water Fishery gives a little bit more protection. There are a limited number of streams which are designated for special protection, either as High Quality or Exceptional Value. In this classification system of the Department of Environmental Resources of Pennsylvania, discharges can lower the water quality down to the stated criteria for a given designation. Any designation other than Exceptional Value allows degradation.

Back in 1985, the Valley Forge Chapter had sought such an upgraded water quality designation for Valley Creek. Seven years later the proposal was still tangled in the bureaucracy.

Joe Armstrong one day in 1992 decided to "go for broke" and seek the highest water quality designation for Valley Creek: Exceptional Value. An exception by definition is rare, superior. Something of value is strong, of worth, useful, and desirable. This designation would not only protect the stream from the proposed sewer plant, but also from other sources of degradation.

A Flood of Paper

How could an Exceptional Value designation be secured? Joe decided to ask the public to write letters and send postcards to the Department of Environmental Resources. Working with several others in the chapter, Joe got in touch with any group which might have some interest in Valley Creek or Valley Forge National Park, including civic associations, garden clubs, outdoor organizations, and patriotic groups. By the time he was through he had collected a list of over six hundred groups, and gotten in touch with everyone. Joe spoke at meetings, made phone calls, and wrote letters. Since personal letters are carefully read and responded to, those willing to do something were encouraged to write to the secretary of the DER. I myself wrote such a letter and received a response stating that the department was completing its study of the stream and expected to submit a stream evaluation report and recommendation to the Pennsylvania Environmental Quality Board later in 1992. Others wrote letters, too. Next Joe and his team began to approach visitors to Valley Forge National Park, telling them about the problem and asking them to express their sentiment. Thousands of addressed postcards were filled out and mailed to the DER. Perhaps the most letters the DER had previously received on the subject of stream classification was a few dozen. Not only did the flow continue, however, but also it increased.

A Public Hearing

Clean Water Action, under the direction of Flo Neilson, saw the concern about Valley Creek as an opportunity to gain widespread public support. News media were contacted, and so were the offices of the state senators and congressional representatives, asking them to support an Exceptional Value designation. Contacts were also made with Chester County political leaders.

On July 24, 1992, the state legislators from Chester County called a special information meeting at Valley Forge National Park on upgrading Valley Creek to Exceptional Value. Over sixty persons came to this forum. Township, county, state and federal political leaders were present. Those who spoke to the meeting expressed the concerns of the Valley Forge National Park, high school biology teachers, Green Valley's Watershed Association, Open Land Conservancy, West Chester Fish, Game and Wildlife, Trout Unlimited, Pennsylvania Sportsman's Federation, Clean Water Action, and others.

Why is Valley Creek of Exceptional Value? Speakers gave clear answers. First, it has geologic and biological worth. Beginning in the 1960s several hundred advanced biology students from Conestoga High School have learned to understand stream ecology systems through studying this creek. Since the Appalachians first rose out of the sea eons ago, the stream has supported life. It is one of the few relatively healthy limestone streams in Southeastern Pennsylvania. Its limestone base supports a large biological community. A class "A" stream for the Pennsylvania Fish Commission has at least 35 pounds of trout per acre. Valley Creek now holds 108 pounds of rare wild trout per acre.

Second, Valley Creek has historic value. The park is sacred to the hearts of Americans, since actions taken here played a major role in the birth of the democracy. What a travesty it would be if the living waters from which Washington's troops drank became a sewer water channel! The Valley Forge National Park superintendent said that he would take all actions to ensure that this trust's resources were not degraded.

Third, Valley Creek has significant scenic and recreational value. Souls go dead without views of trees, grasslands and flowing water. Parks, nature centers, conservancy lands have maintained much open space along Valley Creek, protecting the water and allowing public access. Over four million visitors a year come to see Valley Forge National Park. Hundreds of thousands of others take delight in hiking, fishing, and many other recreational activities related to the stream.

Fourth, Valley Creek has value as a source of drinking water. Statistics showed in 1984 the Valley Creek basin exported 630 million gallons a year from its water table, resulting in a substantial loss of normal stream flow. Its limestone aquifers are a critical, and continually threatened resource. Constant interchanges occur between the stream and ground water. Over the past fifty years dedicated work by government agencies, volunteer groups, and individuals, has restored the water quality of Valley Creek to its present state. The sewering system alone cost over $60 million, and the cleanup of the EPA Superfund Site in Paoli has cost millions more. Giving Valley Creek an Exceptional Value designation would be a further step in the direction already taken.

Fifth, Valley Creek has economic value. Studies by the Pennsylvania Fish Commission show that every trout in the rivers and streams of the state generates $18.50 in retail activity. Because of catch-and-release fishing the trout population in the creek is not depleted. Its class "A" character draws more and more anglers from throughout Pennsylvania, New Jersey, and Delaware. These visitors along with the millions who come to Valley Forge National Park spend hundreds of millions of dollars each year.

Real estate values along Valley Creek have increased much more than other parts of the Tri State area, due to the scenic and open space advantages Valley Creek affords. As one Chester County commissioner noted, the scenic land, hills, and valleys with their meandering streams have drawn many people and corporations to Chester County in the past decade. Continued economic prosperity depends on preserving the quality of the natural life around us.

Sixth, the value of the fish and wildlife must not be neglected. The presence of a naturally reproducing wild brown trout population in this densely settled urban area is miraculous. Insect life in the stream is abundant, furnishing food for the natural chain. Birds and mammals of many species are found along the banks of the stream. Indeed, Valley Creek has great ecological value. Our biological destiny is shaped by our mutual relations with other organisms in an environment we share in common. A healthy stream has everything to do with every living and breathing creature in the area. If we cannot preserve this stream running through Valley Forge National Park, what prospects do we have for human survival?

Finally, Valley Creek has cultural value:

> By cultural, I mean the characteristic attainments of a people or a social order. Is it conceivable that our everlasting logo, our legacy which we leave evidence of what we were will be typified by what we do to protect our world? Right here and now we should think about Valley Creek and its welfare versus conspicuous consumption. From the song bird whose feet clasp a branch atop the state champion walnut tree whose roots are nourished by the ground water, to the protective case of a caddis worm under a stony riffle, Valley Creek today is a rare testimony to mother nature. It has been treated shabbily at times, but like the Timex watch, it has "taken a licken" but it keeps on ticken." Like the watch, however, being struck by a steam roller or a series of sledge hammer blows will finish it. (Address by Carl Dusinberre, July 24, 1992)

But It's Polluted!

How could Valley Creek be of Exceptional Value? Critics argued it has PCBs and other pollutants in it. Speakers responded to this question by pointing out that the millions of dollars spent to clean up Valley Creek are showing considerable effect. Malfunctioning sewer plants in 1992 provided less than one-eighth of one percent of the total stream discharge, and shortly the two worst offenders' discharges would be stopped entirely. The PCB cleanup of the Paoli railroad yards was well underway, as were plans to remove contaminated soils from the three most polluted tributaries. Should more pollution be allowed because somebody in the past had been a bad steward? Instead, efforts must be taken to protect the stream from further pollution even as a great deal has been done to restore it.

Political Leaders Speak Out

The House of Representatives delegation from Pennsylvania had videotaped the informational hearings. Written transcripts were sent to the Department of Environmental Resources as input to its designation on Valley Creek. Organizing efforts went into high gear.

Both U.S. senators from Pennsylvania wrote to the Department of Environmental Resources requesting an exceptional value classification. Letters also went from township and county leaders, as well as leaders of groups throughout the Philadelphia, New Jersey and Delaware area. Letters and postcards were flooding the Department of Environmental Resources.

The big day approached, when the Pennsylvania Environmental Quality Board was to hold its hearing. What would happen? Prior information was that the Department of Environmental Resources would refuse to recommend Exceptional Value classification, instead offering a lower classification which would not protect the stream from pollution. We waited with great concern.

Phone calls continued to go back and forth between members of the coalition. One political leader wrote a very important letter stating his support for an improved water quality designation for Valley Creek. The letter, however, left out the key term, "Exceptional Value!" More work was required to make sure that the Department of Environmental Resources knew that he was in favor of this designation. Similar efforts had to be carried out with other state agencies, making sure that they did not undercut our efforts.

Meanwhile, the Rouse Company lawsuit continued to drag along in court. In early September 1992, we received a legal bill of over $7,000, in addition to what already had been spent. Since all other participants except West Chester Fish, Game, and Wildlife Association and Valley Forge Trout Unlimited had dropped out of the effort, these bills were falling entirely on us. We would have to raise more money, but at the same time we felt that money expended on the suit had been worthwhile. It remained a critical part of chapter strategy, giving time for people to organize to protect the stream. A year after the infamous township meeting, Valley Creek was still running clean, unpolluted by the immense amount of treated sewer water that would have come from the Rouse Company development.

The Environmental Quality Board Hearing

Finally, in September 1992, the first decisive day arrived. The Environmental Qualtiy Board was to receive the recommendation of the Pennsylvania Department of Environmental Resources regarding stream classification designation of many Pennsylvania streams. Persons from the chapter and other leaders from Chester County attended the hearing. After the board convened, State Senator Brightbill spoke. He gave ten reasons Valley Creek should get Exceptional Value status, summarizing the testimony given at the earlier hearing. Then he directed his remarks to the Secretary of the Department of Environmental Resources, moving to accept the Department of Environmental Resources recommendation on the classification of the twenty-five stream proposal package, with the exception that Valley Creek receive Exceptional Value status.

Senator Brightbill reversed the Department of Environmental Resources' recommendation, which was to give a lower status to Valley Creek with a possibility for upgrading following public comment. Such a recommendation from the Department of Environmental Resources would have been hard to change later, no matter how much public comment was given. Next he asked the Director of the Bureau of Water Quality Management if he had any objectives to giving Exceptional Value to Valley Creek. The director said, "No".

Margaret Bunce, a long-term environmental activist, immediately seconded Brightbill's recommendation. Then she asked the Secretary of the Department of Environmental Resources how much correspondence had been received on Valley Creek. An admission that he had received a few hundred was met by a more pointed question from Margaret. He then admitted that perhaps they had received a thousand (Margaret knew that the Department of Environmental Resources had by then received about 5,000 letters and postcards). Next, she asked if the Department of Environmental Resources had received any letters from industry. Meeting a negative response, she stated before the Board that as a matter of fact she knew they had received such letters and that they were in favor of Exceptional Value. She said that citizen and business support combined should lead to giving Exceptional Value designation to Valley Creek.

The legal representative on conservation of the Republican party to the state legislature, who had attended the meeting held in Chester County, stated he was in favor of Exceptional Value, and so were many state legislators and representatives.

The Secretary of the Department of Environmental Resources then put the motion before the board. Thirteen voted for it, none opposed, two abstained. The Environmental Qaulity Board vote immediately went into effect. Valley Creek was temporarily classified Exceptional Value, and from that time on could not be degraded. Of course, hearings would still be held, with possibilities of change in classification. The war continued, but a major battle had been won.

Is it possible to preserve the waters which give us life? Is it possible to stop living today in such ways that we destroy tomorrow? Can citizens take better care of land and water which are essential to the well being of themselves and their children? In the face of determined and well-financed efforts to turn Valley Creek into a sewer, grassroots effort answered these questions in the affirmative. As more and more citizens wrote and spoke, indicating their support for protection of Valley Creek, political leaders saw what was happening and did what they were asked to do to gain an Exceptional Value classification for the stream.

Nowhere else in the country, probably in the world, is there a stream with so much public access, such a high trout population, this close to a large city. Valley Creek is truly of exceptional value. The struggle would go on. Funds would have to be raised to pay off the lawsuit. New efforts would be mounted to make sure that the Exceptional Value classification was not overturned. Bigger efforts to preserve and restore the watershed would have to be made, but for now the chapter could get in touch with all of our friends with letters and words of thanks. Valley Creek was still alive and well. There was hope.

CHAPTER 15

Turn Them Loose

Many of the active members of the Valley Forge Chapter fish with a passion. Nights after work they are out on the stream. They get up early in the morning to fish the morning hatch. There is something strange, however, about these avid trout fishers. They turn loose every fish they catch! Each fish is carefully unhooked, and released to go about its activities. You can imagine all the questions; "Why do you go fishing, since you don't keep the fish?" "What is the point of catching fish if you don't kill them and eat them?"

One of the most skilled fishermen in the chapter, Jim Clark, goes a step further. Sometimes he doesn't even try to catch the fish in his backyard. One day as I was fishing for trout in the James Clark Jr. Memorial section of the stream he came down and watched. He made the comment that he hadn't been fishing for awhile, because "they have been pestered enough." Jim gets a great deal of enjoyment out of watching trout.

There is a great deal more to fishing than catching fish, and certainly more than killing fish. It is the same with any sport. Why do people go golfing, since they can't eat the ball? Why do people hike, raise flowers, and engage in activities which are pleasant, yet provide one with nothing to eat?

Fishing for trout is a complex sport. Sneaking up on a feeding trout, perhaps even crawling on your stomach so that you will not be silhouetted against the sky and frighten the fish, has its own excitement. Your skill can be matched against the acute senses of the trout, as you cast again and again to a feeding fish. Care must be taken not to scare the fish, and to match the type of fly rising from the water. Sometimes a careful fish will be fooled and will rise to grab your feathered offering. Then there is the thrill of a smashing strike, followed by the fight.

All these thrills and more may be had without killing a trout. Indeed, when you release a fish, you are left with a good feeling of having left a fish for someone else to catch, perhaps even yourself. A few weeks later, often you do learn that one of your friends may have caught and released the very same fish. Like people, each fish is different, and for that reason recognizable. Some have notches out of a pectoral fin or an entire fin may be missing. Others may be scarred in some unique way or have other identifying marks. A person who fishes a section of stream very frequently has named many of the fish in that section. There is a good feeling which comes from knowing Scarhead or Old Fighter is lying right where it should be.

In water that is very heavily fished year round, most of the fish will be quickly removed unless people restrain themselves. Indeed, a fishing club once publicized a special fishing contest for West Valley Creek. They placed a few large trout in the stream. Unfortunately, the day of the contest coincided with a rainstorm. The water was high and muddy, making it easy to catch fish. People came out to catch and kill trout. At the end of the contest much of the stream was scoured of its fish.

Urban streams are subject to tremendous fishing pressure. If everybody killed all they caught, our streams would soon be empty. Therefore, we need to learn to be less greedy.

One temporary solution to fishing pressure has been to stock trout. Fish are carefully reared in hatcheries, then placed in the streams for people to catch. The Pennsylvania Fish Commission expects that most of these fish will be caught, killed, and taken home to be eaten. Indeed, one of the reasons for the popularity of trout fishing in Pennsylvania is the stocking program. Many people go fishing only when they learn that a certain stream has been stocked. They enjoy catching fish easily and, of course, a good meal of fresh caught trout is very tasty.

No doubt trout stocking programs throughout the state will continue, but there are certain problems that go along with massive stocking of trout. One is the increasing cost of rearing trout in hatcheries. There are limits to how much money can be derived from license fees to support stocking programs.

Secondly, the crowds which flock to the streams on opening day often leave the surroundings strewn with refuse. Most anglers exercise good stewardship, but with large opening-day crowds, there are always a few who show no respect for the rights of landowners and sometimes abuse and destroy property. Landowners are often forced to clean up worm boxes, beer cans, and soda bottles left scattered in their backyards. Some close their property to fishing because they do not like the abuse and litter of a few. If fishing could be spread throughout the year rather than being concentrated in a few weeks, everyone would be better off.

A third problem with stocking programs is that when stocked trout are placed in a stream where there are native ones, they increase the pressure on native trout in the stream. Natural reproduction suffers and there is probably a degrading of the biological stock. Of course within a few weeks most stocked trout have been caught, since they have been reared in conditions where they are taught to eat whatever human beings feed them.

Fourth, those who become dedicated to trout fishing, going out more than once or twice a year, begin to appreciate more and more the value of wild trout. The beauty and grace of a wild fish makes it seem almost a different species from the sluggish and not-too-bright hatchery trout. Wild trout are also much more difficult to catch, increasing the challenge.

Fifth, research is demonstrating that healthy streams can maintain significant populations of native trout, even with heavy fishing pressure. If one's objective is restoration of coldwater streams, catching and releasing trout makes a lot of sense.

What about the survival of fish which are hooked and then released? Don't they die? Careful research has been devoted to answering this question. In studies made in Yellowstone Park, it was determined that fish hooked with flies tied on barbed hooks had a better than 95-percent survival rate. With barbless hooks an even higher percentage of the fish survived being caught and released. Trout caught on spinning lures also had a very high percentage of survival, but not quite as great as those hooked on flies. One would expect that fish hooked on live bait would swallow the bait or be hooked in the gills, giving a lower survival rate. Yet even trout caught on live bait had a better than 70 to 80 percent survival rate. When fish hooked deeply in the gills or stomach are released by cutting off the hook, thus leaving it inside the fish, their survival rate goes up.

Most fish released do survive. In Chester County streams we frequently see and recognize fish which we have released. We also have noticed that fish once caught do get smarter. It gets harder and harder to catch them as the season goes along. Some fish only with barbless hooks, and do not even need to lift the fish out of the water to release them. They merely release the pressure of the line and slip out the hook. When a fish is caught on a barbed hook, it is grasped firmly, but not squeezed. The hook is slipped out, and the fish immediately returned to the water.

Sometimes a trophy fish is placed on the bank for a moment, and a picture is taken. Then the fish is returned to its native element. Pictures are a way of having your cake and eating it too. You can prove you really caught the "big monster." Yet that monster is back in the stream, where you or someone else may have another chance to catch it.

"Why do you go fishing, if you don't keep the fish?" That is a very good question. It makes me think about why I love trout fishing. I love to wade wet, feeling the water flow against my legs on a hot summer day. I like to talk with friends after an interesting day, comparing experiences and laughing about amusing things which happened. I get deep satisfaction out of seeing all of the living beings which inhabit a stream. I may come upon a blue heron, stalking along watching for an unwary frog or minnow or perhaps even a trout. I regard herons as honorary members of our Valley Forge Chapter. Even though they do not release the fish they catch, they give me a great pleasure.

I love to see the blue sky overhead on a bright spring day, the fragrance of grasses and trees in bloom as earth and water are released from frost to live again. I have always been delighted by thunderstorms. I find a protected place where I can sit under cover and watch the lightning flash and the rain pound down. There is nothing like the odor that comes when the first drops of rain hit the earth on a dusty summer day. Then there is the color of fall, when the variety of shrubs and trees along a trout stream gives a continuing variation of color.

Of course the center of it all is the living stream. There is something deeply pleasing about being in and close to water. Every human being is attracted to and fascinated by rivers. Perhaps in our deepest selves we know that once our ancestors came from the water, and that our body fluids themselves are water. I love to be near the water and derive deep delight from its sounds. I fish for trout because of what I see and hear when I am out in the stream. If I catch a trout or two during the course of the day, so much the better. But the main reason I go is to be outside and experience all that is there.

What's Good for Trout Is Good for the Country

The chief executive of General Motors once made the now famous statement, "What's good for General Motors is good for the country." He was referring to the degree to which the prosperity of the auto industry once was linked with prosperity of the whole American economy. Of course, he was also trying to link the narrow interests of General Motors with the general well-being of the whole country, a more debatable point, particularly since the expansion of the automobile industry has played a major role in depleting the energy and other natural resources of our country. At any rate, I would like to make a case that what is good for trout is good for the country.

I do not mean that having trout in our streams in the narrowest sense may be particularly good for the country. One can imagine people so committed to trout that they kill all nonhuman predators they can find. After all, herons and snakes catch some trout. So do other natural predators. Yet part of the delight of fishing comes from seeing these fellow predators at work. We know, furthermore, that with good habitat, there are plenty of fish for human and natural predators to eat, provided that we human beings exercise some restraint.

I am not talking, therefore, about preserving trout in a very narrow sense as being good for the country. In the broadest sense, however, I would like to make a case for the trout as an indicator of national well-being. To begin with, trout play a role like that of canaries in a mine. Remember how miners used to take a caged canary down with them into the mine? They knew that these sensitive birds would be affected by the presence of dangerous gases before they would be. When the bird got sick, it was time to get out. In like manner, trout demand cold, clean water, with plenty of oxygen. When the water becomes warm and polluted, they cannot live. When trout are living in streams we know that the water is pretty good.

In urban areas we have expanded upon Roman water supply models, drawing fresh water through aquaducts from faraway rivers and also dumping sewage into the rivers close to hand. We pay little attention to the well-being of our urban and suburban watersheds. Today we are learning that there is only so much water. Big cities like New York and Philadelphia for the most part have tapped all of the watersheds they can. We must more and more live with what we have. That means we must pay much more attention to the purity of water within our urban and suburban areas. When the headwaters of our coldwater streams are destroyed, the quality of our drinking water will soon suffer. Trout thus are a canary-type indicator, their absence or presence showing us what is happening to our water.

Clean water is good for the country and it is certainly necessary for trout. There is a second sense in which what is good for trout is good for the country, and that relates to recreational enjoyment. In Philadelphia, people love to get out to the Adirondacks, Poconos, or coldwater streams of upstate Pennsylvania. Some feel they don't need to pay any attention to what is happening to the streams at home, because they can always go away and fish someplace else.

Streams in other parts of the state and Eastern Seaboard are being afflicted by many of the same problems we find at home. Escape becomes more difficult. On the other hand, it becomes more expensive to get away for a few days. That makes our streams in places like the Greater Philadelphia area more and more important. If we can preserve these streams, our children may have the enjoyment of going fishing for a day, and seeing geese feeding along the banks, and perhaps surprising a flock of ducks which burst into the air ahead of them. They can have the pleasure of seeing a pheasant break out of cover right next to the spot they are fishing. They too can see signs of rabbits and muskrats along the bank.

If we are able to keep trout, a very sensitive fish, in the stream, we will also preserve much of the total ecosystem. To learn just how important that is take one of your children or grandchildren out to a trout stream. Watch them and see what they do. They will lay their fishing poles down and begin to lift up rocks to see if they can catch a crayfish. Or they may become fascinated by the insects which creep along the bottom of the rocks. If your know the names of some of those insects, or perhaps even have a stream guide in hand, they will watch in fascination and try to classify all the different kinds of life they are finding. They will play hide and seek behind trees and high grasses. Or on a hot day they may plunge into the water, delighting in the coolness of the pool. Early memories of such experiences are often unforgotten at the close of life. One thinks back to the times that one's friend was walking along the bank, and slipped on a muddy spot and fell in, or of the time that one finally caught a trout after fishing vainly for weeks and weeks.

Trout are indicators of water quality. Trout and their streams are sources of enjoyment. Restoring degraded coldwater streams so that they can support trout is a highly beneficial activity. Coldwater streams are small enough, furthermore, that even limited human effort makes a difference. Perhaps if we can understand what makes for a healthy coldwater stream, we can supply what we've learned to bigger problems and settings.

One small step each can take is to return trout we catch unharmed. Let us "turn them loose."

Raindrops Falling/ Wading Upstream

A stream is made up of drops of rain. Imagine what happens when rain falls. In a healthy watershed, tall trees catch the force of the falling rain. The highest branches and leaves break the impact. Water runs down branches, drips off the leaves, and eventually hits the forest floor.

Perhaps you've experienced being in the woods in a heavy rainstorm, and stood under a large tree for a considerable period of time without getting wet. Then after the storm was over, however, when you walked through the woods you continued to get spattered with drops of water.

The forest floor is covered with old leaves, broken branches, wood from decaying trees. Ferns, shrubs and small trees flourish. When water falls upon the forest floor, it seldom runs off, but slowly trickles into the soil. Much of it soaks down into the subsoil to replenish the underground water supply. Small brooklets run clear in the ravines. Even hurricanes fail to muddy the water in an undisturbed watershed. It takes a long time even for the water from a torrential downpour to find its way into the brooklets. A healthy stream flows from a healthy watershed.

As the brooklets flow downstream, they frequently slip through swampy ground. Swamps are critically important to a healthy stream. They keep the water table high and during heavy rains hold the water. What silt is in the water tends to precipitate as the current slows and backs up over the swamp. The meanders of a natural stream perform similar functions. Each bend slows the force of the water, giving more chance for it to drop its load of silt on the flood plains.

Most are aware that at one time the eastern part of North America was covered with a dense forest. Following prevailing European patterns of agriculture, settlers cut down the trees in order to farm. Raindrops then began to fall on grasslands and on the bare soil of croplands. The effects of clearing the forests were immediate. The streams ceased to run clear, and became marked with colors of the soils of their respective watersheds. Today it is unusual to see a clear stream.

A raindrop falls out of the sky with tremendous force. Even when it hits soil that is covered by grass there is considerable erosion. But when raindrops fall on bare earth each drop splatters upon the soil, creating a miniature explosion of water and earth. Sometimes a raindrop throws particles of soil for several feet. As the soil is displaced by the force of the rain, little rivulets of water run across the surface of the land. Since there are no leaves, shrubs, or decaying trees on the surface to inhibit the flow of the water, most of it runs off of the fields into the streams. Erosion occurs.

In many places erosion has gotten worse since World War II. Being able to use big machinery has encouraged farmers to clear and farm huge fields. "Clean" farming has destroyed hedge rows, leaving less protection to the soil. The continual cropping of corn and soybeans without rotation result in heavy loss of topsoil. Because farmers are working bigger and bigger acreages, they have found it increasingly necessary to plow fields in the fall in order to make sure that crops are gotten in. This means that the surface of the soil is left entirely exposed to erosion for much of the year. Someone has estimated that in Wisconsin alone the amount of soil lost by erosion in one year would fill a line of trucks from the earth to the moon and back!

The kind of farming that is done in this country, in short, tends to leave streams silted, choked with sediment and rubble. In many areas water is polluted by chemical fertilizers, pesticides, and herbicides. Grazing which allows cattle in the streams is also a serious problem. A natural stream has many deep holes, and long stretches of clean gravel where fish may lay their eggs. In heavily silted streams, however, natural reproduction slows and often stops entirely.

Roadbuilding

In most parts of the country, however, agricultural impact on streams is only the beginning. Mining takes its toll, but the vast networks of roads which cut across our country have a terrible effect. When rain falls, even upon a cornfield, some of it soaks in. On concrete and macadam pavement, however, nothing trickles into the soil. Instead, the rain rushes off in little floods, and is concentrated in culverts where it dumps into brooklets or into the streams themselves. Whatever is on the road surface is washed off into the stream. Every road contributes to our water supply its share of oil, gas, lead, and whatever other substances happen to be spilled on the road surfaces.

Building roads is immensely disturbing to streams. Roads go straight, and they cut through hills and fill in valleys. A huge amount of erosion comes from constructing a four-lane highway. In the 1950s Valley Creek, the stream which flows through Valley Forge National Park, was populated with beautiful brown trout. I have seen pictures of strikingly colored native fish which weighed three or four pounds. The building of Route 202 through the Great Valley dealt a near-knockout blow to this stream. It has taken twenty years for the fishery to recover.

Development

Once roads are built, houses, industries and shopping centers spring up. Each removes a certain amount of cover from the watershed as do new streets. The parking lots and roofs of shopping centers pour floods of water into once-tiny tributaries. Storm and wastewater sewers are constructed. In these sewers, in effect, we now have alternate stream systems. As a sewer system is constructed, engineers seek to use gravity to maximize the flow. This means that sewers often follow the courses of existing streams. The effect of sewer construction upon the stream may be very negative. In more outlying areas, septic tanks are used to collect human waste. At least the water from these septic tanks replenishes the watershed. Where the systems do not work well though, human waste itself finds its way into the waters.

Universal Solvent

The first blow to a healthy stream is usually erosion and sedimentation. The second punch is pollution. Human beings do not only build roads and houses. Since the beginning of the industrial revolution water has been used to carry away wastes of industrial activity. Today some of this pours into the stream through the sewer system. Despite environmental legislation, many factories still dump their waste directly into the streams (often as treated effluent). Given the increasing size of the industrial plants and of the scope of their activity, pollution has become a larger and larger problem across the United States.

As chemists know, water is a universal solvent. Almost anything will dissolve in it. Almost everything *is* dissolved in our streams today. No matter how sophisticated the water treatment system, it cannot remove everything from the water. Consequently, all of us are drinking water that is less and less pure.

Fuel oil from the sewage pumping station leaked into West Valley Creek from a township holding tank. Gasoline contaminated the spring along Whitford Road, coming from leaking fuel tanks at the Sunoco Station. Drums of spent cleaning fluid were dumped onto the ice of West Valley Creek. From time to time both pesticides and herbicides have contaminated its water.

Valley Creek, flowing through Valley Forge National Park, has experienced even more serious abuses. Chem-Kleen Corporation, in processing hazardous wastes, contaminated the underground water supply with the carcinogenic degreaser TCE. Knickerbocker Landfill poisoned the stream with leachate containing a number of noxious chemicals. A bit further downstream, a large steel plant leaked cyanide, killing all the fish from that point down to the mouth of Valley Creek where it flows into the Schuylkill River. A broken water main poured drinking water into Little Valley Creek, the chlorine in it causing a substantial fish kill. Chemical lawn fertilizer trucks draw water from the stream and from time to time backflush pesticides, herbicides, and fertilizers into the stream. Runoff from lawns contains chemical fertilizers high in nitrates and phosphates.

Though the construction of the regional sewer system has reduced the amount of raw sewage that enters Valley Creek, enough still is present to cause high fecal coliform counts at certain times of the year. Significant amounts of fine limestone particles from Warner Quarry contaminate the stream during rainstorms. A bit farther downstream, PCBs from transformers in the Paoli railroad yards have polluted much of the stream's ecosystem.

Air Pollution

One may add to these horror stories the effects of air pollution. Acid rain, produced by burning fossil fuel at points far away from where the rain falls is reducing the pH of water, particularly in the Midwest, Northeast and Canada. The effects on trout and stream life are particularly severe when the snow melts. Sulphur dioxide and other polluting substances fall throughout the winter and are stored in the snowpack. When it melts, they go into the water in one huge surge. In limestone streams the effects of acid rain are buffered by the large amount of lime in the water. In watersheds which do not have lime, however, the effects are increasingly serious.

Junk Dumping

Another blow to the stream comes from people who dump junk onto its banks. Along the quarry section of West Valley Creek, people have dumped bedsprings, mattresses, bottles and cans, household garbage, and even a wrecked snowmobile. Groups who do stream cleanups collect dump trucks full of trash.

From Stream to Ditch

The full story of the effect of destructive human activity on our streams has still not been told. When a stream becomes ugly and polluted, children can no longer swim in it. When the fish are gone, or only the most resilient rough fish remain, people do not go fishing any more. Then those who wish to "develop" the land that the stream runs through present their plans. They wish that the stream flowed in a neat ditch, straight and deep, since this makes far easier laying out *square* housing and industrial developments. When the inevitable floods come, they then present plans to dredge the stream, "to end flooding."

When a stream is dredged, it leaves a greatly shortened channel. We estimate that West Valley Creek may once have been twice as long as it is today. Dredging reduced its ability to hold fish. It also reduced the ability of the stream to remove silt and sediment from the water. A naturally meandering stream slows flood water. At every bend, eddies and backwaters allows sediment to drop from suspension. When high water flows over the banks, vegetation plays a similar role. Marshes fill with muddy water, and the silt precipitates, providing new fertility.

Dredging a stream does not end floods. The water shoots downstream all at once. Problems are passed on to the people downstream.

Perhaps even worse for the long run, the natural fertility provided free to river bottoms in times of high water is lost.

Streams are made up of raindrops which have fallen to earth, and have percolated into the riverbeds. The character of a stream is determined by the quality of its watershed.

Four hundred years of careless human activity: trees cut, fields cleared, corn lands eroded, stream banks broken down by livestock, roads built, houses erected, shopping centers constructed, fields paved, sewage polluted, cold water removed by quarries and replaced it with warm, junk dumped on river banks, stream channels dredged and ditched.

The end is still not in sight. There is the continuing threat of more destruction of the stream and its watershed. Can streams be saved and the life forms in them preserved? Or will we experience new acts of ecocide?

A Way to Health: Stream Restoration

Years ago a great American theologian and social ethicist, Reinhold Niebuhr, wrote a prayer which has now become famous:

> God, give me the serenity to accept the things I cannot change,
>   The courage to change the things I can,
>   And the wisdom to know the difference.

When faced with massive human-caused destruction, this serenity prayer suggests a way to peace and health. Accept what you cannot change, and with courage change the things you can. When faced with plans to turn West Valley Creek into a sewer-water stream, what could a little group with four or five thousand dollars to spend do to stop a "world class" developer with political ties in the highest places?

We could reach out and mobilize our entire membership, and we did. We could form a coalition that would seek to preserve the stream, and we did. We could seek to publicize the threat and inform the people of better ways of doing things, and we did. We could keep right on with out efforts to restore West Valley Creek, and we did.

All these efforts were essential parts of what proved to be a successful effort. Stream restoration that helped West Valley Creek heal itself, however, played a particularly dramatic role in efforts to change corporate and governmental plans affecting the stream and its watershed.

"I WOULD LIKE THE MEMBERS OUT SUNDAY AFTER-
NOON FOR A WORK SESSION, TO MOVE SOME STONES."

Planning a Workday

Why has restoration played such a key role? First, stream restoration got us in the water. To help the stream heal we had to get involved with the little sections of the stream in which we could make changes. We got wet. And by getting wet, we entered into a constructive relationship with a living body of water. From that time on we were identified with the stream's well-being.

Many little successes move a movement along. Second, in doing the restoration project, we started out where we could, with what efforts we could mount. After even a short work day, we could see that our efforts had made a difference in the stream. In small ways we were making things better, and each involved could see immediate results.

Third, to guide the project, we had to set goals and objectives. The overall goal of Trout Unlimited, preserving, restoring, and conserving the coldwater streams and their watersheds took on a sharp focus. Our task was nothing less than restoring this little part of the land/human community. As our goals became clearer to us we could communicate them better to others.

Fourth, we learned to know a tough character, West Valley Creek. Some of our learning came through action, trying things out and seeing what happened. That led to asking some big questions, like "What is a healthy stream?" or "What can we do to restore West Valley Creek to health?" We read about what others had done. We learned from the Pennsylvania Fish Commission. I made a visit to Wisconsin to learn from a master biologist, Bob Hunt. We brought in Ray White, a specialist in stream restoration, as our consultant.

Ignorance destroys. Again and again watershed, streams, and wetlands are ruined because the people running machines or developing the plans do not know what they are doing. By studying and learning as much as we could, we learned many different ways to work with nature.

We learned ways to put science and technology together for healing purposes. Old tools like hammers and saws were used for construction of deflectors. Rocks were moved manually with pry bars. We used backhoes and trucks to move rocks dug by modern machines out of the adjacent quarry. Thermometers measured water temperature. State-of-the-art science was used to study the stream and its invertebrate life. We learned how to construct point bars through the use of triangles. We built deflectors, used half logs, created silt-catching porcupines, added spines to deflectors through use of Christmas trees, and built sills and jack dams. We evaluated our efforts. Did what we attempted actually help the stream to heal? Was it beginning to restore itself? Learning is essential. Those who learn to restore are able to speak with authority. Not that we know everything, but some of the things we have learned are valuable.

Fifth, we did things that were "impossible." Biblical prophets, like Isaiah, knew the value of symbolic acts for the well-being of their people. Isaiah did things that most of the citizens of this day thought were crazy. One of the craziest things of all is to change the things that one can. In the face of a system where making money determines what is done and what is not, the very idea that a few folks would go out on a Sunday afternoon and move 85,000 pounds of rock in one day—that is hard to believe! Reestablishing stream-bred trout in West Valley Creek after centuries of neglect, with imminent ruin of its entire watershed at hand—what a crazy thing to try to do! Yet we did it. We set a goal to reduce the water temperature in a one-half mile section of a little limestone stream next to a huge quarry. What a strange thing to try to do in the face of trees being cut down throughout the entire watershed, and when more paved lots would heat thundershower rainfall and pour it directly into the little stream. Yet, we were able to reduce water temperature.

Restore meanders in a stream which have been dredged and ditched (following accepted practice in cities throughout the country)! "Everyone knows" run-off should go into a straight ditch, be gotten rid of as quickly as possible. Who would ever think of restoring natural meanders to a ditched stream? Yet we did it. Deepening and narrowing a stream in the face of scouring floods pouring off a paved watershed. Who would try to do such a thing? Who would try to make the silt and sediment load work for the health of the stream? We did it.

Restoring a stream in an area which is "progressing" and "developing" seems like an impossible task. "You can't stop progress," they say, and we did not try to stop the urbanizing development of Chester County, Pennsylvania. We did raise a vision of progress that would leave children a legacy of clean, healthy streams and fertile watersheds. When we entered the stream and began to restore it, we placed ourselves on the side of nature itself.

Working Up a Sweat

For fifteen years the work days have gone on. During years of intense activity more than one a month were held. In the late 1980s we might go for several months before someone would take hold and organize a work day, but we never stopped. From hot July to cold January, we were out with sledgehammers and shovels working up a sweat. Sometimes we did the work together as a team. Those days we got a lot done. Other times a few of us worked alone. Whether alone or together, we would try something, back off and evaluate, and then start over.

Looking back, I can see three phases in restoration, beginning on the James Clark section roughly from 1978 to 1981. Work in this section has continued since that time, but during the early days it was the center of our effort. From 1981 to 1986, our attention was concentrated on the General Crushed Stone Quarry section. We were able to narrow the stream and had initial success in deepening it, followed by a gradual loss of depth as the newly formed pools began again to silt in. The third phase of the work, from 1986 to 1992, has been to enable the stream to dig and maintain deep holes and to stabilize the stream's return to an increasingly healthy state.

Praying for Healing

As Reinhold Niebuhr taught, serenity, peace, wholeness, healing, all these come through true prayer, that is, letting go of efforts to control what is unmanageable. True prayer keeps the focus on ourselves. For we, ourselves, are major contributors to the destructiveness which we all too easily see acted out in others. I, for instance, hate tyrants, and yet I am constantly tempted to seek security by controlling others around me. The pain of loss, the fury of seeing others senselessly destroy what one loves, the fear of more ruin and loss, all these may be met with an attempt to control persons and events about which one can do nothing. Those who would heal and destroy indeed are constantly tempted to cut down and destroy the destroyers. If they try to put us down and attack our integrity, why don't we do the same? It is easy to caricature a greedy and ignorant human being who pretends to be a savior of humanity, but with our own feet of clay would we wish to have the same treatment applied to ourselves? As Al Frankel so clearly taught years ago, I had to be willing to let "my" stream conservation movement die if people didn't support it.

One day I remembered that West Valley Creek had been flowing through these very hills since the time the Appalachian Mountains had been formed. Imagine the changes this little stream had seen. Glaciers came and went. Forests grew and died. Creatures multiplied and became extinct. Yet the little stream flowed on for millions of years, fed by cold springs emerging from deep limestone aquifers. The creek still lived because it was in touch with raw creative power.

Behind the creation, alive, fertile, dangerous, beautiful is a living Creator. Though the wrong is oft so strong, this Creator is still the ruler. We can, therefore, let go, let God, and with courage change the things we can.

Wading Upstream

A few years ago I had an opportunity to fish a big trout river in the Adirondacks. It took effort to wade in that river. The current was always pushing and splashing against me. It was hard work wading upstream. I looked downstream and thought about how easy it would be to bounce along the bottom a little ways, letting the current push me. Fishing downstream is always easier than wading upstream.

There is a very good reason to wade upstream, however, for if you allow yourself to bounce downstream, before very long the shallow water comes to an end, and water changes color to a dark blue. One step more and you are over your head, swimming to get out. Wading downstream in a big river is fast, easy, and risky. Wading upstream is slow, hard, and safer.

In 1976, we started a movement of people who have been wading upstream ever since. On a little stream as West Valley Creek you can learn a lot by wading upstream. In the early days of the restoration project, after a big flood had come and gone Joe and I would go out to the stream and wade up it. I remember our first big success. Behind a structure the stream was running blue. A hole about a foot and a half deep had appeared where a few days before it had been only a few inches deep. What a success.

Before and after work days we would sometimes spend a little time wading the stream observing and planning. I remember other times when we walked slowly through the water, looking at what worked and what didn't. Intrigued, fascinated, sometimes delighted, sometimes baffled, we looked, learned, and made new plans.

After seven or eight years I began to go out to the stream during big rains. The riffle and pool sequence was then very different. During the big rains I could see what the flood waters were doing. From the flow of the water I could tell which structures were working, and which were not. I could also see why rocks and sediment were being deposited where they were.

Fishing trips provided another opportunity to wade upstream. For several years I fished nowhere else than in West Valley Creek. The reason I fished there was to find out which of our structures were working and which were not. It was a big thrill to catch a trout where the year before no self-respecting fish would have been. I also discovered that some pools that were beautiful in appearance somehow lacked what was needed for fish to move in and live.

More and more frequently we began to take guided tours. My favorite time for a tour was on a hot summer day. If I were the guide, I would put on tennis shoes and an old pair of jeans, splash right in, and get wet. Slowly we would walk upstream. In the lowest part of the restoration project there was a section which remained in its dredged state. The water was a few inches deep, exposed to the sun, with no fish evident. Then we would enter the restoration area. Immediately we could see a narrower stream. Quiet waders would discern fish feeding. Again and again we would see trout.

As we walked along a constant stream of questions and answers flowed. "Why did you do this?" "This bank is undercut!" "You mean this little meadow was once a stream one or two inches deep!" "Did you move all the rocks here by hand?" "Wow! What a beautiful pool!"

By the end of an upstream tour, visitors saw that human beings could indeed work constructively with a stream. Degraded water could become healthy again.

A Stream Is Not a Resource

As I took at our stream conservation work in Chester County, I wonder, what is our relationship with nature? This question was raised pointedly at a meeting of the Pennsylvania State Council of Trout Unlimited. Speakers again and again referred to coldwater streams as "the resource."

Troubled by this way of speaking, I pointed out to my friends that I did not feel that streams were a resource. Almost nobody agreed with me. The discussion, though, did start me thinking. What is a stream? What should be our relationship as human beings to streams and their ecosystem?

I began to think about what I have learned from stream conservation experiences. Streams are far more than "resources" or even "fisheries." They are *living water,* beautiful, alive, mysterious.

Why We Think of Streams Only as a Resource

Why are our understandings of human relationships to streams so narrowly "use oriented?" A careful reading of the history of Western civilization shows that in the seventeenth century there was a narrowing focus on how a given plant or animal could be useful. Increasingly nature was viewed as a *resource* to human beings. There was a "natural selection" of ideas and ways of living. More and more leaders of the expanding industrial society saw nature as a dead and lifeless machine, the source of endless materials necessary for human well-being. Other ideas dropped away.

A new and rapidly expanding industrial civilization was created. Our ancestors never would have expected that we would live in an industrial order which extends over the entire planet. Nature has been harnessed, controlled, channeled, domesticated, and almost overwhelmed. Human beings, when we can afford it, live in hermetically sealed buildings separated from the natural order. Most of us do not grow our own food. We have no relationship to the animals whose meat we eat.

We fear the last part of the biological process, refusing to accept that we, too, are mortal. Aging, death, and the decay essential to the fertility cycle are fought as though they were the enemy. Casual viewing of television shows our obsession with cleansers, designed to keep our homes "spotless." We forget what happens to the "cleansers" when they go down the drain. We are unaware of what the detergents, bleaches, industrial solvents, and other high-powered cleaners do when they flow from the sewers into the rivers and estuaries.

We have almost forgotten from where our drinking water comes, and where our sewage goes. Not so long ago, the human beings who lived on the North American continent drank the water from the streams where they lived. When people settled in cities, clean water ceased to be something people could take for granted. Following inventions perfected by the Romans, decisions were made to create reservoirs and aqueducts to assure a clean supply of water to people in cities. The other side of diverting streams into reservoirs and then carrying the water to the cities through aqueducts was that immense amounts of dirty water became concentrated in cities. Again following Roman practice, sewers were created, which at first collected all of the used water and dumped it into the river below the city. Later, sewage treatment plants were built to remove some of the most offensive human waste from the water.

A few years ago I walked through a park in New Jersey. Down through the center of the park flowed a little brook. This brooklet, however, was an above-ground sewer. Beneath every little waterfall was a huge mound of soapsuds. The stench, even on a cold day, was obnoxious. No doubt a few very tough fish still lived in the water. By contrast, all around were single family houses and well-maintained apartments and condominiums. Everything was neat, orderly, and well-maintained except the stream which flowed from the city.

People Live Downstream from Each Other

If all people could be first users of water, then we might not need to worry quite as much about the fact that we see our streams only as a resource. In countries populated by hundreds of millions of people, however, the water intake from one city tends to be right below the place in a stream where the sewer outflow enters.

Think of a society which can be characterized in a poster I once saw exhibited at the Stockholm Conference on the Environment in 1972. It pictured a huge, open human mouth, with everything else shrunken to insignificance. Into that cavernous opening was being shoveled all kinds of food and drink.

When people think of themselves only, or primarily, as eaters and drinkers, everything gets mixed up. We create a society which is unstable because we lose awareness and respect for the "otherness" of nature. We forget our limitations. Our ability to control streams and land for our use has allowed us to multiply like the lemmings. We dimly sense the ecological fact that when any kind of species multiplies in an unchecked way, the day of judgment is coming. Disease, famine, war, or some other catastrophe enters in to break the back of the population explosion, and reduce things to a more steady balance.

We know it is possible for human beings to reduce once fertile ecosystems to permanently lower levels of fertility. This happened in ancient Greece, and medieval Palestine. In more recent history, anchovies on the Pacific Coast were overfished, and even today the vast schools of anchovies have not reappeared.

Human beings are thinking creatures. Can we study what is happening to our streams so that we grow in understanding? Will we modify our over concentration on use? Will we be able to change our ways enough to avoid collapse?

A Stream Is Beautiful

Before human beings existed the streams flowed from their headwaters through the mountains and plains into the oceans. After human beings are gone streams will continue their journeys. An intentional, conscious decision is necessary for a stream to become a resource. We have to *decide* to take the flowing water, and begin to use it for human purposes. One such decision, for instance, is to build an aquaduct to bring water to where we want it. We use water. It is vitally important to us, but every stream has an existence apart from us, also. It would be sad if we only thought of streams as resources.

One of the reasons I am a trout fisherman is that it gives me an excuse to get up early and go out to the stream. I remember one August morning when I climbed out of bed around 5:00 am. and drove to West Valley Creek. Ground fog blocked off the early rays of the rising sun. As I climbed down the bank and slowly put my rod together, I stopped and looked. Mist was rising from the surface of the cold water. Each willow leaf had a drop of dew at its point. Tiny drops of water adhered to each long blade of reed canary grass. In the stream a pair of geese craned their necks to look at me, interrupting their grazing on the seeds of the canary grass. They edgily began to move away from me, and suddenly I saw scurrying upstream several snowy goslings. A bird sang.

Soon I, a human predator, was part of the natural scene. My rod bent, the line floated out, the fly landed gracefully on the surface. Before long the sun broke through the mist, and it was time to pause and look at the early light refracted in colors of the rainbow in every droplet of dew.

This day's fishing again revealed an astounding truth. Each pool, each riffle, every tree, each living creature I saw was different. If I could see with microscopic eye, as do some of my scientist friends who study streams, my awareness of diversity would only expand. Constantly changing, delighting my senses, when I left the stream I was a little bit more human than I was when I came.

Human Beings Belong to a "Natural Family"

Several years ago I was fortunate to be able to hear an address by Russell Means, the Native American political philosopher. He stated that many of our current difficulties stem from the fact that "white men" think in straight lines. The world of nature, on the other hand, is curved, circular. The seasons move round and return again. The sun and moon are round. All of life, indeed, moves in cycles.

As human beings, furthermore, we are part of a "natural family." Wolves, deer, fish, and coyotes: all are brothers and sisters. We are related to all creatures, just as we are related to members of the human family. Means went on to observe that perhaps we needed to take some lessons from the "original landlords" of North America. While they were living on this continent the natural order remained pretty much in balance. Generation after generation lived and died, leaving unscarred landscapes and fertile ecosystems for their descendants.

After only 500 years of living on this continent the record of white people is painfully sad. I have reflected on what Russell Means said. Human beings are *creatures*, and therefore one with nature. We are not alien beings who have come here from some other planet. The natural order is a part of our human nature. As we can see in our salty blood and watery flesh, streams flow through our veins as well as through the watercourses.

On the other hand, for thousands of years, probably since the beginnings of human consciousness, people have realized that in some ways we differ from animals and other creatures. We are aware and able to speak about what we see, hear, touch, smell, and taste. Furthermore, each human being is *named*. That fact is most significant, as is our classification of all forms of life with formal and informal names.

In many religious traditions, the fact that each human being is unique, with a distinct identity, has been explained by saying that each person has a soul. When this teaching has been interpreted to mean that there is some kind of non-material essence characterizing human nature, it has often gone along with looking down on the physical dimensions of one's own identity. The spirit is seen to be "good" and matter "bad," to be escaped by practices of self-denial and spiritual disciplines.

As a matter of fact, much human history can be explained by observing the driving fear of our physical, animal nature. We have often come close to believing that it is sexuality which is the source of evil.

Such beliefs may have played a role in creating an industrial society in which residential and business structure were almost entirely separated us from the natural order. Work environments were sealed off from the outside by energy expensive air-conditioning and heating systems. Our hospitals reflected our passionate attempt to kill germs and make ourselves sterile. Perhaps the attack on insects and weeds in our agricultural system stemmed from the same root.

Underneath much of contemporary life is fear of death. It is almost impossible for us to see that death is necessary to life. Without existing creatures coming to an end, their bodies cannot be recycled to provide new sources of fertility for the next generation. Indeed, burial customs attempt to prevent our mortal remains from returning to dust. In a strange way we seek to preserve these remains, thus frustrating even the last stage of the process of death and decay. Yet in nature, without death there can be no new life.

By refusing to fit into the natural order we are paying a terrible price. Because we fail to understand our oneness with nature, because we fail to see that human beings are a part of the "natural family," we are destroying the very nature from which we draw our life. Who would dump deadly poison into the bathtub of one's baby? No right-thinking parent, that is sure. Yet we dump dioxin, knowing that eventually it will seep into the water in which our children bathe. We are strangely blind to the effect of our actions, perhaps because we do not see that we are part of nature, an integral actor in the stream ecosystem.

Preservation, Conservation, Restoration

Streams will live again when we see and act on preserving, conserving, and restoring streams. By seeking to preserve relatively undisturbed streams and their watersheds, we respect natural systems which are not defined entirely by our own use. Wilderness faces us with realities other than those we create as human beings. Only when we immerse ourselves in the ecosystem of a living stream can we sense what a degraded stream once was and might again become. The presence of wilderness is a sign that we have not yet lost respect for the Great Spirit, who makes all creatures give praise to the One who created them.

Conservation is a second premise for right relationships to streams. Human beings, as part of nature, do use water. Streams are essential to humanity. We should restrain that use, and do it intelligently. There is no reason to pollute streams with waste. We do not have to create roads which rip through undisturbed landscapes, leaving erosion and sedimentation in their wake. We do not have to cut corners to make quick dollars, so that our short-term improvements are actually long-term losses to the human family. If we could learn to draw on streams for our use without breaking their eco-systems, we would be far better off economically, in the long, and often short-term.

A third premise of right relationships to streams is restoration. Many streams have had the worst done to them. They now exist as bodies of flowing water which are polluted and sedimented. A stream, however, has amazing abilities to cleanse itself. If we discover what a healthy stream is, drawing on the best scientific and naturalist observation, we may be able carefully to intervene and restore streams to beauty and productivity.

The three premises of preservation, conservation, and restoration are mutually supportive. They provide us with the central objectives of Trout Unlimited. We are, therefore, conservationists, preservationists, and restorationists.

A Stream Is Not a Resource

There are realities in our world which cannot be understood only in categories of use. Just as respect for another person is the basis for a right relationship, so also respect for streams and the natural order of which they are a part is the beginning point of right relationship to nature. We correctly shy away from people who would relate to us only because they think they can get something out of us. Respect for the identity and worth of other living beings is necessary if we are to be truly human.

We derive power and energy and insight from a pristine stream which cannot be understood in categories of "resource management." Indeed, there is a form of spiritual renewal which comes when we open ourselves to realities beyond us, or, indeed to the natural realities within our very bodies. A sense of joy at a beautiful moment is remembered as long as one lives.

Perhaps recognizing the wonders of nature will help us overcome our fear of death, which seems to drive so much of our destructive madness. It is not so bad to think that we, with all other creatures, are born, grow, carry out our purposes, age and die, with our bodies returning to the soil and water which nourished them. Nor is it so bad to think that our bones and blood will one day sustain the life of another creature.

CHAPTER 18

Looking Ahead

Senator Gaylord Nelson, founder of Earth Day, once raised this pointed question: "Must we destroy tomorrow in order to live today?" Development as it is currently being done in Chester County answers this question with a resounding "yes."

The purpose of development is to build a city for human beings to dwell in. In order to have a city, citizens work. The purpose of industry is to build and maintain a productive, safe, and fulfilling life for each citizen. Prophets and civil leaders tell us that civilization truly occurs when each works together for the good of all. Therefore, when a person or corporation makes money from a development project, that is fine as long as it contributes to building a beautiful and just society.

Contemporary developers appeal for support to the citizens who make a country go, the average working and middle-class people. They promise jobs, lots of jobs for Chester County. Yet the housing they build does not include much that is affordable by working and middle-class people. And what kind of jobs will there be for average people when the road building and construction are finished?

One thing is clear from our experience in Chester County: the bottom line of development is whether or not someone who has money can make money. If a project is a moneymaker, every effort will be expended to make it happen, and if it looks like a money loser it will not be done.

The big problem with modern development is that it seeks cheap, easy, quick short-cuts. As Joe Armstrong has been pointing out for years, however, there is a right way and a wrong way to do everything, and if you do it the wrong way it is never going to turn out right.

Many living in Chester County have been benefiting from rapid economic development. Townships are keeping taxes low as they add new revenues. The fast-food places are advertising for workers. If you want to see what Chester County will be like in thirty years, however, after the development is over, look at center city Philadelphia. In north and south Philadelphia there are acres and acres of abandoned industrial sites. Many are contaminated by toxic and hazardous wastes. It is very expensive to redevelop an old city which was poorly built in the first place.

A little book on stream conservation can't answer a big question as what makes for a beautiful enduring city. We can only fill in one little piece, namely that relating to streams and water. First, an enduring city must have sources of clean water. Try going without drinking for a week! Knickerbocker Landfill has polluted Valley Creek with its leachate since it was started. The developers of this profit-making enterprise paid no attention to contaminating the drinking water. The planners of Churchill, in like manner assumed that there would be a vast supply of water for drinking and industrial use. Without water their ambitious plans would collapse.

Second, water used by human beings must be safely returned to nature. In natural systems water is continually recycled. The fertility which is introduced sustains fish and aquatic life. Ecologically, streams are not intended to be sewers, and when they are overloaded with wastes there are devastating consequences to human health as well as to the health of the entire stream system. Looking only at water demand and use, development in Chester County is ruining the health of our streams. Those who come after us will pay the price of irresponsible construction.

Third, development must not replace natural beauty with human created ugliness, but instead enhance it. Paved parking lots, square glass buildings, roads overloaded with cars, noise, and dirt create the kind of environment from which people want to escape. Once where Route 352 intersects with old Route 30 there were several ancient spreading linden trees. Today they are gone, sacrificed to develop another ugly shopping center. Throughout Chester County hundreds of thousands of trees have already been chopped down, removing their ability to purify the air, removing the greenness, removing life itself. Rain is intended to fall on eye pleasing, sweet smelling watersheds with trees and grasses, not on parking lots and asphalt roofs.

Development, fourth, must preserve fertile agricultural land. How vulnerable is a city's food supply when all of the highly fertile land adjacent to it has been paved and covered with buildings? Great Valley once was a agricultural region, with highly desirable limestone soils. Now almost all of this gardening and farming land is lost.

Must we destroy tomorrow in order to live today? Unfortunately many citizens, developers, and governmental leaders answer in the affirmative. Like the past owners of the Knickerbocker Landfill, they would like to leave the problems they created to the future. Once they have made their money they will be gone. To live today, to make money, they are destroying tomorrow.

When We're Through, Will the Trout Be Gone?

Human beings can become callous to destructiveness. Like a great glacier industrial society creeps across the entire planet. Vast forests are cut down in a few decades. City populations explode. Automobiles multiply. Given the scope of such worldwide activity, what difference does another road or office building make?

It took millions of years to form the valleys and watercourses through which now flow West Valley and Valley Creeks. Within a day a bulldozer can tear to pieces what took eons to create. It is no wonder those who see what is going on become furious at the destructive power which modern machines and science give to human beings.

Rethinking Progress

Even though we have seen movement toward stream conservation, we recognize that the overall effect of our work has been only to slow down the destruction of local streams. Progress for most seems to mean more industries, shopping centers, and housing developments. Development means more jobs, and a bigger tax base for local and regional governments. Who wants to fight progress?

The way development is done today, however, ruins the watersheds and eventually the streams themselves. When raindrops fall on roofs and pavement, water does not soak into the soil to replenish the stream. Trees and grass are still the best cover for watersheds.

Oddly enough, continuing suburban and city development depends on ample, clean water supplies. For the most part, water is taken for granted. "After all, has not clean water always flowed out of our faucets? Why shouldn't the flow continue? Even when Chester County streams and underground acquifers become polluted and undependable, can't we still bring in water from other places?" After years of stream conservation efforts, I am driven to conclude that most do not worry about preserving the watershed, though they will limit some destructive development practices when pressed hard enough. Small parcels of land will be set aside for parks and nature preserves. Nothing will be done to restore watersheds—that would mean planting trees, re-establishing market gardens and small farms (with good soil conservation practices), and, in general, seeking to enable nature to heal itself.

The bottom line of the development process continues to be the dollar sign. If someone can make money *today*, a new mall or industrial development is feasible—if they cannot, the project is dropped. When dollars are involved those who would conserve are told, "You can't fight progress!"

We need big changes in our idea of progress. Heavier and heavier demands are being made on the surface and underground water of Chester County itself. New wells are being drilled in the West Valley Creek watershed. Wilmington and Philadelphia continue to draw on streams which originate in Chester County. Other sources of surface water outside the immediate Philadelphia/Wilmington metropolitan area, moreover, are being negatively affected by the same development practices that afflict local watersheds.

Effort and money are spent to use and get rid or water. Like farmers who plowed the hills, we live today at the expense of tomorrow. In Chester County alone, millions of dollars are invested in water-related recreation: fishing tackle, boats, trailers, campers, RVs, cottages, etc. Investment in restoration of streams is minute.

Billions have been spent on new sewage systems which have indeed resulted in cleaner rivers. The conservation efforts of the late 1930s did result in restored watersheds. We need to learn from these effort, applauding their achievements and analyzing their shortcomings.

Beyond this, we must state our understanding of true progress. First, future development must take ecological realities seriously—a project should make a given ecosystem more healthy. Healthy streams and land are necessary for human well-being. A stream and its watershed are a living body, of which we are a part. Environmental impact statements should not only assess, "How bad will it be," but also "In what ways will this make things better?" Conservation and restoration of local streams is vital, for it is here that we live and work, here that our destructive and creative activity has its greatest effect.

Taking local ecological realities seriously, second, suggests policies of designing with nature. For several hundred years, progress has often meant warfare against nature. Now that humanity dominates nature almost everywhere on earth, change is needed. Biologically, unchecked expansion of a species leads toward population collapse, as the carrying capacity of the environment is overstressed. To illustrate how such danger may be avoided, consider the objective of establishing self-sustaining wild trout populations in a fishery. Such a goal moves away from increasingly expensive hatchery trout stocking as the solution to fishing pressure. For this new policy to be effective, however, the catch must be limited to what a given stream can provide. Human activity, then, designs with nature, not depending on some outside source of supply to bail us out.

Real progress, third, makes decisions about streams and watersheds which consider the good of the entire human family. By blood and by need we are bound to each other. As the American Revolution, Civil War, and Civil Rights movement should have taught us, when oppressed, enslaved, and poor people advance everyone eventually benefits. When a stream is accessible to all, some will act to watch out for water they benefit from and for which they care.

Human work, fourth, should be an investment in the future. A job or development project cannot be evaluated only as to whether or not it makes money. Work should not only provide the means for a decent living, but also build human communities that leave local streams and their watersheds more healthy and fertile.

Restore a Watershed

We have learned much by seeking to restore a section of West Valley Creek. Imagine how much more could be gained by attempting to restore an entire watershed. That is how we could get progress back on the track. Such a project would require commitment to uses which conserved, and to preservation of remaining relatively undisturbed areas. The center of attention, however, would be restoration of the degraded parts of the watershed.

From our experience thus far, several planning objectives can be identified. To begin with, we would aim at stopping erosion and subsequent stream sedimentation. To do this, we would seek to allow rainfall to soak into the watershed. Trees, shrubs, and grasses common to local ecosystems would be replanted. Size and number of roads and pavements would be reduced as much as possible. Roof and pavement drainage systems would be rebuilt to allow run-off to seep into the soil. A long-term aim might be to close off the storm sewer system, since it would be no longer needed. Farm, construction, and other earth disturbing activities would be studied, and new practices developed. Sewer and garbage system would be modified toward returning water and fertility to the land (which, of course, would require removal of toxic waste).

At the same time as we moved to stop erosion and recycle fertility, we would need to clean up pollution. Local discharges and emissions of poisons would be identified, and steps taken to see that they were stopped. Toxic wastes and spills would be located, and efforts made to clean them up, or buffer their worst effects. The thought of digging up and cleansing a "sanitary" landfill impregnated with toxic wastes boggles the mind, and yet people have done larger projects. Given the fact that much pollution may now be recycling in a human/animal/plant ecosystem, with toxic wastes stored in bones and bodies, new research will be needed. Of course, many effects of airborne and systemic pollution could be corrected only by regional and national efforts.

Another aim would be to remove human habitation from the flood plains. When floods wipe out businesses and houses, it should be a clue they were built in the wrong place! Disaster assistance should be given to help people relocate. Wetlands would be re-established where they should be.

A living green belt should be replanted along stream banks. Where they were dredged, in-stream work should seek to restore a natural, meandering channel. Coldwater springs and tributaries would be located and carefully preserved. I suspect that a serious effort to restore an entire watershed would develop goals we could not anticipate. Economic, political, cultural, and religious changes needed to carry through such a project would be massive. Yet little seeds germinate and grow into plants. Seemingly unthinkable changes may come to seem small when taken step by step, particularly when pressed forward by necessity.

Legislate and Enforce for the Good of All

Tyranny, the imposition of order by a few on many, and chaos, lack of order, are in reality very close. Both are destructive. We do not have to fall into either one. Past generations have often imposed restraints on their actions. We can do the same.

Let us look, for example, at laws which are now taken for granted in the United States and many other countries as well. To fish, people need a license. License fees go to support wardens, provide money for habitat restoration, purchase fish and game lands, and pay for research. These laws are enforced in ways which maintain access to sport and food by the entire people. Unlike in some countries, where game and fish were kept for the private sport of the landed gentry and the monarchy, in the North American democracies everyone has a right to fish and hunt.

In order to have fish to catch and animals to hunt, however, it became evident in the nineteenth century that people could not catch and kill according to their whims. Laws were conceived, debated and passed which set limits on what could be taken. Federal and state agencies with independent funding and leadership were created to enforce the law. Licensing and catch regulations have been so widely accepted, and for the most part have been so effective, that we tend to take them for granted. Our own experience shows, therefore, that it is possible for people to limit themselves, and support laws which restrain the exploitive few.

The laws have not worked perfectly. Particularly in areas where they have been imposed by outside forces, poaching has continued as a semi-accepted way of life. In general, however, conservation laws are accepted and enforced. As a result of the formation of fish and game departments, and voluntary associations aimed at preservation and restoration of threatened species, we have seen the gradual return of many species to their former habitats. Wild turkeys, for instance, are now fairly common in many parts of Pennsylvania. Geese have returned in large numbers to their flyways. Limited killing plus habitat restoration has often led to amazing results.

Fish and game laws have worked because of widespread social support. Where did the momentum for conservation laws come from? They came from a handful of people who believed in the common good and worked for it. These leaders loved the American out-of-doors, and saw what was happening. Undoubtedly they were deeply pained and many must have given up in despair. Some probably were destroyed in their efforts, but others studied and spoke and organized. Probably early conservation leaders were not many in number, but their efforts bore fruit.

We can also learn from the environmental movement of the 1970s. Though masked by controversy about the Vietnam War, public opinion polls in the 1960s showed increasing public concern about water and air pollution. An unfamiliar word "ecology," began to be heard. Throughout the world awareness was increasing that the natural environment was critical to human survival. Issues were dramatically presented, and further defined, in the United Nations Conference on the Global Environment held in Stockholm in 1972.

New organizations were formed, such as Friends of the Earth and Greenpeace, active in other countries as well as the United States. Laws were passed mandating clean-up of water and air pollution. A federal agency, the Environmental Protection Agency (EPA), was created to implement the new national legislation. Billions of dollars were appropriated to build sewage treatment system. Billions more were spent by industries, state, and municipal governments.

Throughout the country, rivers and streams benefited greatly. When pollution occurs, there are legal recourses available which were not there before 1970. EPA and DER staff have helped local efforts in significant ways.

Times change. When a widespread social movement realizes some of its objectives, people redirect concern to other matters. Desire for easy economic growth and personal profit has led to relaxing of standards and enforcement in some areas. New concerns arise: sedimentation, toxic waste, acid rain, ozone layer breakdown, and global warming.

We must not forget, though, that the conservation and environmental movements have given us an enduring legacy. We are stronger today because of their efforts.

Doing the Truth

Human beings not only have the ability to form visions out of their deepest thoughts and feelings, but also to speak of what they see to others. We can communicate. It is no accident that in English the root of the word "communicate" is the same as that for community. Speaking creates commonalty. A truthful vision thus leads to speaking out for the good of all (the common good). Since the arrogant, greedy, and ignorant few often gain control of social institutions, manipulating them to realize their narrow self-interests, speaking out will be lonely. One stands up against the odds for streams, watersheds, and all the people who depend on these sources of life.

Out of vision emerges a sense of direction. A goal, however, is only partly expressed in spoken messages. As we have seen in this book, there are four legs on which a stream conservation movement walks: education/communication, starting an organization and keeping it going, seeking institutional changes in public policy and practice, and restoring streams and their watersheds. These four legs must move in harmony together.

We are contending with powerful enemies. They exist within as well as outside us. There is *greed*, the desire to get ahead, no matter what or who gets hurt. Forming a voluntary association which seeks changes in policies and practices of agencies, corporations, and communities for the good of all overcomes greed. How does this work? No one who volunteers gets paid for it. Though we are not perfect, we show by our lives that decisions should be made for the well-being of all.

Ignorance is met with learning and speaking the truth. One sees what is there, feels what is happening, and tells the story. Science and technology assist us. Careful research helps us understand what is happening. Then education can help grown-ups and children grasp what is happening to streams and their watersheds, how human beings are involved, and also learn better ways of doing things (as the seminars we have organized on storm water runoff and management).

Truth comes by learning and by doing. As we do the truth, learning comes painfully through trial and error. We seek help from others so we do not make the same mistakes twice, thereby benefiting from what they have already learned.

Knowledge is based on manual as well as mental work. Stream restoration is important because it puts us into physical relationship with human beings, and with streams and all living creatures in them.

Other enemies we face are *arrogance* and *violence*, the refusal to acknowledge our finite created nature as human beings. Denying limitedness is arrogance, as is the violent will to power which crushes down all who oppose it. Wisdom allows the seeds we are planting to fall into the earth and die. When death and destruction we can do nothing about is accepted, with all of the horror that brings into awareness, only then does hope spring up which endures, only then does warm confidence arise which can carry us through the deepest waters.

Thinking Like Beekeepers and Rivermasters

In order to move forward, we need new ways to relate to streams. Beekeepers and rivermasters can give us pointers. Once I went with a friend who was buying a hive of bees. As the beekeeper gave instructions, he stated:

> You know, bees are not like animals. They only live a few months and then die. You can't train a bee. You have to find out how bees live, what they like and don't like, and then you try to be clear about what you want. You are able to accomplish your objectives by helping the bees to do best what they do. A beekeeper is successful when you fit into the bee's environment.

Rivermasters of English trout streams know well the lesson taught by beekeepers. The rivermasters work with his or her particular stream to increase its fertility and productiveness. A host of techniques are used to sustain and enhance the stream and its fishery. For instance, a rivermaster in a weed-choked stream will use a scythe to cut weeds in one place, while in another place allow them to grow. The current is channeled almost invisibly, providing more food and cover.

In order to be a beekeeper or rivermaster, an intimate working knowledge of ecology is necessary. Human well-being is understood to be dependent on the well-being of the local ecosystem. Instead of fighting nature, such leaders seek to enhance, not disintegrate, the natural order. Human beings thus fit into nature in ways which allow them to accomplish their objectives.

Overcoming Despair

Responses to the destruction of streams are varied. Those who have cut themselves off from the natural world may be almost unaware of what is happening, but the ones who love the streams of our country suffer deeply. Those who have fished from childhood know what I mean. So do hikers and naturalists. Families who have enjoyed an outdoor picnic on the bank of a clean, flowing river understand.

A few moments beside a tiny brook is refreshing. Seeing children play in a clean stream is a delight which can be remembered forever. Watching the rain splashing upon the branches of an undisturbed forest, and hearing it trickle and drop to the ground is part of what it means to be human. Such experiences fill us with delightful memories, and become part of our very identity. A human being is made of water and soil. Our very bodies and minds are formed from the land and water which gave us birth.

Think Like a River Keeper

How can we not suffer when the living waters which brought us into being and continue to nourish us are turned into poison? Some cannot stand to see what is happening. They care and feel deeply when they see a dying stream, but they do not see anything they can do. In despair they turn away; hopeless, they give up.

Not everyone gives up. Others who likewise cannot stand any more decide to do something. They, too, feel overwhelmed by the forces of destruction. They see clearly that the little bit that they can do probably will have little effect, since the whole society is committed to "progress and development." Conservationists realize that most people believe our way of life requires the control and often destruction of nature. Paving watersheds and polluting streams is taken for granted by those who make decisions about the future of our society. When challenged, they recite the old slogan, "You have to break a few eggs if you are going to make an omelet!"

Those who wish to conserve are a small minority, but their number is growing. Unmaking creation creates despair and hopelessness. No conservationist is without days in which she or he feels alone and ineffective. The odds against us are tremendous. Yet tremendous destruction also creates the seeds of a new movement of hope. Some see that it is one thing to break eggs to make an omelet, another to kill chickens which are laying those eggs. Thoughtless "development" drives people to become active, struggling to do something to stop the destruction of the living water which they love. Destruction, and the threat of more, is the source of many recruits to stream conservation. Anger which emerges from what is happening to one's favorite stream can give energy which will result in action.

Unfortunately despair can also result in a form of suicide. When we can no longer face the pain we feel which comes from ruining that which we love, we may turn away, in effect committing suicide. We can allow acts of destruction and the threat of more "progress" make us give up. That of course allows the destructive forces to move even more forcefully. In effect, when we despair and give up we do to ourselves what we fear may happen by other's hands.

There are no guarantees that becoming a conservationist will save any given stream. Nor is there assurance that we can turn the destructive development process around. We have discovered, however, that we can do something which does make a difference. We do what we can, and this at least changes for the better the areas we touch.

The forces of destruction are not all powerful and unlimited. Though it may not appear to be so, they are entirely dependent upon the water which they unthinkingly use, waste, and pollute. Their own destructive activities limit their days of power.

Hope lies in respecting and fighting for the streams. It lies in acting on the impulse to care for a little brooklet or a big watershed. It is strengthened as one learns to live with fellow environmentalists who may be irritable, short-tempered, abrasive. It feeds on each little victory and learns from painful defeat.

The Creator who shaped the streams and watersheds has not gone on strike nor abdicated to another solar system. The sun still shines, the clouds drop rain, and the streams still flow. If we learn to know and protect living waters, they will cleanse themselves, and become fertile and productive again.

PART III

A Handbook for Organizers

In Part I of *Living Waters* we told the story of the formation, development, and revitalization of the Valley Forge Chapter of Trout Unlimited, and highlighted some of our successes. In Part II we considered the vision out of which this organization was born and its development as we have gone along. Part III summarizes practical things you can do. The lessons are drawn from what we have learned in our own concrete experience in stream preservation and restoration. They will be stated, however, in ways which allow you to apply the learnings in other settings. For instance, our focus has been on streams and their watersheds. Yours may be on gardens, on maintaining fertile healthy soil, or you may be concerned about preserving and replanting forests. When we talk about streams and watersheds, therefore, insert your own goal.

ORGANIZING A MOVEMENT

Remember that learning is always specific to a person, group, time, and ecosystem. Your setting will be different. We think you can learn from us, but be aware that you already know and will learn new things we do not know.

Each begins where one is. As I was writing the last part of this book, a man came to me for help. At his request I went with him and looked at a stream about which he was concerned. He had noticed that pools were filling with rubble and silt, and he wanted to restore them. The stream was part of a privately owned fishing club and semipublic park. The manager was receptive to stream restoration activity. No one else in the club, however, seemed interested except my new friend.

A Logical Approach

"What should I do?" he asked. If I were giving "How To" tips in terms of logical step by step development of an effective stream conservation organization, this is what I *might* have said:

1. *Let yourself have a big vision.* You already see and hear what is happening to the stream and you know things are not supposed to be this way. Talk with others. Ask what is a healthy stream? What is a healthy watershed? Read Part II of this book carefully. Let your own feelings about the enemies of streams emerge.

Think about what you might do to overcome ignorance, greed, and human arrogance which are unmaking creation.

Expect a goal to emerge, perhaps to preserve, conserve, restore your own stream and watershed. In other words, begin with a vision which gives you the big picture, and wait for a sense of direction. The greater the willingness you have to face the destructive realities and allow yourself to feel them, the stronger will be the sense of direction when it emerges.

2. *Set a goal for your efforts.* Out of vision will emerge a goal. Then you can decide what you are going to do. Remember how I had to choose whether or not to do something and whether or not to organize to do it. If you decide to move forward in the direction your vision leads, you have a goal (for me calling into being and sustaining a democratic voluntary association to preserve, conserve, restore streams and their watersheds).

3. *Form a group to carry out the goal.* You will need yourself and one other person to start. For over nine months, up to the organizing meeting of the chapter in the spring of 1977, Chuck Marshall and I were the only two who were thinking and planning together to form such a group.

4. *Explore, visit, and learn from others.* See how those working with similar goals are doing their work. Look at the four task areas we have marked out, organizing, restoring, educating, and communicating, influencing public policy and practice. Find out about others' efforts.

Discover what organizations exist with which you might affiliate. We looked at three before deciding on Trout Unlimited, feeling that the latter was an aggressive conservation organization in Pennsylvania which could help us in realizing our overall goals.

5. *Officially incorporate.* Get an official charter. Elect officers. Start moving.

6. *Do the basics.*
   - Begin your own restoration project.
   - Get involved immediately in the arena of influencing public policy and practice.

- Start attending township and agency meetings where decisions are being made. Meet the developers.
- Continue to learn from what you are doing. Use your goal to evaluate. Begin telling your story to others. Educate and communicate.
- Build up your own organization, its membership, treasury, and internal climate.

Beginning Where You Are

Few start moving forward logically. Most begin where they are. Particularly in the world of organizing voluntary association for the common good, everything depends on motivation and willingness to do something. I began, therefore, with my new friend's willingness to do something. Here is what I *actually* said.

STEP 1
Develop a plan and find at least one other person to help you carry it out. Since in this case you are interested in stream restoration and have landowner and Pennsylvania Fish Commission written approval, do a project or two.

STEP 2
Find a consultant, someone who can help identify restoration project options to help you understand what you can do (in this case it was me).

STEP 3
Complete a small state-of-the-art project. This means you will have gotten official approval for an in-stream restoration project through the landowner with the Pennsylvania Fish Commission. Second, following approval, you and others will have gathered together the materials to complete the project, following the plan you have in hand. Next complete the project. Then stand back and evaluate what has happened and learn from it.

STEP 4
Choose whether you will seek to work for the well-being of the entire stream and its watershed. If you do not, in an area which is rapidly

developing the stream will surely be ruined and your fishing club will finally go out of business.

In this example, a volunteer steps forward interested in only one aspect of organizing for the well-being of a stream and its watershed. That is his beginning point. By plunging in as far as he can go, this person will learn by trial and error, hopefully will become stronger, and then will face the decision of what to do next.

Starting Out

1. Movements start small; my decision to do something for the stream was the beginning of a stream conservation movement in Chester County. A decision by one person—you—will make a difference.
2. Be sure about your decision before you start. It took me a great deal of effort and considerable number of trial-and-error failures before results began to show.
3. Affiliate with a conservation organization that has national and regional connections.
4. Adopt a sound organizational structure.
5. Pull together enough people to organize a steering committee. Yourself and one other person is the minimum number.
6. Hold a well publicized kick-off meeting. Record names, addresses and telephone numbers of all who attend. Form a governing board from these volunteers.
7. Find an inexpensive, attractive meeting place (try churches, libraries).
8. Hold regular meetings (we decided to meet the third Tuesday of each month). These general meetings should be recreational and inspirational in tone, designed to attract new people. Do business at a board meeting a week prior to your general organizational meeting.
9. Present options on important decisions for chapter discussion and vote. Elect officers. With a new group, don't worry about jobs on an organizational chart that no one is willing to do. Start out with what you can get volunteers for. Wait until someone volunteers. Don't try to force anyone to do something he or she does not want to do. That will give bad results. Keep calling people's attention to what needs to be done. Sooner or later someone is going to volunteer if the task is important.

10. Begin to plan for restoration work and attend a few local government meetings right away. Don't wait until the chapter gets strong to become active. Give primary attention, however, to building the chapter and its membership. To begin with, view activity in the community in carrying out your conservation goals as primarily for learning.
11. Hold board meetings at members' homes. We did so for the first few years. It established good relationships very quickly—you learn a lot about someone when you visit where he or she lives.

In the First Year

1. Lift up your goal clearly. For instance, our goal was to preserve, conserve, and restore the cold water streams in our specific geographical area.
2. Create a positive climate for your organization. Pay attention to communication. Make sure people learn to *listen* to each other and say what they are thinking and feeling. Work to make the organization open to everyone, women as well as men, people who are not well-off as well as those who are, people of different racial groups, etc. The broader the base of the organization, the stronger it will be in the long run. Work toward shared leadership. Don't build the organization around one person (as yourself). Establish a commitment to research and learning.
3. Find ways people can get to know each other. Have a picnic. Go on a stream walk. Schedule a fishing trip.
4. Get to know your territory. Don't focus on only one stream or one part of a stream. Fish different streams. Visit nature conservancy and watershed areas, or local parks.
5. Make connections with other conservation groups. Invite leaders to speak. Go and visit them. Learn as much as you can from others. Build on their successes; avoid their mistakes.
6. Conduct orderly meetings. Meet regularly, at the same place, at the same time. Present interesting programs. Build up your treasury.
7. Start a small-sized restoration activity. By doing physical restoration work together you can build a group rapidly.
8. Plan a year's schedule of meetings. Start your plans for September. Look for movies and other available programs that are enjoyable and educational. Invite leaders from other groups that relate

to your goal. Ask them to speak about what is most important to them, and make sure they know that they have a limited amount of time. Try some meetings featuring things like fly tying or rod building. Chop business to the bone. Start the meeting on time and end on time. Keep reports brief, and ask those reporting to summarize them. Don't forget reports of the treasurer and secretary. Do your main business at board meetings prior to chapter meetings, and keep the latter enjoyable and recreational in tone.

9. Teaching is very important. Every organization should encourage young people, tell the story of how healthy streams work and challenge people to decide to get active in working for the good of all. You can begin to get your message out through slide presentations, letters, and public speaking to churches, civic groups, planning bodies, and local governments.

10. Encourage religious leaders to connect faith with action. Go to the local ministers' association and tell the story of what you are doing and ask for help.

In the Second Year

1. Try new things, make mistakes and learn from them. Then try again. Trial and error is essential in learning to build a movement.

2. In trial-and-error learning it is important to start small. Make sure the areas on which you work are small enough that mistakes do not destroy the trust between those who are getting to know each other and becoming involved in action.

3. Discover your own limitations as a leader. Learn what you are good at and what you are not. Keep your limits in mind. Know your weaknesses and strengths. If you are not afraid of your weaknesses, others will come in and help fill in the gaps.

4. Remember that a conservation organization is a *voluntary* association. People become involved because they feel they ought to or want to be active. Build on their motivation. It is the key to effectiveness.

5. When anyone new comes to a meeting, make sure they are warmly greeted, introduced to others, and that their names, telephone numbers, and addresses are recorded. Get in touch with them after the meeting.

6. Enjoy the new friendships which will form. One of the main

rewards you are going to get out of your voluntary work is enduring friendships.

7. Learn how to create interesting programs. Evaluate which meetings sparked interest. Reschedule ones with similar topics and formats.

8. Listen to new and old members. Try asking, "Why did you come tonight?" "What would you like to do?" "What don't you want to do?" Be prepared to suggest to each a job that fits that person's skills and commitments.

9. Form an action committee. Don't expect quick results. Support the one who agreed to chair the committee, but let him or her have the responsibility. Check plans with the board before acting.

10. Go back to your goal, evaluate what has happened and use the goal to start new action.

11. Prepare a plan for yourself. Ask, "What should we be about next year in preservation, restoration, conservation?" Learn from other groups about how they put plans into action.

12. Be willing to let go. Release is essential or you will kill what you are trying to build. Don't take the whole thing on yourself.

In the Second and Third Years

1. Learn as much as you can about streams, watersheds, stream corridors.

2. Your credibility and effectiveness depend on knowing what happens when rain falls on the watershed of your local streams. Learn the major factors which are threatening streams in your area. This knowledge will sharpen your ability to concentrate on what is important in your planning and organizing. For instance, we discovered that erosion and sedimentation were the number one problem in Chester County, with pollution running second. This meant that we needed to concentrate on getting water to percolate into the watershed so that there was less runoff. Pollution events were important but secondary.

3. When you speak in public, draw on what you know. People will listen to what you have to say when you know what you are talking about.

4. See the connections between rainfall, watershed, and healthy stream life. When you understand these connections, it will help you form coalitions. For instance, the Valley Creek Watershed

Coalition was formed when we pointed out that all the groups had a common concern, cleaning up the landfill.

5. Don't be discouraged by "failures." Use low periods to prepare. Don't quit. Continue to wait for an opportunity. One is going to come.

6. Form a coalition to deal with big problems. Over the past two years you will have gotten to know leaders.

7. Remember that obvious poisonous pollution can generate media attention and spark citizen action. Don't despair when something awful happens. Instead, use the trouble to motivate yourself and others to do something to correct the difficulty.

8. Evaluate successful efforts and tell people about them. Honest evaluation will strengthen your organization.

9. When discouraged remember that the forces of the universe are creative. Destructiveness can tear things apart, but you can work with the Creative One who wishes to put things back together right.

In the Third and Fourth Years

1. Find an editor and begin to publish regularly a high-quality newsletter. Make sure that articles are truthful. Credibility is earned by hard work and honesty.

2. Plan and publicize a special event featuring a well-known speaker. Begin to raise funds through such an event or through holding a yearly banquet. These events increase the visibility of your organization and also raise necessary funds for its ongoing work.

3. Elect new leaders. Let the old ones step down.

4. Take "before and after" slides of your work projects. Use them to prepare a talk or slide presentation which communicates respect for streams and the natural order of which they are a part. Check to see that your presentation covers the following:

   - Beauty motivates everyone. For instance, people become patriots because they love the land in which they grew up. Furthermore, beauty delights and revitalizes the soul. Show the beauty of streams and watersheds as you challenge listeners to become active conservationists.

   - A stream is alive. Therefore, those who ruin a stream are killers.

- Degraded stream ecosystems become increasingly inhospitable to human beings. For instance, mine the underground water table and drought will come. Pollute the water and drink poison.
- Overuse of streams threatens human well-being.
- Human beings are part of the "natural family." By refusing to fit in, we unmake creation. By working with a stream to enable it to return to life, we become part of the family again.
- The Creator speaks to human beings through streams. Living water shimmers with the Divine Presence for those with eyes to see. The proper response to a stream, therefore, is awe and appreciation. When we are thankful, we become more careful and responsible. Point out to religious leaders that right religion supports stream conservation.

Over the Long Haul

1. Keep centered on your purpose. Our purpose was to preserve, conserve, and restore the coldwater streams of Chester County. We were not a fishing club, and throughout the years we have kept that in mind. Sometimes we overdid it, as Carl Dusinberre pointed out in our failure to be able to hold entertaining chapter meetings. By returning to the reason for our existence, again and again new life has broken out in the chapter and in the community through our work.

   Keep your plans goal-oriented, and after you have acted, evaluate events in terms of your purposes. Voluntary organizations have a continuing shift of membership. Like a river they constantly change. Keeping the purpose in mind to evaluate what you have done helps you learn from successes and failures, and grow stronger. Our goals keep us moving in the right direction, stirring us up when we get complacent and encouraging us when we feel despair.
2. Be honest. Greed is destroying the streams. The corrective is being persons of integrity, giving your time and money for the long term well-being of your community and its streams. Tell the truth and don't be bought off.
3. Be reliable. Do what you say, and don't say more than you are able and willing to do. Reliability is almost as important as hon-

esty. People will cooperate with a group that they know they can depend on.

4. Plan for and then celebrate many little victories. Small frequent successes pull a movement along. For instance, after a restoration work day everybody can see a small change for the better in the stream. A fund-raising project is something in which everybody in the chapter can participate, including the newest members. Everyone can take pride in spending money raised to better the stream. A well-run board meeting makes people feel good, and so does a chapter meeting with an interesting program. Speaking up at a chapter meeting can leave a person feeling better. A stream clean-up can be done anytime, and it always makes things look better.

5. Tackle big issues in ways that give you a chance of winning. When the Rouse Corporation decided to dump its treated sewer water in West Valley Creek at the head of the restoration project, it provided us with a dramatic issue we could use to raise support. The contrast between a little group of citizens struggling to pick up trash and restore a degraded stream, all on a voluntary basis, and a huge, "world class" developer planning to kill a trout stream gave us a good chance of winning a battle which would determine whether West Valley Creek would live or die.

6. Concentrate your efforts. The Valley Forge chapter of Trout Unlimited often has been effective because we centered on conserving coldwater streams and their watersheds in Chester County. We did not try to stop "progress," because we figured we could not do so. We did think we had a fairly good chance of holding a goal of ecologically responsible development before townships and corporations. We knew that this meant accepting many losses, as trees were cut down and the watersheds paved. We hoped we could gain enough respect for the streams and their watersheds to preserve them.

When we became involved in a controversy, we tackled plans that would have ruined the stream. Some issues cannot be avoided even if prospects for victory are bleak. We could not allow continuing pollution of Valley Creek by PCBs from the Paoli railroad yards. Neither could we accept the destruction of Crabby Creek as a coldwater fishery. When the Rouse Corporation threatened to dump its chemical effluent into West Valley Creek we had to fight.

8. Be informed. Citizens who start volunteer organizations which

seek the well-being of their community and country often begin with very limited skills and knowledge. If motivated with a passion to do something for the good of all, in the process of organizing a group it is possible to learn an immense amount. You only have to avail yourself of opportunities. Find out what is being written in your area of work. Gradually you will become knowledgeable, and though you will not be an expert, you will have all the expertise at hand to do what you need to do.

The opposite of ignorance is being informed. Conservation leaders must learn what makes for a healthy stream and its watershed. In short, we have to learn both conservation theory and practice. When I started I didn't feel I knew very much about stream conservation. After two years of trying to organize a stream conservation chapter, I knew I didn't know very much! Since then I have observed that new recruits to the conservation movement generally feel they don't know much and often feel inferior to the "experts." After four or five years as a conservationist active in public life, I guarantee that you will know as much as any specialized "expert." Ask the experts! Their job is to teach the rest of us what they know, so that we can be better informed citizens. If you listen carefully you will learn more and more about the characteristics of a healthy stream and its watershed, and from your organizing efforts you'll learn ways to get stream conservation goals put into action in corporate, township, and public agency planning.

9. Demand that official leaders *lead*. Years ago, Pennsylvania Trout Unlimited gave each chapter an acid rain testing kit. They asked chapter leaders to sample the acidity of rain in their area and use the results to get universities and others responsible to gather such data and to begin to do so and publish their results. The purpose of the Trout Unlimited research was to get the official researchers to do their jobs. In the same way, the purpose of forming a voluntary association for stream conservation is to get public agencies, corporations, and governmental bodies to do their jobs. There is no way a stream conservation organization *by itself* is going to preserve, conserve, or restore any stream and its watershed. That is too big a task for any little voluntary group. We can do enough, however, to get those who should be doing the job to take it on.

10. Listen, listen, and listen some more. Dialogue is an old word for two speaking together. All too often we take for granted the art

of communication. One listens, the other speaks, and then the
flow reverses itself. Good communication is the basis of good
organization. One can learn skills in listening and speaking.
Such skills build self-confidence and also bring out information
which otherwise would be overlooked or lost.

Never assume that what you know someone else knows, or
vice-versa. If something can go wrong, it will. Therefore, work
at staying in touch and checking things out. It always pays off.

For instance, in 1990 when we were tiring out, we asked for
help from national Trout Unlimited. We listened to Sal Palatucci, and acted on his suggestions. By listening, new energies
were released.

11. Learn the art of communicating. When your group comes together, find out why people came to the meeting and what they
expect to learn or have happen as a result of being there. Listen
to what they have to say, and take notes if possible. If as a leader
you can get people to begin to listen to each other, you will be
half way toward accomplishing your goals.

Don't neglect public speaking. Put together a slide presentation and go out and tell your message to other civic groups,
schools, and churches. By doing so you begin to inform public
leaders. Speak to township meetings, country and township planning committees.

Develop contacts with newspapers and television, and also
with relevant radio programs. Get to know who writes articles
that deal with conservation. Use interest in trout fishing to build
bridges.

Feed news of all sorts to these writers. Remember they need
information from you to stay in business. Then when a crisis
occurs, you'll know who to call, as we did when it was necessary
to publicize the Rouse Corpoation's plans and their ecologically
devastating consequences.

Keep your sense of humor. Carl Dusinberre's cartoons have
been very effective. A funny cartoon is often worth a thousand
words in helping people see what is going on.

12. Expand your communication through a regular chapter newsletter. The articles in the *Banknotes* newsletter have proved to be
invaluable. Hundreds of people every year are informed about
what is going on through this newsletter. It is one of the rocks on
which the effective action of the chapter was built.

Being editor of a newsletter is hard work. People do not give articles. You have to dig them out. But a newsletter keeps in regular touch with everyone on the chapter rolls and builds support. When a crisis comes, as happened with the Rouse Corporation's plans to dump treated sewage water into West Valley Creek, we were able to do special issues of the newsletter to inform constituencies. Then we could make these articles available to the media. A newsletter is an excellent way of communicating.

13. Encourage and back potential leaders. Always assume that every person you meet is a potential leader. Never neglect nor look down on anyone. Some of the best leaders in our conservation work have been persons who are self-educated and who work very hard to make a small living. Also note that each of the major Valley Forge Trout Unlimited efforts were begun and spearheaded by only one person. The job of leaders is to maintain centers of accountability who make sure that work is done when people volunteer to take on a task. A good leader has to be willing to do anything you ask anyone else to do, but you should never get to the point you feel that it is easier to do the job yourself than ask someone else to help.

Use a buddy system. Remember it is in helping someone who has been through it that a new person learns the skills and the confidence necessary to go on to be a leader themselves. It takes most potential community leaders three to five years of trial and error learning and apprenticing before they are ready to take on big struggles.

As you look for leaders, include anyone who is willing to work for the common good. Don't rule out people in advance. A person who is handicapped may be able to do something nobody else can. People without much money often can do things nobody else could do because they've had to do a lot on a very little. Don't let race, class, gender, or family prejudice rule out anybody. When we all work together for the good of all, we all benefit.

14. Organize your movement for the long haul. Encourage leaders who get tired to reduce their activity and perhaps even drop out for a while. Several years of constant effort will exhaust anyone. Let leaders take a break.

Make sure that your best leaders concentrate on the big conservation tasks. Many housekeeping details which are necessary to run and maintain an organization will take care of themselves if you don't forget them, but instead allow them to be caught up in your big efforts.

15. Create an encouraging chapter climate. A person with a vision needs support to bring it into being. Accept the fact that there will be many things which ought to be done that are not going to be accomplished because there is nobody to work on them. When somebody does get a great idea, make sure that they check it out with the chapter before going into action. In a supportive climate checking out a strong idea makes it stronger.

16. Include anyone. A climate conducive to encourage people to volunteer is essential. When someone new comes to a chapter meeting, introduce yourself. Ask each why he or she happened to come, what they liked from the meetings, and listen carefully. When somebody wants to do something, give them a way to sign up. Most people take several years before they will tackle big projects. Therefore it is good to have projects that beginners can take with a good chance of success.

17. Focus on more than one stream. The focus of some local conservation organizations is too small. Keeping the entirety of Chester County in mind as our area of concern helps us be aware of what is happening in many places. Though most of our efforts have centered on Valley Creek and West Valley Creek, because we have had to keep a bigger picture in mind we have been helped to see more clearly what is going on. It has also put us in touch with planning agencies which cross township and county boundaries.

18. Build around several leaders. If a movement is to be sustained, it takes more than one to do it. Many a conservation organizations is started by a vital leader who becomes like the dominant fish in a pool. As the big fish grows older, it defends its territory and keeps all of the young energetic fishes out of it. Dominating leaders are often threatened by new ideas and new volunteers. Indeed, sometimes they seem like a walnut tree in a forest. The juglone poison a big walnut secretes keeps other forest trees from growing in its shade, even little walnut trees.

George Washington is featured in the cartoons in this book. When he was offered the position of president for life, he turned it down. He didn't need the "glory" that many would have sought. He also knew that if a democracy were going to take root, his job was to bow out when he had finished his term of service and let others take the lead.

It's hard to get a new organization started or revitalize an old one. A leader is tempted to take everything on himself or herself, but in the long run it is much better to open up doors to others. If one wishes to sustain a movement, rather than having it die out when one dies or gets tired, build a chapter around several leaders.

19. Keep board and chapter meetings separate. In the *Cookbook* prepared by Ken Sink for chapters of Pennsylvania Trout, Sink recommended that chapter business be done at board meetings, and that chapter meetings be recreational times which would draw people together. This format has proven a wise one. As we have learned, revitalizing chapter meetings brings new life into the entire chapter.

In like manner, a strong sense of direction exhibited in board meetings and a willingness to make hard decisions can and does take the organization forward.

20. Watch for unexpected innovations. From time to time someone gets a new idea. Those ideas should be encouraged and checked out. Life comes into an old movement as people get inspired and are willing to take the responsibility to do something new. It really does take only one person to make a big change for the better.

GUIDELINES FOR ORGANIZING RESTORATION PROJECTS

B ased on what we have learned, the following suggestions should help you start out.

1. Pick an accessible, visible stream which needs help.
2. Select a project area which is large enough to make a difference but small enough to be manageable.
3. Develop a plan with clear objectives.
4. Discuss what you want to do with those who have authority over this stream and get their approval (in Pennsylvania, the Pennsylvania Fish Commission).
5. Do research and learn as much as you can about streams and how they work.
6. Find a project manager who will take responsibility for planning, recruiting and organizing.
7. Start with small projects, and let the stream teach you about what works and what doesn't.
8. Take before and after pictures of the project area.
9. Gather benchmark information so that you can assess the effectiveness of your work. Measure stream width and depth. Find data on trout population from prior surveys—if none exists, find out who is authorized to do electroshock surveys, and schedule one for the project area. If possible also do a survey of insect populations. Ideally a thorough initial benchmark study should be done professionally, so it could stand up in court. Most

groups beginning a restoration project lack resources for such a study—do the best you can.

In the Second and Third Years

1. Begin asking yourself questions about whether your stream is healthy, sick, getting better or worse.
2. Observe the stream weekly throughout the year. Learn the effects of different seasons on the stream and its ecosystem. For instance, we learned that July and January were the stress points for trout in southeastern Pennsylvania. Hold stream walks.
3. Go out during storms and see what is happening. Storm events are good times to identify erosion from poorly managed developments and from farmer's fields. Look at your restoration structures in times of flood. Are they performing as you would have expected during high water?
4. Report to appropriate authorities instances of erosion and sedimentation. Most states have regulations designed to prevent erosion and stream pollution through sedimentation. Also keep an eye out for other types of pollution. Immoral people with toxic and hazardous wastes sometimes dump them during storms figuring that nobody will notice. Keep your eyes open.
5. Read research reports, go to symposiums which deal with stream restoration, invite guest speakers from groups which know about problems you are dealing with. Make field visits to learn from experts. Read the best books and manuals in the field.
6. Sit and watch. See what the stream is doing. Think about it. Ideas often come when you take time to reflect.
7. Talk with people who remember the history of your particular stream. Also think about streams you have known which are healthy. Draw on your memories as you seek to make changes.
8. Consult with a master at restoring streams to health. If possible, have her/him come out and walk the stream with you. Write down what the expert says and draw on it in your further work.
9. Having wild trout in a cold water stream is a prime objective for conservationists. They are a sign of good, clean water and a healthy watershed. The presence of wild trout is also an indicator of your community's well-being. When restoring a coldwater stream to health, therefore, it makes sense to preserve or reestablish a wild trout population.

10. Given a cold, clean flow of water, wild trout can be reestablished. We had good success with a Whitlock-Vibert Box program. Another way might be through special regulations, such as a catch and release program. Teach people who enjoy angling that fishing is recreation. In an urban setting, restraint is required. If everyone killed the fish they caught, none would be left to reproduce.

After Three Years and More

1. Hold at least one work day every month (including winter).
2. Bring experts in to help (draw on your state fisheries division and also on independent consultants). Have them walk the project section with you. Take notes and review them afterwards.
3. Evaluate the effectiveness of your work by keeping careful records. Review learnings. Make corrections.
4. Organize for the "long haul" (it takes five to ten years before efforts really begin to make a difference).
5. When your work runs into difficulties, do research. Find out and define your problem, ask experts, read research reports, and then experiment. When something works well, perfect it.

INTRODUCTION TO
STREAM RESTORATION

The first years of work on West Valley Creek were guided by what I learned from Bob Hunt in Wisconsin. From him I received *Guidelines for Management of Trout Stream Habitat in Wisconsin* by Ray J. White and Oscar M. Brynildson (Madison, Wis: DNR, 1967, 1979). Produced out of thirty years of professional study, experimentation, and evaluation, this handbook deserves much of the credit for whatever effectiveness we have achieved in stream restoration.

Guidelines begins with a one-page summary of principles in managing trout stream habitat. After a decade of effort, these principles seem even more sound than they appeared when I first read this handbook:

> *Tailor habitat management to the individual stream.* This requires thorough examination of the stream and its trout, by diagnosis of problems and a plan for the 'cures' before the work is done. *Preserve and restore the natural character of streams and their landscapes.* This is essential to the quality of angling. Meanders and/or riffle-pool 'stepping' characterize all natural water courses. Both appear to result from the same hydraulic processes. Through such horizontal sinuosity and vertical undulation, the channel meets some of the trout's life requirements. Pools at meander bends or at the foot of riffles or other plunges, provide protective depth. The riffles serve as spawning grounds, nurseries and food producing areas. (*Guidelines for Management of Trout Stream Habitat in Wisconsin*, page 1)

> Provide the most favorable living conditions possible for trout *without destroying natural beauty*. Better living conditions will mean that the stream will support a greater abundance of trout through better survival, better growth, and perhaps through better reproduction. Survival, growth and reproduction requires shelter against predators, fertile water, sufficiency of living space, favorable water temperature, and gravel stream bed for spawning. (page 4)

A healthy stream is the main aim of habitat management. Such a stream has "the capacity for self-repair." The task for human beings, therefore, is to work with the stream to enable it to become more healthy.

Quick and easy approaches to stream restoration are self-defeating. Carefully study the streams in your area. For instance, if you are in an area of high-gradient streams, marked by hilly or mountainous terrain, creating stair step pools may be an appropriate objective. In a low-gradient urban stream dams are disasters.

Healthy streams in balance with their watershed should be left alone. Restoration is called for when human destructiveness has left a stream in a mess. Over the eons, of course, the stream will heal itself. But with some help from its friends, that healing process may be speeded up, if the healers understand streams and know what they are doing.

White and Brynildson also state that protection and control of stream bank vegetation will often help maintain favorable trout habitat: "The trout sheltering characteristic of natural channels are enhanced by the right kinds of vegetation, mainly the low stream edge plants that drape into the water."

They go on to say that the basic rule of in stream alterations is to make the current work for you. For low-gradient streams that means keeping the water moving, removing dams and other obstacles to flow (but not removing meanders!). High-gradient streams lend themselves to making plunge pools. To aid spawning, naturally occurring streambed gravels should be protected and enhanced, rather than trying to bring in and deposit new gravel.

In urban and suburban areas, townships and counties are often worried about flood control. White and Brynildson offer the long-term cure: "Combat floods by reducing overland runoff back in the drainage basin above the stream, not solely by reinforcing stream banks" (page 1).

If you want your stream to be more healthy, therefore, there are three general objectives: One, protect and improve the watershed; two, protect and restore the riparian zone, that area immediately adjacent to the stream to which it flows; and three, seek to renew the structure and vegetation of the stream itself.

What Not to Do in Streams: Armstrong's Rules

Joe Armstrong, drawing on his professional background in engineering, produced designs for the structures we built. After a few years of observation, he set down some rules for what *not* to do:

1. The worst thing is to build a low dam. It silts up the stream, and spreads the creek wider.
2. The next worst thing is to make a downstream pointing "V" deflector, with an opening in the middle. It digs at the corners, and widens the stream. It silts in the center, and produces an island in the middle, if given enough time.
3. The third worst thing is building a peninsula deflector from one side. It will dig at the base, widening the stream (as predicted in the *Guidelines for Management of Trout Stream Habitat in Wisconsin*),

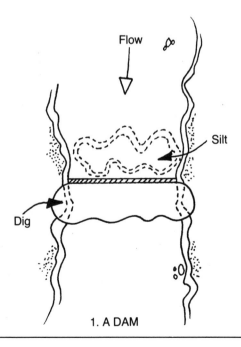

1. A DAM

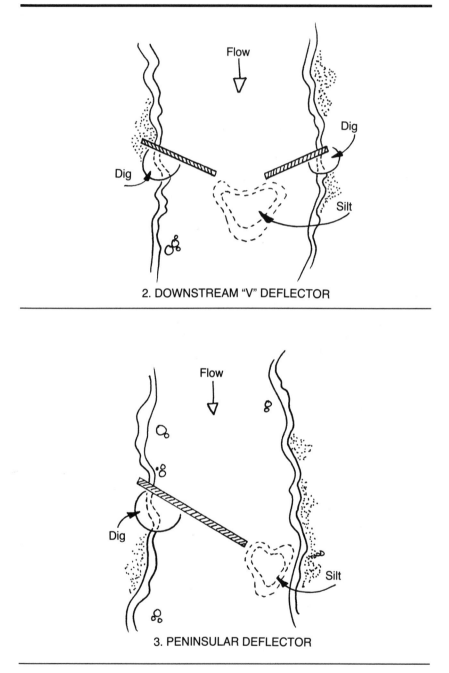

Flow

Dig

Dig

Silt

2. DOWNSTREAM "V" DEFLECTOR

Flow

Dig

Silt

3. PENINSULAR DEFLECTOR

but also it will silt at the opening, which would not have been expected.

4. Ray White and Oscar Brynildson, in *Guidelines for Management of Trout Stream Habitat in Wisconsin* (Technical Bulletin #39, Department of Natural Resources, Madison, Wisconsin, 1967: reprint 1979), give further information about what not to do. In addition to cautioning against "V" deflectors and "I" deflectors, they also warn against an "A" deflector, which is an inverted "V" deflector, with its point upstream. It widens the channel and leaves an island in the middle. They further state: "Concrete, ugly and artificial, has at present no place as a material for devices in trout streams. It can never be used as exterior material without ruining the natural appearance of trout streams." (White and Brynildson, 36)

Where to Start

The logical thing to do in restoring a stream would be to begin with revegetating the watershed, allowing rainfall to soak into the ground and replenish the water table. The next step would be to restore the stream corridor itself, and only after that make whatever modifications were necessary in areas of the stream which had been extremely abused. Unfortunately, however, for the citizen concerned about stream restoration, the most that one can usually start doing something about is a small instream restoration project. Two or three people can make a difference if they choose a particularly visible and degraded section of stream, seek official approval and guidance, build the project according to plan, and evaluate the results by what the stream does.

Every state has its own approach to restoration. Some have professional teams who are doing stream restoration. Others, as in Pennsylvania, provide authorization and guidance for restoration planning and work. The volunteer conservation organization begins restoration by getting in touch with state leaders, learning about what can be done, and developing a plan for a project area one selects. Permission of the land owner is essential, as is that of the official regulatory body. Be sure to get written permission in advance before beginning any project.

As White and Brynildson observe, for the habitat manager there is tension between increasing productivity and developing natural beauty. A beautiful stream is unique, abounding in the sounds and sights of nature. It allows solitude, letting the angler feel that for a few hours at least one has a peaceful corner of the world to oneself. The waterscape is varied, with swift runs and riffles alternating with slow dark pools. Woods and meadows offer different challenges. The person concerned for restoration will respect the stream and its identity, working with what is present to enhance both beauty and productivity (page 4).

In planning a restoration project, therefore, follow nature's lead. Do not construct devices just because they are in a cookbook, but let nature call the shots. Treat your stream as an individual. Then, keep the whole stream in mind—when working with a specific section be aware of how this section is part of the total stream. Finally, preserve natural character by building structures as inconspicuously as possible.

We started as rank beginners, knowing nothing about the art and science of stream restoration. If you are starting out at the same place as we did, start small, and then give yourself plenty of time to look at what the devices you place in the stream do. Keep in mind indicators of a healthy stream as to reduce the width of this dredged section of stream, increase the depth, restore natural meanders, encourage bank-side vegetation and cover.

An increased trout population in the restored sections of stream said to us we were moving in the right direction. So did charts which showed that over the first six years of the project the depth of the stream had increased and the width had been narrowed. We also became aware of a new problem. Though the depth was greater than when we started, we were beginning to see many evidences of new sedimentation and reduced depth. Clearly, new efforts were required.

We wanted to make our stream become more healthy by digging deep holes at key points in the stream bed. The dredged section of West Valley Creek we were working with had once been a meadow stream with low gradient. Steep mountain streams have high gradients, with water dropping rapidly from one level to the next. High-gradient streams have great ability to dig stair-step pools. In our stream, gradient would be of limited value in helping us accomplish the objective of gaining increased depth. We used floods, therefore, to accomplish this objective.

Every stream or river develops its own riffle/pool ratio, which can be determined by taking the average width of the stream, multiplying it by six, and thus determining where the riffles will be (this ratio is affected by volume of stream flow, gradient, substream composition, riparian vegetation, channel pathway, and other characteristics).

You may have the same problems that we did in determining the correct riffle pool ratio for your stream or streams. Ours had been so much altered by years of corn farming and by episodes of dredging that it was almost impossible to form an assessment of what West Valley Creek had once looked like. Flood flows established riffle/pool sequences very different from those obtained in normal flow conditions. Our task, which might also be yours, is to measure, assess, and form judgments about what a correct riffle/pool sequence would be for one's own stream. Based on this assessment, the structural suggestions in the next chapter may help in restoring your stream to a degree of health.

When I was a boy fishing in Wisconsin, I loved to float night-crawlers into the deep holes under the banks of the stream. One limestone creek had a very low gradient, and a smaller stream flow than West Valley Creek. Yet it had holes that were four feet deep. Why?

Reflect on such a meadow stream. The current pushes against the banks, gradually creating an undercut bank and continually scouring the bottom. In a stable stream with a protected watershed over thousands of years, the stream assumes the characteristics of a classic meadow stream: large meanders, undercut banks, cover from grasses and shrubs hanging over the water. Can urban streams again assume such a character? If meanders are reestablished, will they be destroyed by the floods which are created by more and more pavement on the upper watershed?

Limited experimentation is clearly in order. The objective would be to increase the depth of the holding water in each pool. Such a restoration objective would be to accomplish something that any healthy stream would do. Given the shortness of human life and the great length of geologic time in which streams work, however, we intend to speed up the healing process. We compete against increasing development. Somehow we have to make the floods work for a healthy stream, rather than against it. Somehow we have to make more use of the vast amounts of sediment coming off an eroding watershed. These forces can work for the stream, rather than against it.

STRUCTURES FOR LOW-GRADIENT STREAM RESTORATION

F or detailed information on planning and building restoration structures, purchase and use a good handbook. In addition, on the
following pages are brief descriptions of structures mentioned earlier
in this book.

Triangle Wing Deflectors

A triangle structure may not look right in the water. Somehow a dam,
going at right angles across the stream, or a downstream "V" seems to
look more natural. A triangle wing-deflector, however, will work well
immediately. Silt and sand begin to build up downstream behind the
structure. At the point water will cut a hole in the bed of the stream.
Fist-size rocks will be pushed downstream to form a new riffle (rocks
of this size are the type mayfly and other insect larva prefer). Stream
width will be narrowed.

The Porcupine

The invention of the porcupine by Joe Armstrong came out of the
peculiar conditions we faced in southeastern Pennsylvania. Though
buffered by the even flow of a limestone aquifer, each year our

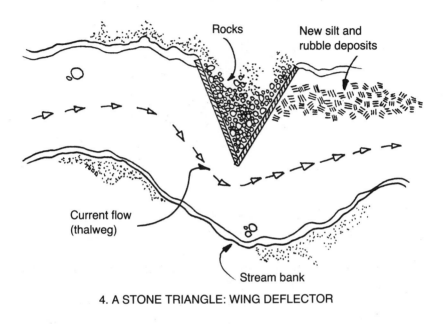

Rocks

New silt and rubble deposits

Current flow (thalweg)

Stream bank

4. A STONE TRIANGLE: WING DEFLECTOR

streams have big floods caused by sudden runoff from paved areas. Masses of soil wash into the water resulting in huge amounts of silt and sand being carried by the current.

We have found porcupines useful in restoring the natural meanders of the stream, and removing silt and sand from the water. They fulfill one of our objectives, which is to make silt in the stream work for the stream's health rather than against it. They encourage the stream to deposit sediment in places where it will be good for the stream and its creatures rather than a liability.

I once thought porcupines were easier to make than rock triangles. That was before I started from scratch to make one. Following the Guidelines for Trout Stream Management in Wisconsin, we cut down small trees growing out of the bank next to the stream (as trees get

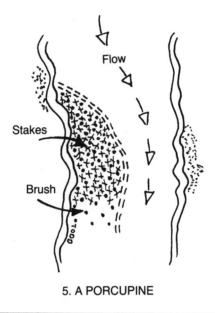

5. A PORCUPINE

bigger, floods often push them over, tearing up the bank and further widening the channel).

Early porcupines were made by driving steel pipes into the stream bed. Now we use straight sections of limbs, sharpen them on one end, and drive them into the stream bottom. Then branches are woven into the stakes. After ten hours or so of work, a porcupine may be completed.

Sediment should pile up on the porcupine forming a new wing deflector and point bar. Unless stakes are driven at least two feet deep into the bottom, however, the next high water will bend them over and wash everything out. After several years our porcupines sported new coats of reed canary grass and bush willows. They looked permanent, but some proved to be easily eroded. What one flood deposited, the next might wash away. Most remained, moreover, only a few inches above water level at their highest points.

Christmas Tree Deflector

Joe Armstrong invented a new device, the Christmas Tree Deflector. On top of the oldest porcupine, in a part of the stream with fairly good

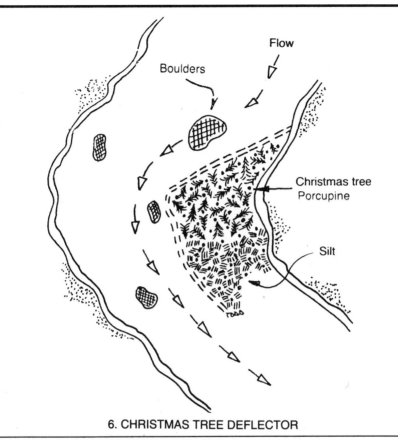

6. CHRISTMAS TREE DEFLECTOR

gradient, he wired together a line of Christmas trees. Silt and rubble were deposited behind the deflector, and the stream was deepened off the point of the device.

Sill and Triangle Deflector Together

An idea by White and Brynildson served as a stimulus for us to put sills and deflectors together. They state: "On a high-gradient stream you can shoot the current beneath the bank cover by means of a subsurface rock wing deflector, angled to let the water fall toward the bank."

Look at the diagram on sill and porcupine together.

First step: place the sill. A log is embedded in one bank at such an angle as to direct the flow against the opposite bank. This diagram is

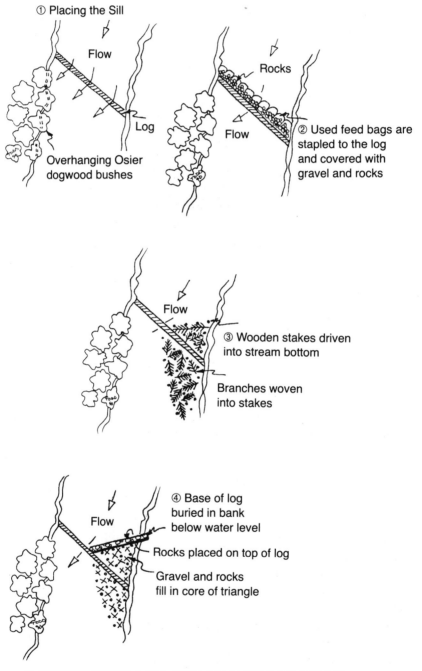

① Placing the Sill

Flow

Overhanging Osier
dogwood bushes

Log

Rocks

Flow

② Used feed bags are
stapled to the log
and covered with
gravel and rocks

Flow

③ Wooden stakes driven
into stream bottom

Branches woven
into stakes

Flow

④ Base of log
buried in bank
below water level

Rocks placed on top of log

Gravel and rocks
fill in core of triangle

7. CONSTRUCTING A SILL WITH A TRIANGLE DEFLECTOR

based on an actual project constructed at West Valley Creek over a several year period. We began with a wide and shallow dredged stream with the deepest place being no more than six or seven inches, certainly not enough to hold trout.

Step two: staple used feed bags to the log, and cover them with gravel and rocks.

Step three: form a porcupine by driving wooden stakes into the stream bottom, interweaving the stakes with Christmas trees. The current flow now is more sharply concentrated against the opposite bank.

Step four: place a second log at the top of the porcupine, making sure that it is well below water level during the driest periods of the year. Large rocks are placed on top of the log to hold it in place and give the structure a natural appearance. Gravel and rocks are used to fill in the core of the triangle. If you wait a year or two after forming your porcupine, and it works effectively, enough silt and sediment should build up so that you will need far less gravel and rocks when you come to fill in the core of the triangle.

Step five: stabilize the top end of the sill with large boulders. Build up the surface of the deflector to at least thirty inches above low-water level. This step must be done with great care. You do not want to create a structure which will cause flooding because it is too high. On the other hand, the surface of the deflector must be high enough to concentrate flood waters over the sill.

Step six: place large boulders in the flow of the current. Space them far enough apart so they do not cause debris to form a dam. The current will dig around the boulders, creating holding water.

Step seven: following the riffle/pool sequence of your stream, determine the location of the tail of the pool, and create a new structure which pushes the current towards the opposite bank. Remember that your goal is to help the stream re-create its meandering pattern, given the limits of the dredged stream structure within which you are working.

Obstructions

As I looked more and more closely at West Valley Creek and other streams, I noted that when a tree fell in the water the stream would often dig a deep pool under or around it. I also noticed the effect of big rocks. Clearly, one answer to what made a healthy stream dig a deep hole is the place and character of obstructions.

With a "come-along" (or hand winch) large rocks can be rolled down into the stream and pulled out into the water. Leave the rock where the current can flow over it, wait for the next big rain, and see what happens. Even in our low gradient section of stream the water had dug three-foot deep holes around rocks. An obstruction in the stream as a big rock can help solve the sedimentation problem. Make sure, however, that rocks are placed so they do not cause dams to form.

Spines

A spine is a structure added to the top of an existing deflector. Its purpose is to concentrate the flow of floodwater so that the energy of the rapidly flowing current may scour the bottom of sediment, and increase the depth of pools at these desired points.

Consider the attached diagram. It pictures a stone deflector. In one such structure tons of rocks had been used to narrow the stream and produce a gently curving stream bank. The structure appeared to be well-designed, and yet the pool below it became sedimented and actually began to decrease in depth. Something was wrong. By adding

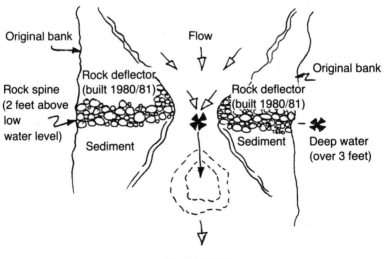

8. ROCK SPINE

a spine of rocks along the top of the deflector and the stone deflector on the opposite bank, a hole over three feet deep appeared below the constricted channel.

High water, instead of flowing over the deflector and eroding the point bar below the deflector, was instead concentrated to flow inside the new stream banks. Floodwater flows now began to scour the bottom below the deflector.

We have used three ways to create spines.

1. The most permanent spine is made of large rocks (as just described). When working with rocks one wants to make sure that the design of the structure is correct. A spine made of rocks and small boulders is not going to be easily dismantled.
2. A less permanent but very effective structure is made of Christmas trees. The trees are anchored in place with stakes. They should not be more than two-and-a-half to three feet above the level of the deflector. Christmas trees exposed to the push of the current often become so completely filled with silt that they are solid enough to walk on. Over a two- or three-year period we have been able to increase the height of some of our structures by a foot or two. The trouble is that Christmas trees must be replaced every year until grasses and shrubs establish themselves and stabilize the structure.
3. Build a porcupine in which the stakes extend above the surface of the deflector by two feet or more. Spaces between stakes are filled with whatever branches are at hand. In a day or two one can build such a structure, and it will immediately concentrate the flow at the desired points. When built in the fall branches will quickly be filled with leaves and will create a very adequate spine. Such a structure, however, tends to last only a year. Without maintenance everything will be washed away, leaving only the stakes.

Spine and Boulders in Combination

Small rocks and boulders create holding water for trout. In a stream undisturbed by fishing, trout might hold in one particular spot for an entire season (and perhaps even longer).

Spines and boulders make a good combination. The spine concentrates the high water flow. When the flow hits the obstruction of a boulder placed in the current below the deflector, it will dig around each side and underneath it, depending on the position of the boulder. Small rocks are less effective than large ones. The bigger the boulder, the greater the effect in digging.

From Porcupine to Meander

Those who have waded and fished meadow streams with low gradient know that one often comes to pools which are over one's boots. Such streams dig deep holes because concentrated current is continually pushing against the bank, gradually undercutting it and scouring the bottom. It takes centuries for a stream with a stable watershed to create the desired U-shaped bottom which casual anglers take for granted.

After porcupines stabilize, they can be turned into meanders. One summer, for instance, I took step one with a shovel, beginning to dig out the stream bottom along the upstream edge of a porcupine. I threw the sand, gravel, and small rocks on top of the porcupine, hoping to speed up the process by which this meadow stream created meanders. I felt that if we could create new stream banks in a meandering pattern, the current flow might begin to deepen the stream beside the new structure.

About that time, in 1985, Ray White, co-author of our guide and a stream biologist skilled in restoration, came and walked West Valley Creek with us. One of the difficult tasks had been to guess the correct riffle pool ratio in establishing these meanders. Ray said he felt that the placement of structures looked to be about right. You may wish similar guidance before taking the next step, which is to place Christmas trees on top of your meanders.

The third step toward forming a meander with undercut banks is to dig a hole about two feet deep on the upstream edge of the meander. Fourth, prepare to sink a log with a diameter of at least twelve inches at the base along what is to become the top edge of a triangle. Dig a hole next to the bank to bury the butt of the log. Then lay the log along what will become the upper edge of the pool. Place large rocks upon the log, securely anchoring it below the low water level. The log is placed under the surface to preserve it from decay (wood which is not exposed to the air lasts for much longer than wood which is exposed to alternate submersion and exposure to air). Sediment and

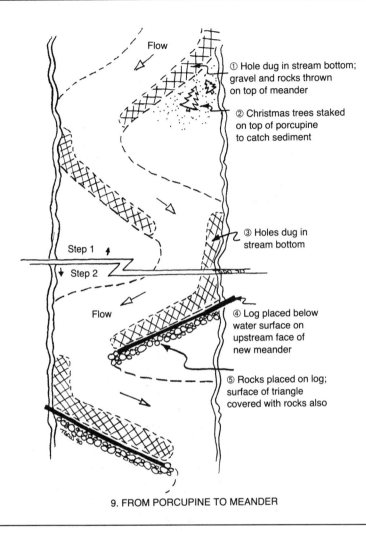

Flow

① Hole dug in stream bottom; gravel and rocks thrown on top of meander

② Christmas trees staked on top of porcupine to catch sediment

③ Holes dug in stream bottom

Step 1

Step 2

Flow

④ Log placed below water surface on upstream face of new meander

⑤ Rocks placed on log; surface of triangle covered with rocks also

9. FROM PORCUPINE TO MEANDER

small stones from the bottom may be shoveled behind the log. Once the new triangle is built up to the surface of the water, more stones and boulders are placed on top of the log.

The fifth step: increase the height of the triangle. Buckets of small-sized stones may be passed by human chain to be dumped on top of the slowly rising triangle. To stabilize the point bar behind the triangle, Christmas trees and small branches can be piled behind the stones and staked securely into place.

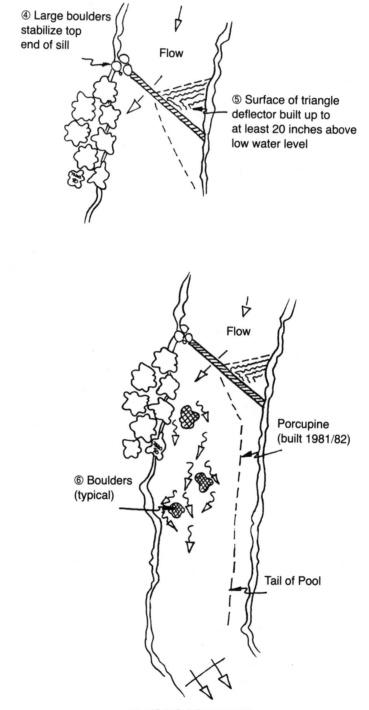

④ Large boulders stabilize top end of sill

Flow

⑤ Surface of triangle deflector built up to at least 20 inches above low water level

Flow

Porcupine (built 1981/82)

⑥ Boulders (typical)

Tail of Pool

10. USING BOULDERS

Summary

1. Use triangle wing deflectors to concentrate current flow.
2. Create porcupines as an alternate way to concentrate stream flow.
3. Turn porcupines into meanders, using below surface logs to form undercut banks.
4. Use a sill to direct current flow and to assist in digging a deep hole.
5. Build spines on deflectors to concentrate flood water flow.
6. Use rocks and boulders to assist in digging, as well as to help create holding water.

Index